YEAR OF THE SWORD

JOSEPH YACOUB

Year of the Sword

The Assyrian Christian Genocide,
A History

Translated by

James Ferguson

OXFORD

UNIVERSITY PRESS

OXFORD

UNIVERSITY PRESS

Oxford University Press is a department of the
University of Oxford. It furthers the University's objective
of excellence in research, scholarship, and education
by publishing worldwide.

Oxford   New York

Auckland   Cape Town   Dar es Salaam   Hong Kong   Karachi
Kuala Lumpur   Madrid   Melbourne   Mexico City   Nairobi
New Delhi   Shanghai   Taipei   Toronto

With offices in

Argentina   Austria   Brazil   Chile   Czech Republic   France   Greece
Guatemala   Hungary   Italy   Japan   Poland   Portugal   Singapore
South Korea   Switzerland   Thailand   Turkey   Ukraine   Vietnam

Oxford is a registered trade mark of Oxford University Press
in the UK and certain other countries.

Published in the United States of America by
Oxford University Press
198 Madison Avenue, New York, NY 10016

Library of Congress Cataloging-in-Publication Data is available
Joseph Yacoub.
Year of the Sword: The Assyrian Christian Genocide, A History.
ISBN: 9780190633462

Printed in the United Kingdom on acid-free paper
by Bell and Bain Ltd, Glasgow

"I am determined to record the martyrdom of a small people, the most worthy of interest yet at the same time the most abandoned, arising out of a great empire of the world's most ancient civilization, whose country, like Armenia, was the stage for Turkish abominations in which men were tragically murdered, women, children and the aged deported into the desert, pillaged, martyred and subjected to the worst atrocities.

This people is the Assyro-Chaldean people."

Joseph Naayem, 11 November 1919

"The persecutions and sufferings that the Nestorians undergo from time to time are similar to those that have been endured by the Armenians and the Jews, and their treatment by the hostile nations is identical. Of the troubles of the Armenians and the Jews, however, we hear quite often, while the Nestorians in Persia and Turkey, probably due to their small number and lack of literary representatives, have excited almost no interest."*

Abraham Yohannan, September 1916

To my paternal grandparents, Yacou Auchana and Mariam, from the village of Khosrava in Persia, massacred by the forces of hatred in 1915.

To my paternal aunt, Angèle, who shut herself in a *tanoura* (a clay bread oven) for a week, trying to escape the carnage. When she emerged from her hiding place she discovered, to her stupefaction, that nobody was left alive in the village. Forced into exile, she followed other fugitives from her community towards Iraq and then Syria, where she was reunited with my father at Hassakeh, in 1933.

To my maternal grandparents, Gaurié and Sara, from the village of Pataver, near Khosrava, who in January 1915 took the gruelling road of collective exodus towards the Caucasus, where they found sanctuary in Tiflis (Tbilisi) in Georgia, together with other members of the family who had preceded them.

To my father Paulus (Bablo), who died in Beirut in July 1974 after a long sojourn in Syria and Lebanon, via Georgia, Argentina and France, always homesick for his native land. Wandering across oceans in search of work, he had not seen the village of his birth since 1911.

To my mother, Bosha, who found her last resting place in Lyon in November 1975. Happy with her children and grandchildren in Syria and Lebanon, she always carried within herself the sadness of having been separated from her parents, whom she never saw again after 1922.

To the Assyrians-Chaldeans-Syriacs, three parts of the same people, who have been ceaselessly migrating since 1915, the fateful Year of the Sword (*farman, seyfo*), which saw half of this resilient nation annihilated by the murderous madness of Ottoman power, driven by a hideous form of unbridled nationalism and by a tyrannical strain of religious fanaticism.

To Claire, my wife, who has been part of this work from its conception to publication. Her presence can be felt within the pages of this book.

CONTENTS

PREFACE

I am delighted to be able to write this preface for an English-language edition of this book. In 2015, mankind commemorated the centenary of the Armenian and Assyro-Chaldean genocides perpetrated by Ottoman Turkey in 1915. Both of these peoples have known the adversity of fate and the iniquities of history. The echoes of this tragedy still sadly persist.

Known under different names—Assyrians, Chaldeans, Syriacs, Nestorians, Jacobites, Arameans, and sometimes, erroneously, Syrians—called *Aïssors* or *Assoris* by the Armenians, *Suriyani* by the Turks, the Assyro-Chaldeans consider themselves the descendants of the peoples of ancient Mesopotamia, the area between the Tigris and Euphrates whose history reaches back 5,000 years. Living since time immemorial in this scarred land, they have always been known as a nation, a people, and for their Churches. Differences in denomination can be traced back to mainly theological divisions in which several factors were mixed (notably the 431 AD Council of Ephesus and the 451 AD Council of Chalcedon), but these no longer apply, since collaboration and ecumenism based on common principles of faith now prevail.

This people of Aramean culture lived on the periphery of both the Persian and the Ottoman Empires, their ancestral territory in the north-west of present-day Iran and in eastern Anatolia—Hakkari, Bohtan, Tur Abdin, Midyat, Mardin, Diyarbakir, Urfa (Ourhai) and Nusaybin—and in the north of Iraq: Mosul and the Nineveh Governorate. The Anglo-Saxon world knows them best under the name of Assyrians—the term used in this book—because of longstanding historic ties between the Archbishop of Canterbury and the Assyrian Church of the East, a link reinforced by their political relations with Britain under the British Mandate in Iraq and before. The British had also established a relationship with the Syriac Orthodox Church from the nineteenth century. British religious, political and diplomatic support was hence important and persists in this people's memory. As a case in point, the Anglican William A. Wigram (1872–1953), a well-known specialist in the Church of the East, enjoyed considerable esteem, and his work, translated into Arabic, continues to attract interest among Assyro-Chaldean and Syriac intellectual circles, not least his short, evocatively titled *Our Smallest Ally: A Brief Account of the Assyrian Nation in the Great War*.

Elsewhere, the material concerning the Assyrian massacres in the official "Blue Book" published by the British government in 1916, *The Treatment of Armenians in the Ottoman Empire, 1915–16*, edited by the MP, historian and statesman Viscount James Bryce (1838–1922) with the assistance of the young historian Arnold Joseph Toynbee (1889–1975), remains a seminal work of reference. In his preface to the English translation of Father Joseph Naayem's book (*Shall this Nation Die?*) Lord Bryce wrote in July 1920: "It was the sufferings of the Armenians that chiefly drew the attention of Britain and America because they were the most numerous among the ecclesiastical bodies, and the slaughter was, therefore, on a larger scale. But the minor communities, such as the Nestorian and Assyro-Chaldean churches, were equally the victims of the plan for exterminating Christianity, root and branch..."

The massacres took place over a large area from January 1915 to July 1918, in eastern Anatolia, northern Persia, the province of Mosul and elsewhere, almost in the same places and in the same way as those inflicted on the Armenians, and according to a similar plan that aimed to homogenize the Ottoman Empire and Turkify the country by eradicating all non-Turkish and non-Muslim groups.

The physical genocide and the seizure of land and property were accompanied by grievous attacks on the Assyro-Chaldean-Syriac cultural patrimony, as is now happening in Iraq and Syria. Historic monuments were destroyed and left in ruins, churches were profaned and schools destroyed. Libraries containing rare books and valuable manuscripts were vandalized and robbed, such as those of the Chaldean Diocese of Siirt or the Assyrian patriarchal seat at Kotchanes, a little village in Hakkari since abandoned, or of the Syriac monasteries of Tur Abdin. In the *vilayet* (province) of Diyarbakir (Amid) alone, more than 156 Syriac churches and monasteries were ruined. Through such sinister methods, an attempt was made to destroy the cultural heritage of a people.

After 1915, a fresh tragedy occurred: the fearful exodus from Persia towards Iraq in July 1918, observed by British military and political representatives and mentioned in a League of Nations report of 1935, which concluded: "In the end, after having lost 20,000 among them, the survivors reached Hamedan and made contact with the British troops." Further disaster lay in the flight from Urfa and the villages of Tur Abdin in the direction of Syria, towards

Aleppo and Djezireh (Hassakeh, Qamishli, Amuda, etc.) in the 1920s.

Since then, the people's history has been punctuated by sufferings and privations, as in Iraq in 1933. Fifteen years after arriving in Iraq in 1918 to escape Ottoman persecution, the Assyrians were again subjected to mass killings widely reported by the international, and especially the British, press. This tragedy unfolded in the village of Simele and in other places in northern Iraq in August 1933. From there, survivors fled to Syria, their second place of refuge.

Now once more under threat—this time from the so-called Islamic State (Daesh)—the children of these refugees live in the north-east of Syria on both sides of the River Khabur, in thirty-five villages between the towns of Hassakeh and Ras al-Ayn, like their Syriac and Chaldean compatriots at Hassakeh and Qamishli. Again under attack since 2014, many have had no choice but to take the road into exile, like those from Mosul and the valley of Nineveh, driven out by the same Islamist, jihadist and Takfiri organization. In June 2015, the Assyrian families of the Khabur and Hassakeh were again scattered.

Yet today, despite such developments, the descendants of those who survived the 1915 genocide are speaking out, asking questions and seeking answers from the political world and international organizations. Many monuments have been erected around the world—from Armenia to Australia—to commemorate the victims. Parliaments are now beginning to recognize the atrocities for what they were, a genocide, and in 2014 the Armenian parliament unanimously voted to condemn the massacres perpetrated by the Ottoman Empire against the Assyrians and Pontic Greeks. On 9 April 2015, the Dutch parliament voted by a large majority to recognize both the Armenian and the Assyrian genocides. Two weeks later, the president of Germany, Joachim Gauck, spoke in Berlin on the fate of the Armenians and Arameans: "Indiscriminately, men and women, children and old men were deported, sent on death marches, exposed to the desert without any protection and without any food, burned alive, hounded, beaten and shot to death."

Other countries such as France have entered the debate, with many different initiatives under way. More broadly, the movement towards recognizing the genocide has assumed global proportions and has thus become the central element of Assyro-Chaldean-Syriac demands for justice. Through the centenary of 2015, publications and media interest have burgeoned; conferences and debates have taken place from Lebanon to Armenia, in Belgium, Switzerland, Milan, Rome, Berlin, Lyon and Paris.

In this context, some words of hope reached us on Sunday 12 April 2015, when Pope Francis, in his speech on the Armenian genocide,[1] referred directly to the Assyro-Chaldean-Syriac experience: "In the past century our human family has lived through three massive and unprecedented tragedies. The first, which is widely considered 'the first genocide of the twentieth century' (John Paul II and Karekin II, Common Declaration, Etchmiadzin, 27 September 2001), struck your own Armenian people, the first Christian nation, as well as Catholic and Orthodox Syrians, Assyrians, Chaldeans and Greeks. Bishops and priests, religious women and men, the elderly and even defenceless children and the infirm were murdered."

On Saturday 29 August 2015, Mgr Flavianus Michael Malke, Syriac Catholic Bishop of Cizre (Jezireh), who was murdered on 29 August 1915 *in odium fidei*, was beatified at the Patriarchal Convent of Our Lady of Deliverance in Harissa (Lebanon) by Patriarch Ignatius Youseff III Younan, following Pope Francis' decree of 8 August, officially recognizing him as a "blessed martyr".

On 2 June 2016, a major development took place in the German Bundestag. A resolution was adopted, almost unanimously, recognizing the genocide (Völkermord) of Armenians and other Christian minorities subject to deportations and massacres perpetrated by the Ottoman Empire in 1915–16. This resolution was entitled Erinnerung und Gedenken an den Völkermord an den Armeniern und anderen christlichen Minderheiten in den Jahren 1915 und 1916, which translates to "Remembrance and commemoration of the genocide of Armenian and other Christian minorities in the years 1915 and 1916". The text of the resolution, though primarily concerned with the Armenians, also explicitly names the Arameans, Assyrians and Chaldeans as equal victims of the genocide.

This resolution had been foreshadowed in a speech given in Berlin on 23 April 2015 by the German president, Joachim Gauck, who used the term Völkermord (genocide) during a religious ceremony marking the centenary of the Armenian massacre; he also mentioned the Assyrian and Aramean genocide, and that of the Pontic Greeks.

Will this ordeal ever end?

Joseph Yacoub
Lyon, June 2016

AUTHOR'S NOTE

The transcription of place names is problematic, as toponymy has varied according to historic periods and political nomination (Ottoman, Persian, Kurdish, Arab) as well as differing between English and French usage. Turkey has also conducted a policy of Turkification, changing many names of villages and towns. The Assyrian people, moreover, have their own toponymy in the Aramaic language. Faced with a plethora of competing place names and spellings, we can only aim for consistency.

Map 1: Anatolia c.1915

Map 2: Eastern Anatolia

INTRODUCTION

A FORGOTTEN GENOCIDE?

"The crime was the crime of the Ottoman nation and of the Stamboul Caliphate, and the criminals are still rejoicing in the success and impunity of their crime."

Rev. William A. Wigram and Sir Edgar T. A. Wigram,
The Cradle of Mankind: Life in Eastern Kurdistan, *1922*

"The Armenians are not the only unfortunates; the Syrians (Assyrians) also have been decimated."

William Walker Rockwell, "Current History", The New York Times, *November 1916*

There are peoples who in the past have met a tragic fate, but who have been brought back to life by contemporary history. This is not yet the case with the Assyro-Chaldean-Syriac people, who have on many occasions endured the vicissitudes of history.

The year 2015 marked the centenary of the Armenian and Assyrian genocides under the Ottoman Empire. In 1915 the Assyrians faced the ordeal of the desert; not that of contemplation and meditation in the tradition of their spiritual Fathers, but a forced desert: that of privation and death.[1] In the broadest sense, the twentieth century will remain for this people, and for its civil, cultural and religious institutions, the century of great tragedy; the extent of the desolation has been vast.

1

Nation, people and churches

History attests to the existence of an Assyro-Chaldean-Syriac nation and people. Living from time immemorial in that wounded land of historic Mesopotamia, they are always depicted in terms of a nation, a people, and of churches. This people existed on the periphery of the Ottoman and Persian Empires, on its ancestral territory to the north-west of present-day Iran, in eastern Anatolia—Hakkari, Tur Abdin, Mardin—and in northern Mesopotamia, the present-day north of Iraq (Mosul, etc.).

Known by different names—Assyrians, Chaldeans, Syriacs, Nestorians, Jacobites, Arameans[2]—the Assyrians, called *Aïssors* or *Assoris* by the Armenians and *Suriyani* by the Turks, are the descendants of the Assyrian, Babylonian, Chaldean and Aramean peoples of ancient Mesopotamia, a land situated between the Tigris and Euphrates rivers whose history dates back more than 5,000 years.

One of the major cradles of human civilization, Mesopotamia contributed significantly during its historical development to the advancement and progress of knowledge and practice in the fields of religion, philosophy, science and politics as well as government. It is notably credited with the Code of Hammurabi (approximately 1,750 BC), a collection of 282 legal articles which represents the first ever legislation concerning social organization. Its traces can still be seen today in the Louvre in Paris, in London's British Museum and in Berlin's Pergamon Museum.

Since the fall of Nineveh, Babylon and the Aramean kingdoms some 2,500 years ago, the Assyrians have been deprived of a state to protect them from age-old persecutions, which often took dramatic form from the Persian Sassanid period onwards. The Eastern Orthodox Church and the Syriac Orthodox Church were thus subjected to massacres and humiliations inflicted not only by the Persians, but also by the Romans, the Byzantines, the Mongols, the Turks and many other conquerors. Indeed, authors who have written about the 1915 massacres have often drawn parallels with the sufferings endured by the same community in previous centuries. Like their Armenian brothers, the Assyrians have become familiar with the adversity of fate and the iniquities of history.

After the loss of their state and the advent of Christianity, the Church was the institution that became the people's protector and the cement that maintained their cohesion. Speaking Aramaic (also known as Syriac), these Christians mostly belonged to one of two Churches. One was the "Jacobite" Syriac Orthodox Church of Antioch and all the East. The other was the Ancient Church of the East; its remnants, the "Nestorians", are also called Assyrians, Syriacs or Arameans, while those former members now in union with the Catholic Church are known as Chaldeans. Both Churches once flourished in Mesopotamia and much of Asia, stretching as far as India and China.

There are some theological and doctrinal differences between the Church of the East and the Syriac Orthodox Church, which have led in the past to Christological controversies. To understand them, we must refer to the Councils of Ephesus (431) and Chalcedon (451), where the Christian dogma was defined and the code of the Christian creed adopted.

The Church of the East has wrongly been called the Nestorian Church. This conflates the Church's doctrine with the Dyophysite doctrine of Patriarch Nestorius of Constantinople (381–451), who identified two separate persons in the Christ (Divine and Human); regarding the

Virgin Mary, Nestorianism used the term *Christotokos* (Mother of Christ), rather than the Ephesus Council's term, *Theotokos* (Mother of God).

Meanwhile, the Syriac Orthodox Church has erroneously been referred to as Monophysite (Christ as solely divine in nature), because it rejected the Chalcedon Council's teaching on the person of Christ (neither separation nor confusion of the Divine and Human natures of Christ), and it called the Virgin *Theotokos*. In fact, the question is more complex, for cultural and political reasons. Both Churches trace their origins to early (first century) Christianity, prior to Ephesus and Chalcedon, and the two Churches reject the Dyophysite/Monophysite labels. Though adherents of the Church of the East feel a certain affinity for the Nestorian thesis, they are not truly Nestorians, and are correctly known as non-Ephesians. Nevertheless, henceforth this book will refer to this religious group as "Nestorians", as the easiest and most unambiguous shorthand.

The two Churches' respective liturgies are distinct from one another, and date back to the first centuries of Christendom. Both Churches pray in Aramaic, which is divided into two branches, Western and Eastern, still spoken both in the Middle East and by the diaspora.

As for links with the Armenians, the Assyro-Chaldean Churches maintain essentially good relationships with the Armenian Apostolic Church. Due to doctrinal positions, the Armenian Church is more closely tied to the Syrian Orthodox Church than to the Church of the East.

The two Churches have differing dogmas and rituals, but ethnically they belong to the same Mesopotamian background. Their Christianity is autochthonous and apostolic; known for their schools and places of learning (Edessa, Nusaybin, etc.), their translations from Greek and their monasteries, these Christians, endowed with their own liturgy, produced a rich literature in many fields of thought both religious and profane.[3]

In the twelfth century, the "Nestorian" Church of the East reached from the eastern Mediterranean as far as Peking and claimed some sixty million faithful.[4] The Church of the East and the Syriac Orthodox Church still have followers in India today.

From the sixteenth century, the two mother Churches— the Church of the East and the Syriac Orthodox Church— underwent internal schisms that led to the creation of separate Churches united with Rome. This was the case in 1522 of the "Nestorian" Church, which witnessed the advent of the Chaldean Catholic Church of Babylon; in 1783 it was the turn of the Syriac Orthodox Church to be rivalled by the Syriac Catholic Church. Moreover, due to the influence of American, British and Russian missionaries, there have also, since the nineteenth century, been Protestants, those close to the Anglican Church and Orthodox worshippers among the Assyrian people.

Despite these differences, it is important to point out that the documentation on the massacres clearly deals with this community as a *distinct* ethnic and religious entity. It exhibits territorial, national, linguistic, cultural and religious characteristics that fit the criteria of a nation.

Despite the oppression and persecutions, this autochthonous nation left a strong imprint on its land, not least through place names and cultural, architectural and religious traces. The land is littered with Aramean-influenced churches. Writing of the district of Hakkari, in the extreme south-east of modern-day Turkey, holy place of Mesopotamian Christianity, the Dominican intellectual Jean-Maurice Fiey noted of Mosul in 1964:

> We found the dioceses of Hakkari well established by the beginning of the fifth century: the shrines with the legends of their saints can be traced back to Christianity's entry into the apostolic era and its definitive spread in the fourth to the fifth centuries thanks to a host of monks. This seems to suggest clearly that the "Assyrian" people already lived in large numbers in these mountains at the beginning of our era.[5]

This sense of a people with deep and long-lived roots was strongly felt at the beginning of the twentieth century and was expressed in the titles of books published on the genocide. For instance, even the subtitle of Assyrian professor Abraham Yohannan's book, *The Death of a Nation* (New York, 1916), is significant: *The Ever-Persecuted Assyrians or Nestorian Christians*. Joel Warda entitled his work *The Flickering Light of Asia*, subtitled *Or the Assyrian Nation or Church*. Father Joseph Naayem of Urfa chose as the title of his book on the 1915 massacres the names of the two victim peoples: *Les Assyro-Chaldéens et les Arméniens*. But in the English-language version, entitled *Shall This Nation Die?*, he refers only to his own community, namely the Assyro-Chaldean (Assyrian) nation. Moreover, reports and published works often interchange notions of religious and national identity, using terms such as "Christian Assyrians".

On the eve of the massacre

In the first decade of the twentieth century the Assyrians were living largely in tribal groups, in their ancestral homeland on the periphery of the Ottoman and Persian

Empires—in north-west Persia (Persian Azerbaijan), in eastern Anatolia (Hakkari, Van, Bohtan, Tur Abdin, Diyarbakir, Mardin, Bitlis and Siirt) and in present-day Iraq (Mosul, the plain of Nineveh and Kirkuk). In Persia, a population estimated at 100,000 (including those settled in Russia and the Caucasus) inhabited more than 180 villages, mainly in the rich and fertile province of Urmia—described as "Persia's promised land" by the Orientalist Eugène Boré—around the salt lake of the same name, from Salmas (Diliman) and Khoy to Senah and Tabriz. The extensive Salmas plain, surrounded by mountains, with its plentiful water and orchards, contained thirteen villages including Khosrova, Pataver, Ula, Chahara, Zilajouk, Satoura, Karilann and Haftvan, the last being mostly Armenian. To the south-east of Salmas, the beautiful village of Khosrova was exclusively Assyrian, with 1,400 inhabitants in 1844 and 2,500 in 1885. The mountains encircling the plateau of Urmia were principally home to Kurds, the Assyrians' nearest neighbours, with whom they maintained a complex and shifting relationship.

Those living within the Ottoman Empire were most numerous in the provinces of Mosul, Bitlis, Siirt, Diyarbakir, Mardin, Shirnak, Van and Tur Abdin. Here, the Syriacs alone accounted for more than 250,000 people. In the Bhotan district they were concentrated in several villages around the town of Jezireh. Forming an enclave within three provinces (Bitlis to the north, Diyarbakir to the east and Hakkari to the west), Bohtan contained some 100,000 Assyro-Chaldeans. The Van *vilayet* (Ottoman administrative province) stretched south from the city of Van to Amadiya, today in the Kurdish region of Iraq. The *sanjak* (department) of Van was home to 4,000 Assyrians, spread between the town and sixteen surrounding villages.

In Hakkari, the second *sanjak* of the Van *vilayet*, the 100,000 Assyrians were strongly concentrated in most of the eleven *kazas* (districts), representing more than a third of the population. This mountainous region had been Assyrian territory long before the arrival of the Kurds and Turks. Kotchanes, a small town near Djulamerk entirely populated by Assyrians (about 1,000 individuals), was the residence of the patriarch Mar Shimun. In a district that spread geographically from Barwari Bala in the south (the border with Iraq) to Gavar in the north (the Persian frontier), the Turkish authorities paid little attention to Hakkari's Assyrian population, who lived in a state of self-sufficient autarchy, deprived of schools and political representation. In the *kazas* of Djulamerk and Gavar, the American Protestant Mission in Urmia had attempted without success to establish several small schools among the Nestorian Assyrians.[6] Education had been declared free under Article 10 of the Ottoman reform decree promulgated on 18 February 1856, the Hatt-i Humayun, and under Article 15 of the December 1876 Constitution, which recognized that all subjects of the Empire were to be defined as Ottomans without distinction, irrespective of the religion they professed (Article 8).

Organized both into independent tribes (*ashiret*, led by *maliks*) subdivided into clans, and dependent tribes or serf clans (*rayet*, mainly subjects of Kurdish *aghas*, or chiefs), the Assyrians of Hakkari had lived for centuries in a compact community. In geo-anthropological terms, they formed a de facto *millet* (autonomous community) with communitarian, religious and civil features, but no judicial status. They enjoyed considerable administrative and territorial independence, but under trust and within limits.

The Kurds, their neighbours, lived under feudal structures governed by tribal chieftains and enjoyed a large degree of autonomy within the Ottoman Empire. Their communities were often present on the land of Assyrian tribes and their villages in close proximity. Foreign visitors wrote of endemic brigandage and the Russian observer Basil Nikitin referred to wild tribes, difficult to contact and understand. Their motives varied and fluctuated according to region, the tribes involved and rivalries. There were periods of peaceful co-existence, but generally hostility and insecurity prevailed, the Christians believing themselves surrounded by enemies. According to Michel Chevalier:

> Insecurity was an essential given in the daily existence of the mountain-dwelling Assyrians ... In reality, the whole life of the *ashiret* and *raya*, isolated within the Kurdish masses or even mixed up with them, was dominated by the problem of their relations with the Kurds ... It is certain that violence was, from the Middle Ages, an integral part of life in Hakkari and neighbouring regions.[7]

Without forming a homogenous group, the Kurds were accomplices in the massacres, and participated in looting for ideological reasons (the Christians were infidels) as well as for personal gain. Used as irregular soldiers by the Turks, there were nonetheless Kurds who, hostile to the Ottoman authorities, chose to defend Christian communities.

The Assyrians evidently formed an autochthonous people, whose territory was distinguished by Christian place names. According to Surma d'Bait Mar Shimun (1883–1975), an influential personality, sister of the patriarch Mar Benyamin Shimun and observer of life in Hakkari, the Assyrians never served in the Ottoman military and the Turks never imposed their customs on them, nor attempted to conduct censuses to measure the size of their population. The taxes that they were obliged to pay to the Ottoman authorities once every three years were, she says, calculated by the Assyrians themselves and sent with a letter from the patriarch. According to Surma Khanum (Lady Surma), a Turk had never entered the Assyrian territory, which she described as "independent".[8] The patriarch was recognized as a prince who governed his people free from Ottoman law, as an interlocutor with the Ottoman authorities and as an internal intermediary in the event of disputes within his community.

This general situation was corroborated by the British Anglican missionary William Henry Browne, who lived in Hakkari during this period.[9] Even so, there were episodes of violent conflict with the Turks between 1895 and 1897 and the carnage perpetrated by the Kurdish Emir of Bohtan Badr Khan in 1843 was alive in the collective memory. In the wake of this outrage, Britain had officially pressed the Ottoman authorities to take steps to protect the Assyrian community.

Conditions worsened in 1878 after the Russo-Turkish War. Embittered by his defeat at the hands of the Russians and by subsequent setbacks, Sultan Hamid II (1876–1909) attempted to impose direct control and absolute centralization on the Ottoman provinces. This included the Hakkari *vilayet*, integrated into the newly created province of Van, with the governor's headquarters established in Djulamerk. A year after its promulgation by Grand Vizir Midhat Pasha, Hamid suspended the 1876 Ottoman Constitution. Thereafter Hakkari experienced a period of assassinations, raids, famines, persecution and pillage.

This repressive policy was accompanied by a desire to weaken the temporal power of the Nestorian patriarch by breaking his independence. In 1870, the governor of Van invited all the tribal chieftains (*maliks*) and other prominent Nestorians, with their patriarch (Mar Rouel Shimun), to a meeting, in which he suggested that the double oocular and ecclesiastical load was too heavy for one man. He then proposed that secular power should be transferred to the father of the patriarch, Benyamin, supported by a gendarmerie composed of elements from the independent tribes, paid by the Turks and working on advice issued by the jurisdiction of the *vali* (governor). The patriarch would still be in charge of ecclesiastical matters. Sensing a trap designed to curtail their autonomy, the Nestorians unanimously rejected the proposal, declaring that they wished to live and die under the leadership of their patriarch and to keep their own laws, independent of Turkish control.[10] There was to be no improvement in relations under the Young Turks (1908–18), who sought to Turkify the region despite promises to the contrary, and when Turkey entered the war against Russia in 1914 in a bid to win back territory lost in 1878, there was to be, said Surma Khanum, no law and order in Hakkari.[11]

In a context of growing hostility, the *rayet* Assyrians were particularly vulnerable, since, unlike their *ashiret* counterparts, they were effectively dispossessed by their submission to the Kurdish *aghas* or to the *mamur* (a representative of the Ottoman government). According to Surma Khanum, there were countless acts of oppression committed against *rayet* Assyrians. Elsewhere, travellers and observers agreed that the Sublime Porte's policy consisted of impoverishing Christians and encouraging their extermination by the Kurds, on condition that this was done discreetly and without attracting European attention. This was suggested by William H. Browne in 1892; his findings, he said, were supported by both Assyrians and Kurds. He conceded, however: "This, probably, is the intention of certain officials; but it would be wrong to attribute such a policy to the Sultan and his government, or to many other officials who have shown indulgence, kindness and patience in dealing with the poor people."[12]

In the nineteenth century, many travellers such as the American missionary Asahel Grant (1839) and the British geologist William Francis Ainsworth (1841) visited these regions, describing the inhabitants' customs and daily lives. In *The Nestorians*, Grant observed the women of Hakkari: "Their dress is neat and becoming; they braid their hair, and wear but few ornaments. Their form is graceful, their expression agreeable, and their complexion (except that it is sometimes affected by more exposure to the sun and the smoke of their dwellings) as fair as that of most Europeans."[13] Most concluded, however, that those living in the mountains and remote villages were isolated, poor and uneducated. Before the arrival of missionaries schools were more or less non-existent and education was limited to members of the clergy and monks.

Social life was patriarchal. The economic structure was agricultural and pastoral, based on self-sufficiency.[14] Food was produced for family consumption, and there was little commerce in the countryside. Those Assyrians living in towns were more involved in trading and small-scale industry and were sometimes employed in local administration as in Diyarbakir, Mardin or Mosul. Their civil status varied, but was always precarious, and always ultimately dependent on the Muslim authorities, which explains why the Church was so central to their lives and identity. Some Assyrians studied in Turkish schools and colleges but were usually banned from government posts. The organization of communitarian affairs was very similar in Persia, Hakkari, Tur Abdin and Mosul, the main differences between the three communities (Assyrian, Chaldean and Syriac) being primarily religious. Their relations with neighbouring Turks, Persians and Kurds were unstable and unpredictable, changing according to circumstance and ranging from peace and truce to tension, conflict and killings.

At the outset of the First World War, the three confessions together numbered around 600,000 people.

The genocide of 1915

The Assyrians were victims of a physical, cultural, religious and territorial genocide of a geopolitical nature that was a prelude to their exile, their uprooting and the sufferings that continue to tear the community apart. The events of 1915 utterly shattered their lives and destroyed their society. Social and religious structures were ruined and completely disintegrated.

These massacres took place over a very wide area—in eastern Anatolia, in Persia and in the province of Mosul—from January 1915 to July 1918, under the same conditions and almost in the same places as those inflicted on the Armenians and according to a similar plan which aimed, according to fixed objectives, to homogenize the Empire, to Turkify the country and to eradicate any ethnically non-Turkish or religiously non-Muslim groups.

This suicidal policy of ethnic cleansing was stirred up by pan-Islamism and religious fanaticism. Christians were considered infidels (*kafir*). The call to Jihad, decreed on 29 November 1914 and instigated and orchestrated for political ends, was part of the plan. Those in power were blinded by a shrill and exclusive nationalism of conquest (pan-Turkism) and by an authoritarian and hyper-centralized state, hostile to local autonomy and reform and suspicious of any expression of aspiration to freedom on the part of the nationalities and religions that then composed Turkey.

The massacres of 1915 did, moreover, have Ottoman antecedents: principally in 1894–96 under the aegis of Sultan Abdul Hamid II, and in Adana in 1909, under the leadership of the Young Turks. In 1895, Habib Jarwé, an Assyrian from Mardin, a town in eastern Anatolia, had kept a daily diary in Arabic on the *Nakabate*[15] (calamities) committed by the Turks and Kurds in the towns of Diyarbakir, Saadiya, Qarabach, Qaterbel, Urfa, Tal Arman, Gulié, Benebil, Kalaat-Mara, Deir Zafaran, Mansuriye, Nuysabin, Tur Abdin, Sbirino, Veran Shehir, Derik, Mardin, Kharput, Sivas, Sason and the surrounding villages.[16] The fate of Habib Jarwé was tragic and symptomatic of that allotted to the Assyrian people. While he escaped the massacres of 1895, he was arrested on 4 June 1915 together with other well-known citizens of Mardin. Six days later, he was led outside the town and executed along with other prisoners.

The 1915 massacres took place in historic Mesopotamia on a huge scale and happened in various phases, starting with Urmia-Salmas in north-western Persia, passing through Hakkari in Van province, and spreading to Diyarbakir province, to the towns of Mardin, Bitlis, Siirt, Midyat, to the area of Tur Abdin, from Bohtan to the town of Jezireh and to many other places, all situated in eastern Anatolia, in the south-east of today's Turkey.

The Assyrian tragedy began in September–October 1914, just before the outbreak of war. At that time, Turkish and Kurdish troops made an incursion into the plain of Urmia, a frontier region situated in Persia, and devastated several villages, murdering their inhabitants. These were the early warning signs of the massacres that were to follow some months later.

Many distressing events and scenes of horror fill this history, during which hundreds of thousands of people were massacred or died of thirst, hunger, poverty, exhaustion or illness on the road to exile or deportation.[17] The objective was to drive them out of geographical zones considered too politically sensitive by Turkish nationalists and, by weakening and deporting them, to get rid of them, under the bogus pretext that these non-Turks and non-Muslims were disloyal and infidels.

The year 1915, from January to November, was dreadful. Massacres took place on several fronts. On the initiative of the Turks and Kurds, under the Turkish *vali* of Van, Djevdet Pasha, brother-in-law of Enver Pasha and commander-in-chief on the Persian border, abuses began to occur again at the beginning of January in non-Turkish territory within the frontier region of Urmia-Salmas in Persia, where dozens of villages were devastated: Goetapa, Ada, Gulpashan, Sopurghan, Khosrava, Salmas, Haftvan, etc.

These attacks extended steadily to Turkish Hakkari, before the flames spread to several more Turkish *vilayets*: Van; Diyarbakir (Amid in Aramaic), notably the towns of Mardin, Jezireh (Bet-Zabdé in Aramaic), and the region of Tur Abdin (mountain of believers); Kharput, with the town of Malatia; Bitlis with the town of Siirt, the town of Urfa (Ourhai in Aramaic); and Aleppo, to give just a few instances. These crimes, writes Joseph Naayem, "dishonour the history of humanity". They were committed, alleges Isaac Armalet, by "enemies of humanity". These two authors came close in their thinking, before their time, to the notion of "crimes against humanity", a concept developed much later.

Contemporary documentation

This genocide is not an unknown field of geographical and cultural research, far less a new area of investigation. With regard to these events and places, we possess a rich array of documentation covering all the territories where the drama unfolded—a range of testimony which springs from authoritative sources, from individuals known for their moral integrity and whose authenticity is unquestioned, and in a wide variety of languages. From January 1915 documents appeared in French, Russian, English, German, Italian, Arabic, Danish and Armenian, and in Aramaic (eastern and western), where the Armenians and Assyrians are grouped and discussed together.

The precision and factual accuracy of these many documents irrefutably confirm the nature of the tragedy. The information, provided by impartial witnesses from different backgrounds and nationalities, historically verifiable, all intersects and overlaps to condemn the Turkish government and the regional and local authorities. All of it shows that these massacres were "combined and concerted" actions on the part of the Ottoman authorities and that it was in no sense a question of acts committed by isolated or uncontrolled elements.

To cite a few examples: the British "Blue Book", *The Treatment of Armenians in the Ottoman Empire* (1916) is a major contribution, bringing together the testimony of eminent and absolutely reliable witnesses and dealing in its original English-language version with the massacres of the Assyrians.

Miss Mary Schauffler Platt (1868–1954), the American author of several books, published at the end of 1915 the daily diary of an anonymous female Presbyterian missionary based in Urmia: *The War Journal of a Missionary in Persia*.[18] The diary tells of the atrocities committed and of the suffering endured by the Christian population between January and June 1915.[19]

Father Joseph Naayem, eye-witness to the massacres, who was imprisoned and narrowly escaped being killed, wrote a work in French in 1920 whose title is highly evocative: *Les Assyro-Chaldéens et les Arméniens massacrés par les Turcs*. This book essentially brings together the accounts and testimonies of victims who miraculously escaped their tragic fate, from Urfa, Siirt, Diyarbakir, Lidja (or Lidje), Kharput, Erzurum and Trebizond.[20]

To these individuals can be added many more. The French-speaking jurist André Mandelstam, in his book entitled *Le Sort de l'Empire ottoman* ("The Fate of the Ottoman Empire"), evokes the small Nestorian community, who "suffered at the hands of the Young Turks a martyrdom approaching that of the Armenians". The French priest Eugène Griselle (1861–1923) titled his work on the massacres *Syriens et Chaldéens: leurs martyres, leurs espérances, 1914–1917*.

Documentation in Arabic is equally important. Isaac Armalet, a priest from Mardin, specialist in the Syriac manuscripts of Deir Charfe (Mont-Liban) and another eye-witness to the tragedy, produced a work entitled *Al-Qousara fi Nakabat Annasara* ("The Calamities of the Christians"). This is a vital and inexhaustible source of testimonies and information on the massacres of 1915, and indeed 1895.

As regards Aramaic, it is essential to bear in mind that a literature exists in eastern and western Aramaic, literary and oral, in its different written forms (*soureth* and *serto*), which is little known and inadequately drawn upon but highly revealing. Most importantly, this documentation in Aramaic defines the events of 1915 as *farman* (massacre), *qtlé* (killings), *rdoupié* (persecutions), *tloumié* (oppression) and as *gounhé mariré* (terrible and cruel happenings). The year 1915 is also fittingly called the Year of the Sword (*seyfo*).

Ethnocide and extermination

During the 1915 massacres more than 250,000 Assyrians of all different religious persuasions—a figure representing more than half of the entire Assyro-Chaldean-Syriac community—perished on the whole of the Turco-Persian territory at the hands of Turks, Kurdish irregulars and other ethnic groups used to this end. Death stalked hundreds of villages, leaving a huge number of orphans, captured children, abandoned individuals, women and girls kidnapped and sold, widows, refugees, those deported and those forcibly converted to Islam.

The physical genocide and plundering of land and property was accompanied by pitiless attacks on cultural heritage. Historic monuments were destroyed and left abandoned, churches desecrated and schools demolished. Libraries containing rare books and intricate manuscripts were pillaged and destroyed, for instance in the Chaldean diocese of Siirt, the Assyrian patriarchal seat at Kotchanes—a small village in Hakkari since abandoned—and at the Syriac monasteries of Tur Abdin. Hakkari was a land filled with shrines dating back to the first centuries AD. The patriarchal church of Mar Shalita has fallen into ruins. Others once contained ex-votos and Chinese vases brought back by Nestorian missionaries from China. The Assyrians thus found themselves dispossessed of a great many of their sites of memory and culture. In all, more than 250 churches and convents were ruined.

In the French daily newspaper *Le Gaulois* of 16 January 1916, Father Jean-Baptiste Chabot, a member of the Académie des Inscriptions et Belles-Lettres, and a scholar and specialist in Aramaic literature, informed the Academy that, according to the British Foreign Office, Turks had set fire to the episcopal residence in the town of Siirt, where an important library housed nearly 200 Aramaic and Arabic manuscripts. The Turks had also seized the Chaldean bishop, the patriotic Mgr Addai Scher (1867–1915), who was to be murdered on 17 June 1915. They took with him a manuscript containing the third volume of his precious Arabic language *History of Chaldea and Assyria*, which covered a period up to the beginning of the nineteenth century.

With this deadly policy, an attempt was made to destroy the cultural heritage of a people and to dispossess it of its identity. This is what ethnologists term ethnocide.[21]

This generalized policy of genocide, conducted under orders, was premeditated and planned at a high level and passed down to local networks. "There was an Ottoman plan to exterminate Turkey's Christians," we read in a Syriac document of 1920. The massacres were systematic. Generally speaking, first came the arrests and imprisonment of well-known citizens, bishops, priests and monks in order to eradicate the community's leaders. The men would then be taken out of the town to be executed. There then followed searches in houses and shops, ransacking and pillaging in homes and in churches and convents—of which there were many in this area—or the extortion of property and money. *Falaka* (beatings administered on the soles of the feet) were commonly carried out. The population was moved out towards unknown destinations and the death convoys set off towards Deir ez-Zor, Aleppo and Ras al-Ayn in Syria or Sinjar and Mosul in Iraq, ending the lives of large numbers of the deported. Many women and children were captured. The former were violated on the road, were sold and sometimes, it is insisted, resold. Among the population were also victims of forced conversion to Islam, with many witnesses attesting to this fact.

Gorek de Kerboran, an Assyrian intellectual from the village of Kerboran in Syriac Tur Abdin, painted a distressing picture in a 1923 lecture at the Institut Catholique de Paris:

> In each province, in each district, the Turkish authorities bring together all the Assyro-Chaldeans. They take all the men aged 13 to 55 or 60, send them into the interior, allegedly to turn them into soldiers, and they are never heard of again. Those who are left are split into two groups. Girls and young women are sold at market or locked up in harems. That leaves only small children, older women and old men. They are given 24 hours to pack some belongings and gather together essentials; then they are directed towards a departure port. Here the Turkish police become involved; they remove gold, silver, jewels, carpets, valuables of all sorts, and it is in this lamentable state that the unfortunate exiles head towards a new destiny![22]

INTRODUCTION

Joseph Naayem, in a lecture given in Paris at the offices of the Comité de l'Asie Française on 30 May 1919, reported:

> There, like everywhere, the Turkey of the Committee of Union and Progress wanted to remove through violence those outsider elements that it could not assimilate. It started with the disarming of the Assyro-Chaldean soldiers who were at the front. They were turned into special labour battalions, put to work on the roads and in the trenches. Many of these men brought behind lines were "eliminated". The local authorities took charge of disarming the civilian population. A certain number of weapons were demanded and the inhabitants of villages who could not supply them were tortured, often in a dreadful way.[23]

Oblivion and its causes

How can this history have been all but forgotten? Why, since it runs parallel to the well-known Armenian genocide, has the Assyrian genocide faded from view?

With this in mind, it is firstly important to correct a certain number of misconceptions that persist regarding the lack of interest shown in the Assyrian tragedy, compared to that surrounding the Armenian genocide and sufferings. Not only is there no shortage of documentation, but the sources and testimonies concerning these events are numerous. Between 1915 and 1925 the attention paid to the Assyrian question was considerable and on a global scale. In my view, the relative invisibility of the Assyrian genocide can be attributed to several factors.

In contrast with the Armenians, the Assyrian people was small in number and suffered from lack of recognition as an independent community. Geographically, the groups

(Assyrian, Chaldean, Syriac) were dispersed and separated from one another, and resided far from urban and political centres. Some lived in inaccessible mountain retreats, and sociologically the population was in its majority rural. Furthermore, abandoned and incessantly forced from one exodus to another, they lacked the strength offered by their own protective and compact national territory, while the Armenians had an independent—albeit ephemeral—state (1918–21) before it was incorporated into the Soviet Union (USSR).

Though the Assyrians had notable leaders and a small urban elite, it is nevertheless true that they lacked both a class of intellectuals and individuals sufficiently educated, influential and experienced to make sense of differing forms of political discourse, as well as articulate spokespeople to argue their case both locally and abroad. This is reflected in a Syriac document dated 1 September 1920, which notes: "Battered and stricken nations like ours do not have enough men to have their voices heard."

To these factors may be added the fact that their tragedy, as we shall see, did not end in 1915. Immediately afterwards and ever since, the persecutions and exile have continued: there is no shortage of similarities between 1915 and 2015.

An international issue

Frédéric Masson (1847–1923), a historian and member of the Académie Française, published an article on the front page of the daily *Le Gaulois* on 25 July 1916 entitled "Ce qui vient de Chaldée" ("Out of Chaldea") in which he observed: "A people small in their ruins yet immense in the glories they claim and remember, the Chaldean people have almost entirely perished without Europe being moved to indignation and without anybody taking any interest."

The Assyro-Chaldean religious and political leadership had expended great time and effort in the capitals of Europe after the end of the First World War, sending between 1918 and 1923 memorandum after memorandum on the sufferings and losses endured during the war and on claims for compensation. Many delegates from Turkey, Persia, the Caucasus, Mesopotamia, Syria and the United States had attended the 1919 Peace Conference in Paris. Others, such as General Agha Petros Ellof and Malik Cambar, were later to come to the conferences at Sèvres and Lausanne (1920–23), and still more during the establishment of the frontier between Iraq and Turkey in 1925. Malik Cambar, concerned about the interests of his people, had sent a letter to the International Court of Justice at The Hague on 25 September 1925, in which he asked bitterly, "Why have all the conferences, which have rendered justice to all oppressed small nations, failed to this day to hear the voice of the millennia-old Assyro-Chaldean people, who have been so unfortunate?"

The very active Chaldean patriarch Emmanuel II Thomas came from Baghdad to Rome in 1920, then visited Paris and London. He had already, at the beginning of 1919, sent a detailed report with illustrations explaining the losses that the Chaldean Church had suffered during the war. In a letter to Benedict XV he wrote:

> For five years I have witnessed with unspeakable bitterness all sorts of misery, the massacres of my children and the ruin of a large part of this Patriarchate and its works. It is my misfortune to have seen during these five terrible years six of my bishops massacred along with more than 50 priests and 50,000 of the faithful, who leave behind them the distressing spectacle of their

ruined homes and a large number of orphans, mostly dispersed among the Kurds or seeking refuge in Mosul, with thousands of refugees reduced, despite my efforts, to the most extreme poverty.

To the same pope, Dr Harry Packard, an American doctor at the Presbyterian mission hospital at Urmia, had sent from Tabriz (Persia) on 29 October 1918 a report detailing the massacres and pillage conducted by Turks and Kurds at Urmia during that year, especially at the Congregation of the Mission (Lazarists).[24] Father Joseph Ghanima, a Chaldean patriarchal vicar, sent a letter from Mosul on 29 August 1919 to the French Consul in Mesopotamia expressing his gratitude for the financial aid that France "was kind enough to offer in support of our poor Chaldeans from the province of Amadiya."

The 12 January 1920 edition of the *La Croix* newspaper announced the arrival in Paris three days earlier of the Chaldean patriarch, who had come from Rome with Mgr Pierre Aziz, the Bishop of Salmas and his two secretaries. In London on 7 March, under the vaults of Westminster Cathedral, the patriarch laid out the Assyro-Chaldean issue: that of a people crushed by poverty. The reaction to his speech was reportedly positive. On 21 March, the Assyro-Chaldean delegates from Turkey, Said D. Namik and Rustem Nedjib, were received in Paris by the President of the Republic, Paul Deschanel. From there they continued their journey to London, where they met the Chaldean patriarch and took part in all the ceremonies organized for him by the British authorities.

Meanwhile, the Syriac Catholic patriarch Ignace Ephrem Rahmani (1848–1929), the author of several works, made representations to the French authorities and at the Peace Conference, as did Mgr Gabriel Tappouni, his vicar gen-

eral. Mgr Mor Ephrem Barsoum, a Syriac Orthodox dig-
nitary mandated by his patriarch Elias III Chaker, arrived
in London in February 1920 after a stay in Paris, made
contact with the Foreign Office and India Office and on
4 February gave an interview to the daily *Morning Post*.[25]
On 8 March he addressed a memorandum to Prime
Minister Lloyd George, in which he explained various
issues that he considered fundamental.

Surma Khanum, a representative of the Nestorians of
Hakkari and from the patriarchal Mar Shimun family, also
came to London, in November 1919, and addressed the
British authorities, including the Foreign Minister Lord
Curzon, on 17 February 1920. Concerned for the future
of her people, she wished to speak at the Paris Peace
Conference. According to the *Times* of 15 March, she had
already met the Armenian patriarch in London.

Father Joseph Naayem, Mgr Jacques Manna, Chaldean
Bishop of Van, and the Chaldean Lazarist Abel Zara, to
name but three, also came to Paris and London to plead
the cause of their people and to seek humanitarian assistance.[26] In London a solidarity committee was formed.
Joseph Naayem spent six months in America, where he
established a support group like that in London, the
Chaldean Relief Committee. Gorek de Kerboran was
equally present and active in France during this period.

Among the political and religious figures contacted
were the following: Stephen Pichon, Lord Curzon, David
Lloyd George, Alexandre Millerand, Raymond Poincaré,
Pope Benedict XV, Cardinal Pietro Gasparri (Secretary of
State at the Vatican), Cardinal Nicolo Marini (Secretary
of the Congregation for the Church of the East), Georges
Clemenceau, US President Woodrow Wilson, Aristide
Briand, the Archbishop of Canterbury Randall Davidson,

Paul Deschanel, Cardinal Léon-Adolphe Amette (Archbishop of Paris), and Mgr Alfred-Henri-Marie Baudrillart (Rector of the Institut Catholique de Paris and member of the Académie Française). Important international jurists and political commentators were also drawn to the cause of the Assyrian people, including the Russians André N. Mandelstam and Basil Nikitin, and the Frenchmen Louis Le Fur and Thomas-Joseph Delos.

On 28 March 1923, *La Croix*, under the heading "The Assyro-Chaldeans", reported on a lecture given by Gorek de Kerboran on 21 February in the lecture theatre of the Institut Catholique de Paris. The newspaper also mentioned another Kerboran lecture on 17 March on the origins of the Assyrian people. The same paper had published on its 14 February front page an article by R. Le Cholleux on the Assyrians entitled "'A nation' oppressed by Islam", which reminded readers that the Greeks and Armenians "are not the only ones to find themselves under the heavy Ottoman yoke", and that the Assyrians were suffering the same fate. He continued: "And on this soil covered with vestiges of a glorious past lie myriad innocents fallen without defence!" As director of the Assyrian Union, Gorek de Kerboran again sent two letters to the League of Nations, on 16 April and 10 August 1925, to denounce "the systematic work of destruction conducted by Turkey in Kurdistan", where local authorities were acting "on the orders of Ankara".

It is thus reasonable to conclude that the Assyrians enjoyed an appreciable amount of international support and that reports of the horrors they faced inspired sympathy among those in possession of the facts. At the same time, humanitarian messages and statements began to emerge from the Vatican, Russia, France, Britain and the

United States, followed by action. Campaigns of solidarity and assistance were started in the Assyrians' favour.

The Russians, through their Red Cross, delivered important aid to the Assyrians by sending clothing, food and medicines. They were the first to publicize the massacres. In the United States, the wartime support committees covered the two communities—Armenian and Assyrian—without distinction, as was the case with the influential American Committee for Armenian and Syrian Relief. On one of their posters was the single word "Starving". The Chaldean Rescue committee was no less important.

In 1925, the Union Catholique d'Etudes Internationales submitted to the League of Nations Council and its international commission of inquiry into the contested Iraqi-Turkish border a deposition from the Assyrian priest Paulus Bédaré, from the Zakho district in northern Iraq; it concerned the perilous situation of Assyrian refugees, driven out of Turkey and deported into this area.

As we can see, in the period between 1915 and 1925 the Assyrian question had become an international issue.

Yet from 1925 onwards, a turbulent period began, preceded by retreats on the diplomatic front. The Treaty of Sèvres, signed on 10 August 1920, had granted the Assyrians guarantees and protection within the framework of an autonomous Kurdistan (Article 62), without specifying the parameters of the territory in question. These measures, however, did not appear in the Treaty of Lausanne, signed on 24 July 1923 by the same powers that had agreed the Treaty of Sèvres. What had happened in the meantime was that the Turkish negotiator had changed political complexion. Mustafa Kemal, known as Atatürk, was in command of the country—and he had rejected the Treaty of Sèvres.

By 1924, there were few Assyrians remaining in Turkey, as those who had escaped the massacres had fled towards Iraq (via Persia) or in the direction of Syria. In 1925, Hakkari was ceded to Turkey and the province of Mosul to Iraq. As for the region of Tur Abdin, it became an integral part of Turkey.

As such, the case of the massacres under the Ottoman Empire was closed—all the more so as, for the sake of pragmatism and political caution, the Assyrian clergy and civil and political institutions were now trying, as best they could, to adapt to the young states created in 1920 (Turkey, Iraq, Syria), reluctant to be too outspoken on the events of 1915. In 1945, they were once again forgotten in the peace that followed the Second World War, despite appeals to the United Nations.

From then on, a cloak of silence covered this community until 1975, which marked a turning-point and the beginning of mass migration towards the countries of the West.

Renewal and memory

Despite this cloak of silence, consciousness of the past has gradually resurfaced and collective memory has not necessarily entirely faded. The diaspora, paradoxically, has been a space in which identity can be reawakened and where memory can be rediscovered.

In 1965, on the fiftieth anniversary of the Armenian genocide, James H. Tashjan was already engaged in recalling the Assyrian tragedy, publishing in Boston a study on the centenary of the massacres in Turkey (1822–1922) of Armenians, Assyrians and other peoples of the region. In his book he spoke of the massacre of the "Nestorians" in the nineteenth century and devoted several pages to the "destruction of the Assyrian nation" in 1915.[27] But it was in the 1980s that the silence surrounding this genocide, long hidden, was broken. After fifty years, a process of renewal and rediscovery announced that the Assyro-Chaldean-Syriac people were ready to return to the stage of history.

Born in 1944 in Hassakeh in Syrian Jezireh, I spent my childhood and youth on the banks of the biblical River Khabur. I knew people who had survived the genocide of 1915 as well as the massacres of 1933 in Iraq, who came from Hakkari, from Urmia-Salmas (my parents), from the Caucasus, from Midyat, from Tur Abdin, from Diyarbakir, from Mardin, from Urfa and from Nuysabin. From the banks of the Khabur to Hassakeh, from Qamishli to Beirut, from Beirut to Lyon, the melodies of the *soureth* and *touroyo* languages still echo pleasingly in my ears.

In France, I gathered together for the first time the oral testimonies of those who had survived the genocide and of their descendants, which were published as an article on 1 September 1986 under the title "Les Réfugiés assyro-chaldéens de Turqie" ("The Assyro-Chaldean Refugees from Turkey").[28] Since then I have continued to collect testimonies in Europe, the United States and Australia.

Today a revival of identity, memory and culture, within the perspective of a recognition of the genocide, is gathering pace in the collective consciousness. Revolt against the genocidal ethnic and religious cleansing that we have witnessed in Mosul (northern Iraq) since June 2014 cannot help but accelerate the process.[29]

Are we witnessing an historic anamnesis, a recollection of a forgotten past? Many signs today suggest so. In an age when discourse associated with minorities has entered the field of social sciences, we are indeed witnessing an awakening of peoples and their aspiration to autonomy and self-determination as enshrined in international law. Such international law prohibits all forms of discrimination and deplores the crime of genocide. It is thus time that a people as suffering and oppressed as the Assyrians should be fully integrated into the conscience of humanity and justice finally handed to them.

The professor of international law Louis Le Fur (1870–1943) wrote as far back as 1926, in a spirit of universalism:

> The sense of human dignity, the belief in all humanity's right to life and to physical and moral freedom, are increasingly viewed by modern consciousness as an indispensable minimum. It is no longer as an exception to the rule but as a universal principle that it is stated that no government and no State has the right to abuse its sovereignty in a flagrant and despicable way as was, and unfortunately still is, the case with the Armenians and Assyro-Chaldeans.[30]

In 1984, *Le Monde* commented above an article I published on the 1933 massacres in Iraq:

> The international community's failure of memory in regard to the Armenian genocide is today in part corrected. In contrast, however, the Assyro-Chaldeans, who in 1915 and in 1933 witnessed the deaths of a large part of their community, are for the time being forgotten by humanity.[31]

On 2 August 2014 the Syriac Orthodox Church issued a statement in which the patriarch Mor Ignatius Aphrem II Karim announced that the patriarchate had decided to commemorate the centenary of the Syriac genocide (*Seyfo*) throughout the world in 2015, in accordance with a resolution of the Holy Synod held in Damascus on 30 March 2014. The slogan chosen for this commemoration was "Lest we forget" ("Pour ne pas oublier"). The year 2015 was one of commemoration and reflection, involving all communities, in many parts of the world. The Syriac Churches' marking of the centenary culminated in an international colloquium held at the Holy Spirit University in Kaslik, Lebanon, in July 2015.

1

WITNESSES TO GENOCIDE

"Reports state that during the massacres in the region of Van and in the Persian districts of Salmas, Urmia and Saoutschboulak no distinction was made between Armenians and Syrians (Assyro-Chaldeans)."

Johannes Lepsius, 1916

A terra incognita?

The Assyrian people have long been studied by academics and students of religion interested in their ancient civilization and important Churches, and are known by modern historians for their role in the First World War. Among the first in-depth reports on these Christian minorities, however, were those provided by American and British missionaries.

In 1830, the American Protestant missionary and scholar Eli Smith (1801–57) travelled with the minister Harrison G.O. Dwight through Armenia and Georgia into Persia before writing a two-volume work on his mission.[1] The American Board of Commissioners for Foreign Missions in Boston had sent them to explore Nestorian territory with a view to converting the community to

Protestantism, and their research introduced the Nestorians and their Church to an American readership. Another missionary, Justin Perkins, continued this work in Urmia, forging links with the Nestorian Church. In 1838, the British *Penny Cyclopaedia of the Society for the Diffusion of Useful Knowledge* already contained a mention of the Nestorians. From 1840, Western missions, contacts and scientific publications began to proliferate.

In 1842, supported by the Archbishop of Canterbury, an Anglican mission to the Nestorians was launched, and the minister and doctor of theology George Percy Badger (1815–88) was sent to the region. In his classic book *The Nestorians and their Rituals: With the Narrative of a Mission to Mesopotamia and Coordistan in 1842–1844*, he proposed that the Church of the East would be willing to reach an accommodation with the Anglican Church. The Archbishop of Canterbury decided to spare no effort in this objective and founded the future mission.[2] A petition signed by fifty-three prominent Nestorians including bishops, priests, deacons and tribal leaders was sent to the new archbishop, Archibald Campbell Tait, in 1868. The appeal, led by the patriarch Mar Rouel Shimun, appeared in the Anglican missionary journal *The Colonial Church Chronicle*, which had published other articles on the mountain-dwelling Nestorians.[3] It highlighted what the patriarch described as "abject" and "deplorable" living conditions as well as spiritual degradation and lack of education, pointing to the main factors that threatened the community's survival:

• The decadence of the Nestorian community, threatened on all sides by Islam and the papacy;
• The spiritual ignorance prevalent among the people;

- The lack of knowledge and education; their ancient books, said the patriarch, had been destroyed, and they had neither the scribes nor the printers to replace them; nor did they have schools to educate the young.

Mar Rouel accordingly called on the Anglican Church alone for spiritual and educational assistance, to the exclusion of Russians, Americans and Catholics, thus inaugurating regular links between the Nestorian Church of the East and the Church of England. He concluded:

> The people of Israel, after a captivity of seventy years, were restored to their own land; but our captivity has lasted 700 years, and yet no one has remembered us; and now we would lift up our eyes unto the hills hoping that help may come. But if we look to the hills of Russia, we discover that they are covered with images and idols; if to those of Rome, we see (the Western) Mohammed holding sway there; if to those of America, the prospect does not suit our views, neither is it adapted to our wants ... But in looking to England we are all of one mind, and find comfort and hope in the anticipation of receiving succour of the great City of London.[4]

In 1886, Edward White Denison succeeded Campbell Tait as archbishop and re-founded the mission. On 2 June he informed the Nestorian patriarch of his plans and of the imminent arrival of two missionaries, including William Henry Browne. The Anglican Church subsequently opened a mission at Kotchanes, the patriarchal seat of the Church of the East, while in Persia schools were built in Urmia and nearby villages and a printing works established. Browne chose to live in the region until his death in September 1910, and, close to the patriarchal family, he educated the future patriarch Mar Benyamin Shimun as well as his sister Surma Khanum.

The Anglicans were also advised to extend their Assyrian mission to the Syriac Orthodox Church,[5] and from 1844 the Church of England had a missionary presence in Mardin, supporting education and printing.[6] The patriarch Mor Ignatius Peter IV (1872–94) received the imperial *firman* (decree) recognizing him as head of the Syriac Orthodox community in 1873, and during a visit to Istanbul he made contact for the first time with the Anglican Church, subsequently travelling to Britain and India between 1874 and 1877. Under his patriarchate, relations between the two Churches were strengthened, and in September 1874 he met Campbell Tait, then archbishop.[7] Between November 1887 and April 1888 Bishop Mor Gregorius Abdallah Sadadi was in London, where he was invited as an observer to the Lambeth Conference before returning with the promise of a printing press for the monastery of Deir Zafaran. The first Syriac Orthodox book was duly published and sent to the then archbishop, Edward White Benson. In a 1906 visit, the patriarch Ignatius Abdallah II (1906–16) met Archbishop Randall Thomas Davidson (1903–28) and Secretary of State Lord Morley.

It was thanks to Britain that non-Catholic Assyrian communities gained some degree of statutory recognition. Under the patriarchate of Mor Ignatius Peter IV, for instance, the Syriac Orthodox community was granted the status of an independent *millet*, giving it a greater degree of visibility. On the eve of the First World War, the Anglican Church had suspended its contacts with both Assyrian Churches, yet by that time the problems and threats facing these communities were by no means unknown in Britain and beyond.

Reporting the genocide

Many written sources confirm the tragedy of 1915. The first of these began to appear immediately after the start of the massacres, from January onwards, often accompanied by appeals for solidarity and generosity. Comparing these documents and looking at them together, it is striking how similar the reports and testimonies are, even though compiled by individuals of different sensibilities, in different places and speaking different languages. This is confirmed by reading reports on the atrocities committed in Urmia-Salmas by Turkish troops and Kurdish irregulars between 2 January and 30 May 1915, reports written by American Presbyterian missionaries, Lazarist missionaries, the Filles de la Charité (Daughters of Charity) or even German Protestants. Take another example: examining their correspondence reveals the same conclusions in the reports and testimonies of Joseph Naayem, Isaac Armalet, Jacques Rhétoré, Marie-Dominique Berré, Hyacinthe Simon, the patriarch Rahmani and Mgr Suleiman Sabbagh in relation to the massacres at Diyarbakir, Mardin, Bitlis, Siirt and Jezireh. Yet another instance, equally instructive, is worth mentioning; although writing in two different languages and geographically distant, the Russian Consul at Urmia, Basil Nikitin, and the Anglican Canon William A. Wigram use almost exactly the same terms when describing the pillaging of the churches of Hakkari and the destruction of their cultural riches.

The religious missions were important witnesses to the massacres, and certain missionaries paid for this with their lives. These included, in particular, Lazarist missionaries, the Filles de la Charité, Dominicans, Capuchins, the Franciscan Sisters of the Immaculate Conception of Lons-le-Saunier, the British Anglican missionaries, the American Presbyterians and the German Lutherans.

Four day-to-day accounts of events in Urmia-Salmas

After the temporary but abrupt withdrawal of the Russian Army from Persian Azerbaijan on 1 January 1915, the Turkish troops of Khalil Bey, commander of the Turkish Army of the Caucasus with Djevdet Bey (*vali* of Van), entered the region of Urmia and Salmas/Dilman in the north of Persia. The Turkish forces, composed of 20,000 regular soldiers and 10,000 Kurds from the region of Upper Zab, remained there until the end of May of the same year, when they were driven out by Russian troops. During those five months, pitiless massacres and unprecedented atrocities were carried out by Turks, Kurds and Persians against the Christian population; on their arrival the Turkish forces had appealed to the Shiite Persian population to forget Sunni-Shiite religious disputes and to join them in the jihad that had already been proclaimed.[8]

There are numerous documentary sources relating to this episode, and it is this ordeal that is recounted in the four following testimonies. The Sisters of St Vincent de Paul from the Lazarist mission, eye-witnesses at the time, wrote a day-to-day "Journal des troubles d'Ourmiah" ("Diary of the Disturbances in Urmia") from 1 January to 30 May 1915.[9] Here is an excerpt:

> 6 January
>
> The Kurds, assisted by the Persian Muslims, have spared nobody: they kill young people and the men: young women and girls are seized, children cut to pieces! ... The night is threatening...

20 January

Urmia is more or less devastated.

12 February

After two weeks of relative calm, once again we're very worried. The Turkish authorities had been told that missionaries were hiding weapons and munitions. Under this spurious pretext, yesterday morning, at about ten o'clock, the secretary of the Turkish Consulate, an officer and a score of troops entered the Mission in order to carry out a search. While their leaders engaged in a fruitless and rather perfunctory inspection, the Turkish soldiers got hold of the men who had taken refuge in the house and forcibly pushed and jostled them into the parlour, where about 150 of them were eventually gathered; they were then divided into groups of twenty and taken away to prison without the missionaries being able to speak a single word in their defence.

21 February

There is clearly a hatred of France evident among the Turks. Today the Mission was again invaded by a group of Kurds, accompanied by Turkish soldiers. They forced their way into a cellar full of the possessions of our Christians and, despite the protests of the missionaries, after throwing everything around, they took away carpets and beds. When informed, the Turkish and Persian authorities were evasive in responding to complaints made against the looters. The Turks' fury is visibly directed against the French Mission.

23 February

This morning, a terrifying piece of news has thrown everybody into consternation ... Our poor prisoners have been executed, in an act of unspeakable cowardice: yesterday the authorities were still assuring us that they would be returned to us, and during the night four were hanged and the others shot! All through the house one can hear nothing but cries of despair, and the pain of the poor women is unimaginable ... Permission to go and bury the dead has been refused. From seven until ten o'clock we saw a great many Muslims heading towards the place of execution as if going to watch a spectacle; eight of the unfortunate were still alive, and the Persians finished them off with stones and knives. They were executed close to the Jewish cemetery, tied together in fours. Among them was a Nestorian bishop and a Chaldean Catholic priest who, at the critical moment, administered the last rites to these poor men.

4 March

The Kurds and local Muslims have finished their sorry task of pillaging the villages: all of them are absolutely destroyed!

15 March

The animosity of the Turks towards the French Mission is becoming increasingly brazen. At eight o'clock this morning four Turkish soldiers came to demand in the crudest way that we open the door to a cellar where they had already taken booty. When questioned by the governor's[10] people, who came straight away, the soldiers responded with insults. Two passions are driving the actions of Noury Bey [the provisional Turkish Consul in Urmia],[11] hatred of Christians and hatred of France…

8 April

The Kurds are still looting more houses, and the Turks are making more arrests in order to extort money. When will help arrive? For three months our life has been so painful that everybody's courage is beginning to weaken.

22 April

The Turkish soldiers who up until now were few in number have received reinforcements: now there are twenty thousand…

20 May

We are trembling with fear at the idea of seeing the Turks come back, and we are told they are not far away. If the Russians do not arrive, all is lost, as the Muslims, who are extremely inflamed, will rise up again against the Christians.

30 May (final entry)

More than 600 people have died at the French Mission since the beginning of the disturbances; the hardship is immense and our hearts are broken at not being able to bring relief for lack of resources! What will become of our Christians, most of them with neither shelter nor bread?

Their colleague, the Lazarist father Abel Zaya (1972–1951), an indigenous priest, also kept a diary of this tragic period. His text, which appeared in Eugène Griselle's book,[12] is a detailed day-to-day account, "reflecting the agonies and the tortures of the unfortunate population exposed to Turkish vengeance during the withdrawal of the Russians from 1 January to 30 May 1915". This report tells how in September 1914 the first symptoms of looting, arson and massacre had appeared in the plain of Urmia and its surroundings. On 1 October, Turco-Kurdish troops had moved down from the mountains and attacked the Christians in the plain of Targavar. The villages on this plain—Mavana, Kourana, Balulan, Chibane, etc.—had been abandoned after looting and mass killings. Having burnt them, the troops had spread out into the plain of Urmia and set fire to all the Christian villages that they came across such as Anhar or Alvach, massacring those left behind. On 4 November war broke out and the Russian troops withdrew.

Abel Zaya then reports on the catastrophic exodus towards the Caucasus that ensued after the Russian troops' unexpected evacuation from Persian Azerbaijan. He also covers the massacres committed in the villages of Urmia-Salmas, then left in the hands of the Turks and Kurds until the Russians returned on 25 May. He writes that he would need volumes to relate everything and takes as an example the village of Ada, situated thirty kilometres north-east of

41

the town of Urmia, which was subjected to atrocities. From 4 to 7 January this village was thoroughly sacked by the Persian Muslims of neighbouring villages. On 8 January, led by a *kaymacam* (district governor) and the Sunnis of Balawe Gadjine, together with Kurdish Beyzades and others totalling 3,000, the Turks took over the village and committed crimes that defy description. All women and girls, including children of six or seven, were raped. Here are some excerpts:

> A well-known authority assured me that forty-two of these poor children had taken refuge on a rooftop: they were all raped and several died at the hands of these brutes. The American Doctor Packard[13] saw some of them and stated that they had serious wounds. A young married woman who was being chased threw herself from a roof seven metres high and was unable to get up again. Eighteen of the most beautiful young girls were selected and taken into the church where they were stripped naked and violated in turn on top of the Holy Gospel.

Having provided further details, Zaya remarks that "there are a thousand deeds of the same sort", and continues his account:

> 17 January
>
> The sight of the villages is lamentable ... Many homes have been burnt. The saddest thing is the number of women and girls who remain in the hands of the Muslims and whom it is impossible to free.
>
> 19 January
>
> The looting continues.
>
> 1 February
>
> Of all the villages on the plain only three are still intact today. Sometimes permission to bury the dead is withheld.

12 February [referring to a search carried out by the Turks]

Quite perfunctory, moreover, it yielded nothing; but the men took advantage of the opportunity, quite obviously planned, to arrest the men who had taken refuge with the Lazarists and the Sisters.

21 February

The looting was complete, but murder was soon to follow and, despite all efforts, the fears of the prisoners' families were soon borne out.

26 February

Permission to bury the dead has been granted to the head of the American Mission. Forty-two corpses were lying on the ground, near all defiled: some had their eyes gouged out, others their ears, lips, noses cut off! Two pits were dug to receive these mutilated bodies.

At the end of his account Abel Zaya asks the following question: why is Urmia in mourning? He answers:

For the hundreds of innocents tied together in groups of five or six, shot in the most cowardly way, stabbed, stoned to death, buried alive, thrown into wells; in the end, it's the mourning of unfortunate mothers who have had their little girls of eight to ten violated by brutes, and many of these died, as we have said, at the hands of their abusers; it's the mourning of our virgins sold at the bazar [market] for prices ranging from 6 *tomans* [30 old francs] to 30 *tomans* [150 old francs], not even the price of a piece of livestock! Again, it's the mourning of those snatched and taken who knows where, but far away! What more can be said? Out of 40,000 people, 10,000 are missing, and the others are reduced to a state of beggary, their houses burned, their possessions taken away.[14]

In conclusion, Zaya observes that, all things considered, the Chaldean nation has suffered more than any other:

Among all the peoples who have suffered because of the war, there is one, reduced to minuscule numbers, a people that reminds us of the cradle of civilization, whose agony has remained unknown to civilized nations and to France ... this is the Chaldean people, of whom there remains only a faint breath of life.[15]

"The War Journal of a Missionary in Persia", compiled by Miss Mary Schauffler Platt and published by the American Board of Foreign Missions, is among the most detailed records of events. Here are several brief entries:

Saturday 9 January 1915

When war was declared between Russia and Turkey, we knew that this meant war for Ourmiah, for we are right on the Turkish border, and only a few years ago Turkey tried to get this section for her self but failed ... At once, as soon as the Russians had gone, with large numbers of Armenians and Syrians leaving at the same time, the evil-minded Moslems all over the plain began to plunder the Christian villages. When the people were trying to flee to the missionaries in the city, they were robbed on the roads of everything they had, even of their outer clothing.

Sunday 10 January

The crowds had begun to pour in at our gates on Sunday; the city people were taken in by night and many others from near by.

Wednesday 13 January

They are hundreds of mountaineers who have no place to go to. Before these affairs, they were distributed among the villages, and we had established a number of schools especially for them. These people had been driven from their homes by the Kurds early in the autumn. Many of them seem little better than animals—dirty, lazy, satisfied with any hole to lie in and just enough bread to keep their stomachs comfortable. Of course, they are not all of this sort, but we have several hundred that are. They are chiefly crowded into the church and our large school-room. The people who are suffering most are those who have been accustomed to the comforts and decencies of life, who are crowded together like cattle, without sufficient clothing or food.

This journal refers also to the massacres at the villages of Ada and Karajalu. "At Ada perhaps as many as a hundred were killed, most of them young men. It is told that they were stood up in line, one behind another, by the Kurds, to see how many one bullet would kill."

Saturday 16 January

The same story of robbery, exposure and horror...

Friday 12 February

Tomorrow completes six weeks of this siege and demi-siege condition. We keep on praying, but see no signs of deliverance. We are shut off from the world, and thousands are held in this bondage by a few hundred Osmanli troops and a few wandering Kurds. I realize now that Persia is dead—or worse; she has no manhood or moral character left.

Friday 13 February

A few days ago the Turkish Consul arrested all the men at the French Mission...

Recorded by the German pastor Johannes Lepsius in his book *Le Rapport secret sur les massacres d'Arménie* ("Secret Report on the Massacres in Armenia"), certain letters are worthy of note: that by Pfander, the German-American pastor of Urmia, dated 22 July 1915, and that written by the former director of the German orphanage at Urmia, Miss Anna Friedemann of the Deutsche Orient mission,[16] who had herself received several letters on these massacres.[17]

The testimony of Pastor Pfander is revealing:

Scarcely had the Russians left than the Muslims began stealing and looting. Windows, doors, stairs, panelling, everything was taken. Several Syrians [Assyrians] had left their possessions and winter provisions and had fled. Everything fell into the hands of the enemy. Fleeing was the best option, as those who stayed met a sorry end. 15,000 Syrians [Assyrians] found refuge within the walls of the Mission, where the missionaries provided them with bread: one *lavash* [thin unleavened bread] per person per day. Illnesses began to appear: the death rate reached 50 daily. In the villages, the Kurds killed everyone they could get hold of.

Even while remaining deliberately silent on all the horrible facts, Pastor Pfander cannot help referring to some scenes of cruelty: "I must mention," he writes, "how the Turks had erected a gallows in one of the main streets near the town gate and how they hanged there many Syrians [Assyrians] and shot others after holding them for a long time in prison."

Miss Friedemann, meanwhile, had received letters outlining the sufferings of the Assyrian and Armenian Christians:

The latest news is that 4,000 Syrians [*sic*] and 100 Armenians have died of illness while with the American missionaries at Urmia. All the nearby villages have been ransacked and reduced to ashes; in particular Goegtape, Gulpashan, Tscheragouscha: 2,000 Christians have been massacred at Urmia and close by; many churches are destroyed and burnt, as are many houses in town.

Another letter tells how "Saoutschboulak has been razed to the ground by the Turks." A third deals with the horrible massacres at Salmas and Haftvan. In the town of Dilman, crowds of Christians were imprisoned and forced to convert to Islam. The men were circumcised. Elsewhere,

Gulpashan, the wealthiest village in the Urmia area, was completely destroyed by fire. The men, we read, were killed and the prettiest women and girls seized and taken away. The same thing happened at Barbarou, where the women threw themselves in their hundreds into the river when they saw that many of their companions had been raped on the roads by Turkish gangs. This letter adds:

> In the courtyard of the Catholic Mission at Fath-Ali-Khan-Gheukl, forty Syrians [Assyrians] were hanged on a scaffold that had been put up ... At Salmas and Khosrava all their establishments have been destroyed. Maraga is in ruins. 1,175 Christians have been killed in Salmas, 2,000 around Urmia. 4,100 people died of typhus with the missionaries. All the refugees together, including those from Targavar, Van and Azerbaijan, are estimated to number 300,000.

The major witnesses: the Assyrians

The French-speaking Assyrian Father Joseph Naayem (1888–1964), chaplain to the Allied French and English prisoners of war in Turkey and Officer of Public Education (Officier de l'instruction publique), was in his parish in Urfa in the spring of 1915. "Urfa was an agricultural town, and my father exported goods from there to Aleppo and Lebanon." He states that from March "convoys made up of women, children and old men were arriving in Urfa in a pitiful state" and that "every day ten to fifteen people were dying". Then the Turks went after his own family. They claimed "that my father was in contact with the enemies and was exporting merchandise through Lebanon". They locked him up "in prison in a cell reserved for those condemned" and finally executed him. Naayem himself managed to escape from Urfa in August 1915, disguised as a Bedouin. He reached the city of Aleppo where, in early November, a telegram from the Chaldean patriarch Mar Emmanuel II Thomas suggested that he go to Istanbul to serve as chaplain to the Allied prisoners of war. He then set off, carrying papers of authorization from the authorities in Aleppo. Naayem writes in this respect that "the pope, Benedict XV, had, after several months of negotiation, obtained from the Turkish government permission for priests to go to the prisoner-of-war camps".[18] He adds, "Only Chaldean priests were allowed to go."

On Naayem's arrival in Constantinople, the Turkish War Minister issued him with official documents and on 15 December 1915 he left for Afion-Kara-Hissar, the concentration camp for French, British and Russian prisoners.

In his work *Les Assyro-Chaldéens et les Arméniens massacrés par les Turcs*, he writes:

> I am determined to record the martyrdom of a small people, the most worthy of interest yet at the same time the most abandoned, arising out of a great empire of the world's most ancient civilization, whose country, like Armenia, was the stage for Turkish abominations in which men were tragically murdered, women, children and the aged deported into the desert, pillaged, martyred and subjected to the worst atrocities. This people is the Assyro-Chaldean people.

He continues:

> How can I not impart the details of the tragic martyrdom of the Assyro-Chaldeans from the district of Jezireh, on the Tigris, and from Midyat, where more than fifty villages whose names I know, mostly prosperous and fertile villages that were soon to be on the route of the great Baghdad railway line and for which a bright future was certain, were totally sacked and ruined, while most of their population was put to the sword.

His book, illustrated with photographs of the individuals he interviewed under oath, begins with the account of a German chaplain, Father Dangelmonier, of the Congregation of St Francis de Sales, with whom he had had a long discussion in Constantinople. This priest had been as far as Mardin and Diyarbakir and had seen, according to Naayem: "the convoys of those deported in the desert, and the terrible state they were in". He had told him of the tragic situation faced by the Christians and had reported the suffering endured by the various Assyro-Chaldean communities. Naayem observes that he would need

> several hundred pages to talk here of the innumerable cruelties that those engaged in massacre have inflicted on their victims. It would make a special chapter in the history of this war; even in the time of the barbarians such acts of cruelty were not committed against the Christians. Here is one example among the many he provides: more than 200 women were led through the mountains, the steppes and the desert until all had perished from hunger and exhaustion; only eighteen managed to survive, and it is from them that we have these details.

There follow other accounts that Naayem gathered from those who witnessed massacres at Diyarbakir, Siirt, Kharput and Loudja as well as the deportations into the desert.

The English-language version, appearing under the title *Shall This Nation Die?* and published by Chaldean Rescue in New York in 1921, is expanded with a third section consisting of two chapters dedicated to the massacres in the regions of Hakkari, Urmia and Salmas. Acclaimed by the Aramaic-language press, it contains the accounts of Mgr Pierre Aziz, the Bishop of Salmas, and of Father Lazare Georges, a Chaldean priest in the village of Khosrava. As a delegate in Paris to plead the cause of his people, Georges, a chaplain to the Russian Army in Azerbaijan, provides testimony on the massacres in Urmia-Salmas, while Mgr Aziz relates his own experience.

Significantly, the English translation contains a preface by Viscount James Bryce (1838–1922), dated 23 July 1920. This eminent British historian, politician and former ambassador to the United States was behind the famous work *The Treatment of Armenians in the Ottoman Empire*. Denouncing the premeditated nature of the massacres, Lord Bryce also alluded to the fate of the Assyrians:

> It was the sufferings of the Armenians that chiefly drew the attention of Britain and America because they were the most numerous among the ecclesiastical bodies, and the slaughter was, therefore, on a large scale. But the minor communities, such as the Nestorians and Assyro-Chaldean churches, were equally the victims of the plan for exterminating Christianity, root and branch, although the Turks had never ventured to allege that these communities had given any ground of offense.[19]

He continues: "In the present volume there is presented a graphic and moving narrative of similar cruelties perpetrated upon members of the Assyrian Church in which about half of them, men, women and children, perished at the hands of Turkish murderers and robbers."[20] He then commends the book and its timely publication to British and American readers who wish to know the extent of the innocent victims' suffering, and calls for continued solidarity.

Lord's Bryce's preface is followed by "An Historical Essay", a contribution on the history of the Church of the East by the Chaldean Gabriel Oussani, from St Joseph's Seminary in Dunwoodie, New York State. In this chapter Oussani stresses the persecutions endured throughout history by this "unfortunate nation", and in particular the massacres of 1915.[21]

Isaac Armalet (1879–1954), a Syriac Catholic priest and scholar from Mardin, was another eye-witness to the tragedy, including the murder, along with 416 others, of the Armenian Catholic Bishop of Mardin, Mgr Ignace Maloyan;[22] he produced a voluminous book of 504 pages in Arabic, *Al-Qousara fi Nakabat Annasara* ("The Calamities of the Christians").[23] Expelled from his homeland, mistreated and persecuted, he lost his brother and other relatives in the massacres, leaving him with four orphans in a "pitiable" state whom he entrusted to the Syriac Catholic patriarchate in Beirut.

In 1919, he settled in the Deir Charfe Syriac Catholic monastery in Harissa, Lebanon, where he transcribed the notes he had secretly taken, recreating the tragic episodes that had plunged the province of Mardin and particularly Tur Abdin into mourning. He then had a copy of his text sent to the Holy See, as he reminded Cardinal Pietro Gasparri in a letter sent from Beirut on 17 July 1923: "On 21 September last year I had the honour of offering to His Holiness a copy of my work *Al Kousara* which I have published without my name as author in order not to risk persecution in the future by the Turks."[24]

Benedict XV had died in the meantime, and Armalet sent his successor, Pope Pius XI, a letter also dated 17 July 1923, accompanied by a copy of the book:

> I know that Your Holiness views Oriental sciences and particularly the Arab language with benevolent interest; if You would deign to look at this book, You will see the various sorts of suffering to which the Christians of Mardin and Mesopotamia, and especially Catholics and their clergy, have been subjected.[25]

He describes his book as:

> A rare document, telling in the greatest detail of the martyring of the Christians in Turkey and Mesopotamia, and notably in Mardin, who bore—with fortitude and bravery—oppression,

aggression, kidnappings, deportations, captivity, massacres and all sorts of crimes, in 1895 and then again from 1914 to 1919.

In his preface, he writes:

This unfortunate country, scene of the most revolting crimes and of the most infamous abominations in the midst of the century of civilization, is still today languishing under the yoke of its executioners; we hope that an end will be put to that human butchery which has depopulated once flourishing regions and that, at the cost of so many martyrs' blood iniquitously spilt, these poor lands will live to see more peaceful times and better days, for the development and spread of Christianity and the triumph of the cross.

Speaking for the Nestorians, the patriarch Benyamin Shimun (1887–1918) made the following declaration at Salmas in October 1915:

My people comprises 80,000 souls who live in Turkey as free Ashiret [tribes]. Like the Kurdish Ashiret, they neither had taxes to pay nor men to send to conscription. Not a single Turkish functionary ever set foot in our regions. Our tribes had been armed from time immemorial and our children are taught from the age of ten how to use weapons so that with our 20,000 armed men we could always defend ourselves against attacks from the Kurds who surround us. When the Constitution[26] was proclaimed in Turkey, we believed in the promises of the government who guaranteed our security, and we sold a large part of our arms as we had been led to believe that the Kurds had also been disarmed. And so our people were left defenceless. After the declaration of Jihad (holy war), the Turks resolved to exterminate us in the same way as the Armenians and had us attacked by their troops and by the Kurds among whom we lived. Our situation became worse when Khalil Bey, after his defeats at Salmas and in the Urmia region, joined in with his defeated army throughout our valleys. At the end of May Turkish forces arrived from Mosul in our regions. Then began the official massacres and the devastation of our villages. Our people left their pasture lands and withdrew to the high plateau of Betaschin, where they remain trapped. They are threatened by lack of food and epidemics have broken out. Only one hope remains for them: that of breaking through the chains of their assailants and fleeing to the Persian border.[27]

Surma Khanum,[28] the patriarch's sister, published a book in which she depicts this tragic period. This is the transcribed story of a woman from the village of Kirmi who, barefoot in the snow and with a three-month-old baby in her arms, encountered Khanum on 13 November 1914 in Kotchanes:

> We were just about to go to bed when a section of Turkish soldiers on their way to Djulamerk stopped in our village. The men wanted to eat. They also ordered us to bring them clothing against the cold such as socks and woollen hats since they were very badly equipped. We did this without flinching. While I was preparing the meal I heard a woman from the village cry out and a man's voice say, "I am your servant but do not take my wife." At this moment my husband came in and shouted, "Run as fast as you can and hide!" I ran towards the cradle to take my baby and I climbed as far as here. I don't know what happened to the others.[29]

Two letters written by Surma Khanum were reproduced in the British "Blue Book" of 1916: one was addressed to Mgr Margoliouth in Oxford and described the poverty of refugees in Persia, while the other, to Rev. Heazell, tells of their dreadful escape across the mountains.

Born in Bakufa in northern Iraq, Mgr Jacques-Eugène Manna (1868–1928) was the Chaldean bishop of Van province from 1902 and later author of an important anthology of Aramaic literature, an Aramaic-Arabic dictionary and a grammar; in July 1915 he accompanied his

Assyrian diocesans on their traumatic flight towards the Caucasus, where he oversaw their settlement.

Russian troops had withdrawn from Van in July–August 1915 towards their own frontiers. Panic stricken, many Armenians and Assyrians, including 2,000 Chaldeans from Bitlis, several dozen among the Syriac Orthodox and three priests from Siirt, were forced to abandon their homes and seek refuge in the Caucasus. A survivor of the massacres and eye-witness of the exodus, Mgr Manna gave this description of events:

> Here was a heart-breaking spectacle! A crowd of 200,000 people, men, women, children, all on foot, going who knows where; all that could be seen along the road were poor wretches with swollen legs, pitiful old men barely able to carry their loads, small children weeping and grieving mothers crying for their dead or lost children. Then from time to time, the Kurds would fall on those who were slowest and massacre them. Finally, after a painful journey of ten days, this wretched population arrived in Russia where many of them died of poverty and sickness. As for the town of Van, it has been almost entirely razed and destroyed.[30]

Dealing also with Hakkari, which was part of the province of Van, he tells of the events that occurred in the two districts of Baskale and Saray. In the Gavar area, the Assyrians occupied about twenty villages in which nearly all the men were massacred. The Assyrians of Hakkari managed to resist the Turco-Kurdish forces from May to September 1915. Retreating in the face of a large Turkish army and several Kurdish tribes, they finally reached Persian territory, leaving only a force of several thousand men to confront the enemy and cover their retreat. This was the result: "Unfortunately all the possessions of Hakkari's Assyrians have been looted, their villages burned and nearly a quarter of them have died of hardships or have succumbed to illness." Among the victims he mentions Mar Oraham, a Catholic bishop who died in the mountains, denied a tomb, and twenty-six priests killed by the sword or by sickness. Referring to the massacres perpetrated in the two districts of Baskale and Saray, he holds the Turkish authorities primarily responsible:

> Presiding over these atrocities was the infamous and barbarous Djevdet Bey, also named commander-in-chief of the Russo-Persian border. It was this Djevdet Bey who wrote to his Muslim friends in Van: "I cleansed the Christians from the districts of Baskale and Saray, and I will also come and cleanse those from Van and its surroundings."

Having surveyed the past and written of "twenty centuries of continual persecutions", he ends his account as follows: "The Assyro-Chaldeans, once freed and returned to the ancient land of their ancestors, will once again be free and able to serve the cause of civilization and humanity."[31] Defending his community and alerting world opinion to its fate, Mgr Manna also undertook long journeys through Russia, Sweden and Denmark; he visited London, Paris, Rome and Beirut, coming to the French capital in 1917 to inform the public about the massacres.

The Chaldean priest Paul Béro, from Constantinople, published a French-language brochure in 1920 entitled *Les Turcs peuvent-ils entrer dans la Ligue des Nations?* ("Can the Turks be admitted to the League of Nations?"), later translated into English, Greek and Armenian. He also contributed in the same year articles to the magazine *L'Action assyro-chaldéenne* in Beirut. In New York in 1921, George Lamsa and William Chauncey Emhardt published a work entitled *The Oldest Christian People*.[32] Dr Lamsa (1888–

1975), an Assyrian from Hakkari, had in 1917 settled in New York, where he was secretary of the American branch of the Archbishop of Canterbury's Assyrian Mission. Emhardt was Europe and Middle East secretary of the National Council of the Episcopal Church in Jerusalem.

Paul Shimun, an Assyrian from Gulpashan in Urmia, Persia, was another witness of what occurred in 1915. He organized the link between the New York office coordinating American humanitarian aid and the mountain-dwelling Assyrians who had come to seek refuge in the Urmia-Salmas area from September 1915. From Persia he went to Britain and to the United States as the representative of Mar Shimun, patriarch of the Nestorian Church, and gave statements to the Armenian journal *Ararat* in London, to *The Churchman* in Oxford and to the British "Blue Book". A graduate of Columbia University in New York, Shimun published a book entitled *Massacres of Syrian Christians in N.W. Persia and Kurdistan* with the university's press in 1916.[33]

Two other Assyrians from Urmia contributed through their publications in the US to awareness of their compatriots' ordeal in Persia. Yonan H. Shahbaz, who was with his American wife at Goegtapa near Urmia during the events, produced a book filled with details. On 25 October 1918 the first edition of his *The Rage of Islam* appeared, offering an account of the massacre of Christians by the Turks in north-west Persia between 1915 and 1917. Another Assyrian from Urmia, Kasha Samuel Nweeya, published his *Persia and the Moslems* in 1924.[34]

On the massacres in Urmia-Salmas we also have the report of Mgr Pierre Aziz, the Chaldean bishop of Salmas and eye-witness to events between 1915 and 1918. "Mémoires sur les massacres survenus dans les diocèses de

Salamas et d'Ourmiah" appeared in February 1920 in *L'Action assyro-chaldéenne*. Another account by the same author is included in the English-language version of Joseph Naayem's book, mentioned above. Yet another resource is Mgr Pierre Abed's detailed survey of the killings and devastation in various dioceses of Mesopotamia.

Testimonies in Aramaic: survivors' stories

There is an important corpus of Aramaic literature dealing with the Year of the Sword, including many accounts and laments (*dourekta*) in the form of poems, in eastern and western Aramaic.[35] Most were written at the time or were compiled later from collected and recorded testimonies. Some of the texts from this period were to be printed and published in the 1980s. One striking feature is that every author, without exception, expresses a sense of shock that Germany and Austria, two Christian countries, could have found themselves on the same side as Turkey during the war.

Mgr Israel Audo, the Chaldean bishop of Mardin, wrote a report on the massacres not only in his diocese but in those of Amid (Diyarbakir), Siirt, Jezireh and Nusaybin.[36] He provides a wealth of detail, especially on the Syriac Orthodox of Mardin and the surrounding area, lists the names of martyred priests and devotes a chapter to the murderous commissar Mamdouh.[37] He stresses the particular horrors faced by women and points to the martyrdom of the Chaldean priest Hanna Chouha; the massacres at Nusaybin, Midyat and its surroundings, Ain Ward, Anhel and Jezireh (where the Chaldean Bishop Mar Abraham Yacoub, 1848–1915, was murdered), Siirt and its dependencies; and to the case of Addai Scher (1867–1915), whom he considers "the most famous of the martyrs of the East", as well as to the question of divine justice. Father Paulus Bédaré (1887–1974), a well-known intellectual, concentrates in his text on the massacres of Christians in the Jezireh district.

Dourekta d'firman ("The Laments of Firman"), by Chorbishop Yonan Bidawid, a native of Bédaré, is a 31-page manuscript dating from 1916. Abraham Shlemon from Barwar tells the tragic story of Hakkari, while Yoel B. Rustem describes the disastrous experiences of refugees from Hakkari to Bachkale (February 1916).

Malfono Abdelmassih Nouman Karabash (Qarabashi) (1903–83),[38] originally from the village of Qarabach in Tur Abdin, a master of the Aramaic language and former pupil of the Metropolitan Yohanna Dolabani (1995–1969) at the monastery of Deir Zafaran, was the author of several textbooks (*Herge d'Keryono*, ten volumes, 1965) used from primary school to sixth form.[39] A grammarian, he also translated from Arabic into Aramaic *The Prophet* by Khalil Gibran as well as pieces by the Bengali poet Tagore, *The Code of Hammurabi* and *The Epic of Gilgamesh*. Among his own writing is *Dmo Zliho* ("Spilt Blood"), a reference to the events of 1915–18 and the suffering endured by the Syriacs.[40] The author looks back to ancient history and to the first persecutions of Mesopotamia's Christians from 64 AD, evoking the 1895 massacres in Diyarbakir and surrounding villages such as his birthplace, Qarabach,[41] and writing at length on the war and atrocities of 1915. His text, constructed around what he saw and what he heard from reliable witnesses, takes the form of a diary beginning in August 1914 in which he traces the historical background of the war, devotes several pages to Enver Pasha and denounces "the wickedness of the Turks".

Memré d'Al Seyfé ("Writings on the Sword"),[42] an anthology of twelve texts by different authors from 1714 to 1915, was published in 1981 in Holland by the Diocese of the Syriac Orthodox Church of Central Europe under the aegis of the late lamented Metropolitan Julius Yeshu Çiçek. It deals with the painful events that occurred in the villages of Tur Abdin in 1714, 1847, 1891, 1895, 1915, 1926, 1935, 1941–42 and 1964. The anthology contains poems by several authors including Gallo Shabo from Ain Ward (1875–1966), two contributions by H. Numan Aydin and pieces on the 1915 massacres by Qashisho Ephrem Safar from Midyat, Dayroyo (Friar) Yohanna Kefry, Yousef Chahine and Khoury Yousef Bilan. In his introduction, Mgr Çiçek sets out the three motives behind the publication: to pay tribute to the villages of Tur Abdin and to the Aramaic language, and to re-establish the truth.

Another manuscript, dated 1975 and written in Midyat, focuses on the history of that town; *Maktabzabno* ("Stories"),[43] by the previously mentioned chorbishop H. Numan Aydin, contains material on the 1915 massacres.[44]

Gounhé d'Sourvoyé d'Tour Abdin ("The Massacre of Syrian Christians at Tur Abdin") by Chorbishop Suleyman Henno[45] is introduced by Hassio Mor Julius Çiçik, who stresses the Syriac nature of Tur Abdin past and present. After fully detailing conditions in the region's shattered villages, often through eye-witness accounts (Keferzi, Hapisnas, Baté, Benebil, Zaz, Kerboran, Hah, Hassan Keif, Deir Salib, Anhel, Arbo, Ain Ward, Salah, etc.), he concludes with observations on the massacres[46] before comparing censuses of inhabitants in seventy-nine localities in both 1915 and 1979, the date the book appeared:

In forty-five villages, there was nobody left at all in 1987. The population of Midyat had shrunk from 1,400 in 1915 to 250, Ain Ward from 200 to 6, Anhel to 82... in other communities, there were even fewer people left. In Baté and Kerboran, 300 and 500 inhabitants were counted respectively in 1915, and not a single person in 1987.[47] A large number of the survivors have chosen the path of exile in Europe and live today in Sweden, Belgium, Holland, Germany and France.

Wounds in Syriac History, written in Aramaic by Deacon Asman Alkass Gorgis in 1980, was translated into Arabic under the title *Jirah fi Tarikh al-Suryan*. The work lists massacres since 1828, referring to texts of the periods involved;[48] it describes those in Urfa (1915), Veran Shehir (1895 and 1915). Derik (1895 and 1915), Kalaat Mara (1895 and 1915), Benebil (1915), Kfar Dis, Diyarbakir (1895), Ain Ward (1895), Hassan Keif (1915), Kerboran, Zaz and so on.

The Syriac Orthodox Diocese of Azakh and Jezireh comprised nineteen villages in 1915, along with the town of Jezireh and the village of Azakh itself. All of them were devastated and left in ruins. Two important documents in Arabic deal specifically with the village of Azakh: *Azakh (Bet Zabdé), Events and Men* contains many testimonies on the massacres and resistance of the inhabitants of Azakh through successive tragedies. Here, and in Ain Ward, the Syriac population had fought valiantly against the Turks and Kurds, and this has remained an integral part of the collective memory. This book was compiled and published in Aleppo by Youssef Jibrail Kass and supervised by Dr Elias Hadaya.[49] Given its importance, it is worth giving its dedication, translated from Arabic:

> To all Azakhians, or rather to all the Syriac people dispersed around the world, who, despite all tragedies, remain attached

to their ancestral origins and to the heritage of their illustrious ancestors; and to all those who defend to the death the right to life of their brother men and the right of all peoples to three essentials: bread, dignity and peace.

The second document, a manuscript, entitled "The History of Azakh, its Massacres and Wars", was written by the Syriac deacon Jibrail Thomas Hindo.

Other articles have appeared in Arabic and Aramaic in the monthly journal *Mghalto Phatriarqueto* ("Review of the Syriac Orthodox Patriarchate, Damascus"). The scholar and Syriac Orthodox Metropolitan of Mardin, Youhanna Doulabani, has also written on the 1915 killings, as have Samuel Abdel Ahad, Yousef Namek, Naoum Fayek and writers for the Aramaic press in the United States. Other authors can be added to this list:, such as Shmuel David, a Chaldean priest from the village of Gavilan (Persia), who published an Aramaic-language book in Chicago in 1923 entitled *The Assyro-Chaldean History*, covering many developments up to the First World War, its causes and its tragic impact on the Assyrians between 1914 and 1921.

Other books written by community leaders and based on witnesses' reports in Hakkari reveal events on a day-to-day basis. Malik Yacou, for instance, son of Malik Ismael (chief of Upper Tyari), published a book in Aramaic (*soureth*) in Tehran in 1964, *The Assyrians and Two World Wars*. Joseph Malik Khoshaba, son of Malik Khoshaba (leader of Lower Tyari), gave his version of events in an Arabic work published in Baghdad, *The Truth Behind Contemporary Assyrian Events* (2000). Yonan, son of Malik Loko Shlimon d'Bit Badawi (1902–77), a leader from Tkhuma, published a voluminous English-language work in Chicago based on the documents amassed by his father.[50]

These accounts constitute a central series of references when considering the massacres. They recount in detail, with striking similarities, the nature of the tragedy and the atrocities carried out by Turks and Kurds from town to town and from village to village, without exception. Some look far back into history, to the distant massacres of the early Christian era, while others concentrate more specifically on events occurring from 1714 up to 1918.

The missionaries

Deported by the Ottoman authorities, the Dominicans Jacques Rhétoré, Marie-Dominique Berré and Hyacinthe Simon spent two years in Mardin (1915–16), during which they were witnesses to unfolding events. Father Rhétoré wrote:

> In December 1914 ... I had the honour of being expelled from Mosul with two companions, Fathers Berré and Simon ... Due to the advancing winter and our age, we were able, through the services of an excellent intermediary, Hilmi bey Mutasarrif [governor] of Mardin, to obtain permission to stay in this town, at least during the period of peace, the winter. We stayed there for two years. I did not regret being expelled, for it allowed me to participate as an eye-witness in the events that occurred in these regions, some of which concerned the ongoing war and others the massacres ordered by Turkey against her Christian subjects...[51]

Hyacinthe Simon, meanwhile, wrote *Mardine, la ville héroïque: autel et tombeau de l'Arménie (Asie Mineure) durant les massacres de 1915* ("Mardin, the Heroic Town: Altar and Tomb of Armenia [Asia Minor] during the Massacres of 1915"), in which he recorded his memories precisely so that events might be remembered. He completed his notes in Mardin in June 1916, finishing his book in Aleppo three years later and dedicating it, "in memory of our shared ordeals", to "my brother in chains", Mgr Gabriel Tappouni, Syriac Catholic titular bishop and Apostolic Vicar of Mardin. The manuscript was entrusted to the Syriac Catholic hierarchy in 1919; Simon said that it consisted of notes collected "here and there" while in exile.

Marie-Dominique Berré (1857–1929) also left his testimony, producing a report dated 15 January 1919, "Massacres de Mardin", in which he writes that the Turks "thought the moment had come to liberate Turkey from the enemy within, namely the Christians".[52]

These three testimonies cast an invaluable light on the tragedy of the Ottoman Empire's Christians during the dark year of 1915 and complement that of Isaac Armalet, who was also in Mardin during the war.

The Lazarists and the Filles de la Charité, whose sisters often accompanied the priests in the land of their mission, collected multiple testimonies while close to the events of this dark period. Present in Persia since 1840, especially in the region of Urmia and Salmas, their rich correspondence, in part recorded through instructive letters in their periodical *Annales de la Congrégation de la Mission*, is damning in its view of the events of the Great War.

The editions of the *Annales* (founded 1834) covering the years from 1915 to 1919[53] are particularly illuminating. On 26 September 1914 Father Nathaniel Dinkha, a locally born Lazarist, was already sensing the disaster about to threaten the Christians when he wrote to Father Villette in Paris: "We are not safe here at the moment. There is much talk of war between Russia and Turkey: we fear that the Christians will be slaughtered by the Muslims."[54] The worst was soon to come. On 23 October, the Alsatian apostolic delegate in Persia and archbishop of

Ispahan, Mgr Jacques-Emile Sontag, recently returned from Paris, wrote from Urmia:

> Scarcely had I returned than the Kurds, under pressure from the Turks, threw themselves on the land. They killed those Christians who had not fled, and looted and burned five villages. We are sheltering 620 people, The Kurds wanted to take Urmia and massacre the Christians. We were not without concern; the Russian reinforcements arrived just in time.[55]

On 25 January 1915, in a brief note addressed to Father Villette to describe the situation, he remarks: "Let it suffice for me to tell you that our Christianity has returned to the days of Decius,"[56] and on 20 May, again writing to his Superior in Paris, he simply says, "The ordeal has been long."[57] On 17 October he sent a detailed report from Urmia to his Superior General:

> The Russians had barely left the country when the furious Muslims, enraged for various reasons, pounced on Christian villages, massacring those left behind, violating and abducting women and girls, taking away anything that could be carried and smashing the rest. Thus, three of our churches have been burned down, and eighteen more looted and damaged to some degree ... In the plain of Salmas where our house is situated at Khosrova the same scenes of pillage and cruelty have unfolded. But while the buildings have been less damaged than at Urmia the massacre has been even more barbaric: one of our priests was skinned alive.[58]

Having accompanied many of the Assyrian faithful on the road to forced exile, Lazarists such as the Chaldean Father Abel Zaya or Georges Decroo described the horrors of the flight towards Russia.[59] As we have seen, others kept daily records of the terrible occupation of Urmia. The weekly illustrated bulletin of the Society for the Propagation of the Faith, *Les Missions catholiques*, also published testimonies by Lazarist fathers regarding massacres in Persia as well as by others such as the Discalced Carmelite Mgr Louis Martin.[60]

Prior to the war, Capuchins from the province of Lyon and sisters from the Franciscan Congregation of the Immaculate Conception of Lons-le-Saunier were present in Urfa, Diyarbakir, Mardin, Mamouret-ul-Aziz, Kharput and Malatya. As soon as the conflict broke out, these religious communities were expelled. Only thirteen individuals, mostly locally born, stayed in Urfa and Mardin and witnessed subsequent events.

The eloquent report of the Syriac Father Bonaventure de Baabdath describes what he saw as well as what happened to him during the war, first in Diyarbakir, then at Urfa. A childhood friend of the Capuchin Father Léonard Melki (1881–1915),[61] himself from Baabdath, Father Bonaventure was arrested, condemned to death and then freed. He disguised himself as a Kurd and managed to reach Lebanon, where he wrote a report in which he described the death of his colleague Léonard as well as that of another compatriot, Thomas de Baabdath.[62]

Father Léonard Melki had been arrested by the Turks in his monastery in Mardin, thrown into prison and tortured. Led out of the town on foot at the head of a column of 400 people, with the Armenian Bishop Mgr Maloyan bringing up the rear, he was executed at dawn on Friday 11 June 1915. According to Father Bonaventure:

> Someone, however, remained behind: our dear Father Léonard ... He had helped the Sisters to leave, but had stayed because at the last moment old Father Daniel, in his eighties, who could not dream of leaving, said to him sadly: "So, are you going to leave me on my own?" Father Léonard had immediately and selflessly decided to stay with this venerable priest ... Father Léonard

was murdered, victim of his own charity. A recent letter of 21 December 1919, written from Urfa by Father Attale, tells us: "We learnt from Qas Youssef, a priest from Urfa, that Father Léonard was killed on 11 June 1915 at Zirzouan near Diyarbakir, having repeatedly refused to become a Muslim, having been beaten with sticks, and after giving absolution to all the Christians who had been taken away with him."[63]

American Protestant missions had been active in Persia from 1830 onwards, with the American Board of Commissioners for Foreign Missions in Boston at the centre of their extensive programme. Many missionaries from this organization, essentially Presbyterians, were hence to be found in the Urmia-Salmas and Tabriz areas during the conflict. The correspondence of some of these was partly included in the British "Blue Book", including William A. Shedd, Robert M. Labaree, E.W. McDowell and his wife Mary Coe, who died on 16 April 1915, F.N. Jessup, Mrs Katharine Cochran, the widow of Dr Joseph Plumb Cochran, Hugo M. Müller, Dr Jacob Sargis, Dr H.P. Packard and his wife Frances Bauley and the pastors E.T. Allen and Y.M. Nisan.

The testimony of William A. Shedd from the American Mission in Urmia is important, indicating that attacks on Urmia by Kurds and Turks began as early as October 1914. Robert M. Labaree, meanwhile, sent an initial report from Tabriz, dated 1 March 1915, on the first exodus from Urmia to the Caucasus. He then left to help the refugees on their way to the Caucasus, describing the deadly seven-day march to reach the frontier of the Aras river. He sent his report to the American consul at Tiflis, F. Willoughby Smith, with other letters following, such as that of 12 March on the massacres at Salmas and Gulpashan.

The missionary F. N. Jessup wrote about the massacres from Tabriz on 17 March 1915, Mrs J.P. Cochran from Urmia on 20 May, and Rev. Nisan on 25 May. Dr Jacob Sargis, an Assyrian Methodist missionary from Persia, who had escaped death by fleeing to Petrograd, sent a letter from that city published by Associated Press on 12 February 1916, which told of the horrors and atrocities perpetrated particularly in Supurghan.

Later, Mary Lewis Shedd, William A. Shedd's wife, who was herself in Urmia, was to write a biography of her husband in which she recorded these events and discussed the aid distributed by the American mission to the refugees.[64]

The range of witnesses

All sorts of individuals—academics, diplomats, religious and military men and women—bore witness and collected information through differing sources and in many languages. There is no shortage of documentation in Aramaic, Arabic, English, German and French, often produced by eye-witnesses. There follow some important examples that allow us to grasp both the scale of the tragedy and the methods used.

The British "Blue Book"

> "But the record of the rulers of Turkey for the last two or three centuries, from the Sultan on his throne down to the district Mutessarif, is, taken as a whole, an almost unbroken record of corruption, of injustice, of an oppression which often rises into hideous cruelty."

Viscount James Bryce[65]

From October 1915, Britain began to take a close interest in the genocide of the Armenians and other Christians
in the Ottoman Empire. A "Blue Book" (an official parliamentary report), *The Treatment of Armenians in the
Ottoman Empire*, was compiled and edited in consultation
with Lord James Bryce (1838–1922), an eminent historian
and statesman, by Arnold Joseph Toynbee (1889–1975),
then his young assistant. Made up of many reports, it deals
with the massacres of the Assyrians; of the 684 pages of the
original English-language edition, 104 pages are dedicated
to them. It is undoubtedly a major work on the subject.

These documents were presented to Viscount Grey of
Fallodon, Secretary of State for Foreign Affairs, by
Viscount James Bryce on 1 July 1916. In its original form,
the text was entitled *Documents Relating to the Treatment
of Armenians and Assyrian Christians in the Ottoman
Empire and Northwestern Persia, Subsequently in the
Outbreak of the European War, Following upon Correspondence between Viscount Grey of Fallodon, Secretary of
State for Foreign Affairs, and Viscount Bryce.*[66] Published in
mid-war, the "Blue Book" then appeared in a commercial
edition[67] before a slightly abridged French edition became
available in 1917.[68] In his preface to the French translation, Viscount Bryce asserted: "It contains all testimonies
that could be obtained up to July 1916 concerning the
massacres and deportations of the Armenians and other
Christians of the East living in Asia Minor, Armenia and
the north-west part of Persia invaded by Turkish troops."[69]

In a speech in the House of Lords on 6 October 1915,
Lord Bryce placed responsibility for these events with the
highest levels of the Ottoman government, declaring:

> That is because the proceedings taken have been so absolutely
> premeditated and systematic. The massacres are the result of a

policy which, as far as can be ascertained, has been entertained for some considerable time by the gang who are now in possession of the Government of the Turkish Empire. They hesitated to put it in practice until they thought the favourable moment had come, and that moment seems to have arrived about the month of May. That was the time when these orders were issued, orders which came down in every case from Constantinople, and which the officials found themselves obliged to carry out on pain of dismissal.[70]

The 104 pages covering the Assyrian massacres are divided into 21 documents of a total of 150, which are covered by Chapter IV, "Azerbaijan and Hakkari". The chapter comprises 19 documents (nos 27 to 45) to which were added two more (nos 147 and 148) received after the book had gone to press. These documents, whose sources are very varied, are based on eye-witness reports from Urmia, Salmas, Hakkari, Bohtan and Tabriz by seven American missionaries, three American consular representatives and one from the American Medical Department in Urmia, two American journalists, one English missionary and four Assyrian individuals. They cover events referring to the first period of the genocide, the 15 months from 2 January 1915 to 14 April 1916, in Persia and Hakkari. Moreover, Chapter V, "The Refugees in the Caucasus", comprising seven documents (nos. 46 to 52) mentions in at least two reports the arrival of many Nestorian Assyrians in the Caucasus alongside the massive influx of Armenians.[71]

In the preliminary memorandum, Arnold Toynbee refers to the sources, nature and value of the documents, and explains the text's structure. Several of the documents were provided by members of the American Committee for Armenian and Syrian Relief,[72] presided over by James

L. Barton, of which William W. Rockwell of the Union Theological Seminary in New York was a member; by the Foreign Missions of the Presbyterian Church in the United States of America; by the Armenian Refugees (Lord Mayor's) Fund; and by individuals such as Mrs D.S. Margoliouth of Oxford or the Rev. F.N. Heazell, secretary of the Archbishop of Canterbury's Assyrian Mission. Among the witnesses, states the memorandum, some were indigenous inhabitants of the Near East, Armenians or Nestorians, "who were either victims of the atrocities themselves or were intimately connected with others who played a direct part in the scenes described".

The list of the main individuals who made declarations concerning the massacres in Hakkari and Persian Azerbaijan includes several well-known personalities and intellectuals, some of whom were experts on the Assyrian people and the Church of the East:[73] William A. Shedd[74] and E.W. McDowell of the American Presbyterian Mission in Urmia,[75] Robert M. Labaree and F.N. Jessup of the American Presbyterian Mission in Tabriz, Miss Mary Schauffler Platt of the Presbyterian Mission in Urmia, Mrs J.P. Cochran of the American Mission in Urmia, Y.M. Nisan, an Assyro-Chaldean priest from Urmia, Dr Jacob Sargis, an American missionary in Petrograd, Paul Shimmon, an Assyrian from Urmia, Surma Khanum, sister of the Nestorian patriarch Mar Benyamin Shimun XXI, Hugo A. Müller of the American Mission in Urmia, the wife of David Jacob, an Assyro-Chaldean woman from Urmia, Philips Price, a journalist at Tiflis, and M.J.D. Barnard, of the Archbishop of Canterbury's Assyrian Mission.

It is important to emphasize that before the publication of these reports Lord Bryce, who "directed the work from beginning to end", decided to submit them to three specialists for their advice on the authenticity of the testimonies. These experts were Herbert A. Fisher, a historian and vice-chancellor of the University of Sheffield, Gilbert Murray, professor of Greek at the University of Oxford, and an American jurist "of long experience and high authority", the ex-president of the American Bar Association, Mr. Moorfield Storey of Boston. In his reply dated 2 August 1916, Herbert Fisher remarked that he was impressed by "the cumulative effect of the evidence",[76] writing:

> Whoever speaks, and from whatever quarter in the wide region covered by these reports the voice may proceed, the story is one and the same. There are no discrepancies or contradictions of importance, but, on the contrary, countless scattered pieces of mutual corroboration.[77]

He added that events were the consequence of a policy decided upon in Constantinople and put into practice by the Committee of Union and Progress:

> There is no contrariety as to the broad fact that the Armenian population has been uprooted from its homes, dispersed, and, to a large though not exactly calculable extent, exterminated in consequence of general orders issued from Constantinople. It is clear that a catastrophe, conceived upon a scale quite unparalleled in modern history, has been contrived for the Armenian inhabitants of the Ottoman Empire. It is found that the original responsibility rests with the Ottoman Government at Constantinople, whose policy was actively seconded by the members of the Committee of Union and Progress in the Provinces.[78]

On 27 June, Professor Gilbert Murray wrote in his reply on the question of veracity that "the evidence of these letters and reports will bear any scrutiny and overpower any scepticism" and that "the undesigned agreement between so many credible witnesses from widely separate districts puts all the main lines of the story beyond the possibility of doubt".[79]

Moorfield Storey, meanwhile, replied on 7 August that, in such a context:

> Such statements as you print are the best evidence which, in the circumstances, it is possible to obtain. They come from persons holding positions which give weight to their words, and from other persons with no motive to falsify, and it is impossible that such a body of concurring evidence should have been manufactured.[80]

On the role played by the Turkish authorities, he wrote: "I think it establishes beyond any reasonable doubt the deliberate purpose of the Turkish authorities practically to exterminate the Armenians, and their responsibility for the hideous atrocities which have been perpetrated upon that unhappy people."[81]

The editor of the work, the young Arnold Joseph Toynbee, observed that if some of the witnesses were indigenous inhabitants of the region involved, Armenians or Nestorians:

> A majority of the witnesses, however, are foreign residents in the Ottoman Empire or the Persian Province of Azerbaijan, and nearly all these, again, are citizens of neutral countries, either European or American—missionaries, teachers, doctors, Red Cross nurses or officials. A few witnesses (and these are the weightiest of all) are subjects of states allied to Turkey in the present war.[82]

Some extracts from the "Blue Book"[83]

When Russian forces withdrew on 2 January 1915, they were followed in their retreat by a section of the population, around 15,000 people, who experienced enormous suffering. Those who remained sought refuge in the town of Urmia and endured all sorts of atrocities during the twenty weeks of its Turco-Kurdish occupation. This is the ordeal, along with those of Hakkari and Bohtan, described in the "Blue Book".

According to William A. Shedd, the Kurds invaded the plain, followed by Turkish troops, while Muslim villagers began looting, massacring and raping. Those villages that failed to defend themselves succumbed alongside those that offered resistance.[84] The missionary Dr Robert Labaree recounted that the wealthy village of Gulpashan was looted by Kurds, the men killed and the women treated in the most barbaric manner; the Assyrians who had stayed in Diliman (the chief town of Salmas), numbering about 800, were tortured and killed by the Turkish troops of Djevdet Bey.[85] Father E.T. Allen from Urmia testified that he had himself buried 161 Assyrians, massacred by Turkish and Kurdish troops, at Tcharbash, Gulpashan and Ismail Agha's Kala.[86] According to the American Medical Department in Urmia, hundreds of women, sometimes young girls, were raped in villages around Urmia.[87]

Around 1,000 Assyrians were killed in the plain of Urmia after the Russian withdrawal by Kurds and Persians. In the space of two weeks, the homes of all 45,000 Assyrians and Armenians in the region were looted, with not a single village escaping. Eighteen villages in the district of Baranduz were sacked, sixteen around Urmia, fourteen near the Nazlu river and three in the district of Tergavar, according to the report of Paul Shimun.[88]

Some 12,000 refugees from the plain sought sanctuary in the American Mission and 3,000 in the French Mission in Urmia. The death rate in the American Mission was at first between ten and twenty-five per day; then 2,000 Assyrians died of epidemics and a further 1,000 were killed.[89]

Dr Shedd estimated the number of those massacred in the Urmia district before the return of Russian forces (end of May 1915) at 1,000, and at 800 in Salmas. He further attested to the rape of hundreds of women of all ages and the pillage of five-sixths of the homes of Assyrians, Armenians and other Christians. He put at 4,000 the number of those dead from epidemics during the Turkish occupation.[90]

The journal published by Miss Mary Schauffler Platt records that the Turkish consul at Urmia extorted the sum of 6,000 *tomans* from Assyrian February in exchange for their safety.[91] A few days later, the same consul imprisoned all the Assyrians who had fled to the French Mission; forty-eight of them would be shot and five hanged.[92] The Turkish soldiers sent by the consul to assure the "protection" of the population in non-Muslim villages raped all the women.[93]

Dr Jacob Sargis recounted how a doctor called Shimun, captured by the Turks in the village of Supurgan, refused to convert to Islam. The Turks poured oil on his clothes and set fire to them, shooting at him as he ran away in flames and cutting off his head when he fell. The missionary E.T. Allen found Shimun's corpse half eaten by dogs.[94]

Thus the distressing pages of Toynbee's "Blue Book" tell of the ordeals faced by the Assyrians. The historian, moreover, retained his interest in this people from their settlement in Iraq in 1919 up to 1934, and his writings serve as a resource on this issue. In May 1917 he joined the Foreign Office's Political Intelligence Department, and in November he was sent as the British delegate to the Paris Peace Conference with expertise in the Middle East. It was in this role that he reacted to the various memorandums delivered to the conference by Assyrian delegations. In January 1919, Toynbee suggested a varied settlement, depending on the context, for the five Aramaic-speaking communities (Nestorian, Jacobite Syriac, Syriac Catholic, Chaldean and Protestant), ranging from territorial autonomy (in the form of cantons) to equality of rights:

> The policy suggested above in regard to the five Syriac [Aramaic]-speaking communities may be summarised as follows:
>
> i) Nestorian East-Syriac Christians (Assyrians): territorial autonomy as a canton of the S. Kurdistan Confederation.
> ii) Jacobite West-Syriac Christians (in the Tur Abdin): possibly territorial autonomy in the Mosul province of Mesopotamia.
> iii) East Syriac Protestants, East Syriac Catholics, West Syriac Catholics: should be given equal rights with other populations in whatever district, province, or State they are found in, but no corporate political autonomy.[95]

Other international publications

Besides the "Blue Book", there is no lack of testimonies on the tragedy of the Assyro-Chaldeans and Syriacs—in English, French and many other languages. Numerous and from many different sources, they ensured that the experiences of this people during the Great War were widely known. Anglican priests such as William A. Wigram, Catholics, Protestants of differing denominations, members of the French and British military—Paul Cajole,[96] Nicolas Gasfield[97] and Herbert Henry Austin[98]—and many other individuals were all determined to give their testimony regarding the atrocities.

On 24 March 1917 in Paris, Father Eugène Griselle (1861–1923), Doctor of Letters and honorary Canon of Beauvais, published *Syriens et Chaldéens, leurs martyres, leurs espérances, 1914–1917*. In this work he describes the massacres according to recollections gathered among Assyro-Chaldeans such as Mgr Jacques-Eugène Manna, the Bishop of Van, the Lazarist Abel Zaya and the Filles de la Charité (Daughters of Charity) of St Vincent de Paul.[99] In this collection Mgr Manna recalls the incendiary words of the *vali* of Van who claimed to "have cleansed the Christians from the districts of Bachkale and Saray", and threatened to also "cleanse" those of Van and its region.[100] Looking at the troubled events in Urmia from 1 January to 30 May 1915, the detailed account of the Filles de la Charité "reflects the agonies and torture of the unfortunate population delivered up to Turkish vengeance after the withdrawal of the Russians," writes Griselle.[101]

The book also contains several pages on the Assyrian nation from a historical and ethnographic perspective, where the emphasis is on the importance of a people who "for thirty-five centuries (from 4000 to 500 BC), first at Babylon, then at Nineveh, ruled the East". Their religious legacy and its impact on world culture is also stressed:

> The religious importance of the Christian Churches founded by them and the power of their apostolate's expansion are perhaps less remembered today. And yet Persia, Arabia, the Indies, China, Tartary, the Caucasus and Armenia were all the stages on which their missionaries worked. Four great schools or universities (Antioch, Edessa, Nusaybin and Ctesiphon) were for several centuries centres of intellectual activity. Monastic life enjoyed its splendid flowering, and the liturgical and linguistic

significance attached to their religious books should keep our attention focused on this Assyro-Chaldean nation which we know now only for its recent and terrible ordeals. And yet the martyrdom it has endured over these last years is but the latest in a series of sufferings that stretch back through twenty centuries to its Christian origins.

André N. Mandelstam, former first interpreter at the Russian Embassy in Constantinople from 1898 to 1914 and doctor of international law at the University of Petrograd, who spent two years in Turkey and was initially sympathetic to the Young Turks, wrote two books on the Ottoman Empire and the Armenian question in which he also dealt with the Assyrians. In his 1917 *Le Sort de l'Empire ottoman* he observes:

> Without the slightest pretext of provocation, the Turkish government put the land of the Syriac Christians of Hakkari to fire and the sword, destroyed their humble homes and forced this poor people to flee abroad. If, thanks to their bravery and to the help of the noble American missionaries at Urmia, some Nestorians escaped the massacre, the odious plan of the Turkish leadership to rid itself of all Christians in the Empire nonetheless appeared here in all its hideous clarity.[102]

In his second work, *La Société des nations at les Puissances devant le problème arménien* (1926), Mandselstam writes: "The Young Turk government could only partly carry out its plan of using the Great War to establish the radical Turkification of the Ottoman Empire. It still succeeded in exterminating around a million Armenians and hundreds of thousands of Greeks, Lebanese and Assyro-Chaldeans."[103] In support of his views, he quotes from the British "Blue Book" (on the treatment of Armenians and from the reports of Basil Nikitin, the former Russian Consul in Urmia).[104]

Five years earlier, George Dubois had published his *La question assyro-chaldéenne* in Paris.[105] The author had visited Constantinople, Alexandretta and Beirut, where he observed at close quarters the officers and soldiers of the Assyro-Chaldean Battalion raised by France at the initiative of General Gouraud. René Puaux's 16-page pamphlet, *La Grande Pitié des Chrétiens d'Orient*, dealing with the massacres of the Great War, was published in Paris in 1922.

L'Asie Française, the monthly bulletin of the Comité de l'Asie Française edited by Henri Froidevaux, published several revealing articles on the massacres. It covered, for instance, the lecture given to a large audience in Paris on 30 May 1919 by Father Joseph Naayem, presenting the French public with five striking testimonies on the sufferings of his compatriots.[106] He described the methods of those conducting the genocide, the terrifying situation in Siirt, the persecutions in Diyarbakir and the "ferocity of the policy inflicted on the Assyro-Chaldeans". The same journal regularly drew attention to the crisis, as in January 1919: "We have repeatedly pointed to the dreadful situation facing the Nestorian Christians of Kurdistan and the North-West of Persia. They have been abominably massacred by the Turks and their associates, the Kurds."[107] In March 1920, the journal's director Henri Froidevaux contributed a long article, "Les Assyro-Chaldéens et la France".

Other French periodicals also took up the issue, such as the *Bulletin de l'Oeuvre des Ecoles d'Orient*, which dedicated several articles to events after January 1915, including the declaration made by Giacomo Gorrini on his return to neutral Italy, regarding the massacres he'd witnessed as Consul General in Trabzon.[108] Similarly, the bulletin of the St Francis Xavier Jesuit Oriental Seminary in Beirut published articles by Father George Hamal, a Syriac Catholic priest from Mardin, while in 1935 *L'Unité de l'Église* featured a long piece entitled "Le calvaire [the ordeal] des Assyro-Chaldéens (1915–1935)".[109]

German religious missions were active in and around Urmia, providing eye-witness reports as events unfolded. Dr Johannes Lepsius,[110] a German theologian, missionary and president-founder of the Deutsche Orient-Mission, published *Bericht über die Lage des Armenischen Volkes in der Türkei* (Potsdam, 1916), in which he also discusses the Assyrians. On hearing of the 1915 massacres, Lepsius had visited Constantinople to undertake an in-depth investigation, gathering testimonies via concerned German diplomats. Deemed an "undesirable", he was deported by Enver Pasha, but managed to smuggle out the documents and return to Germany in February 1916, completing his report. Even though the German government confiscated the text and banned it, copies found their way into the hands of certain individuals. A French version was then published, with a preface by the historian and academic René Pinon, entitled *Le Rapport secret du Dr Johannès Lepsius sur les Massacres d'Arménie*.[111]

The report describes events in the *vilayet* of Diyarbakir: "Between 10 and 30 May 1,200 more of the most prominent Armenians and Syrians [*sic*] of the vilayet were arrested." When the orders of the *vali* were not followed, local leaders like the *mutasarrif* of Mardin were removed from office: "At Mardin, too, the mutasarrif was deposed because he did not want to act against the Armenians, as the vali wished. After he left, first 500 then 300 more well-known Armenians and Syrians were forced on to the road to Diyarbakir. The first 500 never arrived; and no news was ever had of the other three hundred"; others, like the *kaymacam* of Lidje, were killed.[112]

Lepsius also collected testimonies from the Urmia region, confirming the atrocities committed by the Kurds and by the Turkish forces commanded by Khalil Bey, Enver Pasha's nephew: particularly those of Pfander, the German-American pastor of Urmia, and Anna Friedemann, director of Urmia's German orphanage from 1900, who also assembled incriminating letters showing how local villages such as Goetapa, Gulpashan, Tscheragouscha and Saoutschboulak had been reduced to ashes. One letter told how in Haftvan and Salmas, 850 bodies had been recovered from wells, headless, because the commander in chief of the Turkish troops had fixed a price for each Christian head.

Lepsius concludes: "Reports state that during the massacres in the region of Van and in the Persian districts of Salmas, Urmia and Saoutschboulak no distinction was made between Armenians and Syrians."[113] Dealing with forced conversions to Islam, Lepsius lays the blame with the Turkish authorities: "The pressure exerted on the Christian population to force it to embrace Islam did not come from the Muslim people nor their clergy, but exclusively from the government."[114]

In 1919, Lepsius, also president of the German-Armenian Society, published a second important work in Potsdam, *Deutschland und Armenien, 1914–1918: Sammlung diplomatischer Aktenstücke*, in which he surveys the writings of German diplomats and returns to the issue of the Assyrians, notably in Mardin and Midyat.[115] The information provided by consuls and other diplomatic staff in Asia Minor as well as the ambassador in

Constantinople, subsequently sent to the Foreign Ministry in Berlin, is highly revealing.[116] In his introduction, Lepsius is unambiguous, insisting that from October 1911 the Young Turks' Committee of Union and Progress had adopted as a government programme nationalist and pan-Islamic principles aimed at promoting the hegemony of the Turkish race:

> It was this pan-Turkic programme that was concealed, even before events in Van, behind the mass arrests and deportations in Cilicia and the vilayet of Erzurum; it also inspired the campaign of extermination led by Turkish and Kurdish forces in the north of Persia during the winter of 1914–15 against the pacific Syrian and Armenian population of Urmia and Salmas. It was this same programme that was at the origins of the systematic persecution of Christians in the vilayets of Diyarbakir and Mosul, where the victims, without distinction among them, were Jacobites, Chaldeans, Nestorians and Armenians.[117]

A telegram of 21 July 1915 (document no. 118) from the Imperial German Consulate in Mosul to the German Embassy in Constantinople and signed by Vice-Consul Walter Holstein states:

> Up to now we have seen about 600 women and children (Armenians, Chaldeans, Syrians) arrive here: all the men in their families have been massacred at Siirt, Mardin and Feishkhabour. We are expecting as many again in the next few days. The hardships endured by these people defy description, their clothes rotting on their bodies: every day women and children die of hunger.[118]

The same vice-consul reported to Ambassador Baron Hans von Wangenheim on the violent atrocities of the *vali* Rachid Bey in Mardin:

> The Vali of Diyarbakir, Rachid Bey, is like an unleashed wild animal in his treatment of the Christians in his vilayet. Recently

he summoned the gendarmes of Diyarbakir to Mardin, who, on his orders, rounded up 700 Christians (mostly Armenian), including the Armenian bishop, and slit their throats like sheep in and around the town.[119]

Other diplomats such as the Ambassador Prince Hohenlohe-Langenburg, concerned for the international image of their country, advised their governments to assume no responsibility for the violence directed against Christians and recommended that it condemn such actions.[120]

German-speakers such as the Swiss citizen Jakob Künzler (1871–1949) also witnessed and reported on such abuses. Künzler, who opened a school in Urfa for Syriacs in 1903, produced significant information based on the accounts of Armenian and Syriac deportees in his 1921 book *Im Lande des Blutes und der Tränen. Erlebnisse in Mesopotamien während des Weltkrieges* ("In the Land of Blood and Tears: Adventures in Mesopotamia during the World War").[121] It reveals the mistreatment inflicted on Christians, notably within the ranks of the Turkish army, where highly educated men such as a schoolteacher quoted by Künzler were forced into the most degrading hard labour.[122]

In September 1916, Abraham Yohannan, an Assyrian from Urmia, Protestant Minister at St Bartholomew's Episcopal Church in New York and Professor of Modern Oriental Languages at Columbia University, published a thoroughly documented book on the atrocities committed against Armenians and Assyrians. He wrote:

> The civilized world has been horrified by the monstrous crimes and most pathetic tragedy in history ancient or modern to which the Assyrians and Armenians have been once more subjected. We are witnessing to-day the greatest and the most ruthless atrocities in modern history. The entire Christian

nations of the Armenians and Assyrians are undergoing the process of extermination, by cruel methods of execution which surpass anything that ever preceded them anywhere. The atrocities that are being committed now against these harmless and helpless Christians in Turkey and Persia are of a long standing character. Sometimes the storm has abated its fury, only to start up again with increased energy, and the present relentless persecutions and brutal massacres are but the culmination of the generations of terror.[123]

That same year, a 72-page publication dealing with the massacres of Assyrians and based on eye-witness accounts appeared, written by a member of the American Committee for Armenian and Syrian Relief, William Walker Rockwell, professor at the Union Theological Seminary.[124] Rockwell appealed for help for a people who, he said, spoke Aramaic, the language of Christ:

> May this little publication be not merely a record of bravery in bearing the cross, but also a call for aid in the rescue of the decimated survivors of ancient communion, which preserves very closely in its liturgies the Aramaic spoken by our Lord. Once pioneers in the penetration of Asia by Christianity, for centuries in their mountain fastnesses they have been loyal defenders of their faith.

Joel E. Warda's *The Flickering Light of Asia or the Assyrian Nation and Church* appeared in 1924, published in Jersey City.[125] Written by a well-known Assyrian, it has since become a classic and a seminal source on the Assyrian people's contemporary history. Warda was president of the Assyrian National Association of America, and his book describes in detail the massacres of his people in Persia up to 1918 and their representations to the Paris Peace Conference, where he was one of the two Assyrian delegates.

The former US ambassador in Constantinople (December 1913–January 1916), Henry Morgenthau Sr., published his memoirs in 1918.[126] James L. Barton, who was extremely active in 1915 in defending Turkish Christians (both Armenians and Assyrians) in his role as president of the American Committee for Armenian and Syrian Relief, later told in *The Story of Near East Relief (1915–1930)* of American aid efforts in the Middle East, dedicating several pages to Turkey and Persia. In this book, ex-Ambassador Morgenthau makes special reference to the Assyrians: "The Armenians are not the only subjects in Turkey who have suffered from this policy of making Turkey exclusively the country of the Turks. The story which I have told about the Armenians, I could also tell, with certain modifications, about the Greeks and the Syrians."[127]

US government archives contain several reports relating to the Assyrian genocide.[128] Responding to a request by the State Department in 1918, two briefings were produced ahead of the Peace Conference,[129] one by Professor David Magie and the other by Abraham Yohannan.[130] The American consul Leslie Ammerton Davis also wrote a vivid account of the Armenian massacre from May 1914 to April 1917 in the region of Kharput, a report that was classified as confidential until 1949.[131]

Besides the "Blue Book", interest in the beleaguered Turkish Christian population was widespread in Britain. The Rev. F.N. Heazell, formerly secretary of the Archbishop of Canterbury's Assyrian Mission, an expert on the Assyrian Nestorians, produced a booklet on their predicament, *The Woes of a Distressed Nation: Being an Account of the Assyrian People from 1914 to 1934*.[132] Canon William A. Wigram (1872–1953), author of several works on the Assyrians and the Church of the East, produced a brief account of their experiences during the First World War, entitled *Our Smallest Ally*. In April 1915, J.D. Barnard published an article on the Assyrian question in the *Anglican Assyrian Missionary Quarterly Paper*, while later that year Paul Shimun contributed a statement to the monthly *Ararat*, the journal of the Armenian United Association in London.[133] In March 1916, the same publication carried an article ("Memorandum about Assyrian Refugees in Paris") by the war correspondent Morgan Philips Price, who had worked for various British and American newspapers on the Caucasus front and had been in Persia when the first Assyrian refugees had begun to arrive in Hakkari in October 1915. More generally, as we shall see later, the British press maintained its coverage of this issue.

Interest in the subject extended to other counties of the Middle East and Europe. Between 1920 and 1921 a monthly magazine, *L'Action assyro-chaldéenne*, appeared in Beirut, describing itself as "the organ of all Assyro-Chaldeans in the Mother Country and abroad" and aiming to act as a link between Europe and the Assyrian nation. It commented:

> At this time when small nations are establishing their autonomy, *L'Action assyro-chaldéenne* demands the creation of an Assyro-Chaldean state in Upper Mesopotamia and Assyrian Kurdistan, where the nation will live under a regime capable of guaranteeing its independence under the aegis and the trusteeship of France.

In *Armenia and the Near East*, by the Norwegian scientist, explorer and diplomat Fridtjof Nansen (translated into French in 1928), a revealing detail appears concerning the Ottoman authorities' intention to eradicate minorities:

> In February 1915, the vali of Van, Djevdet Bey, Enver Pasha's brother-in-law, made this statement at a Turkish assembly on the subject of Urmia's Assyro-Chaldean Christians (here called

Syrians). "We have made tabula rasa of the Armenians and Syrians in Azerbaijan, and we must do the same thing with the Armenians at Van."[134]

The Norwegian delegate to the League of Nations after the First World War, Nansen concerned himself with the repatriation of prisoners and the problem of refugees. The High Commission for Refugees, under Nansen's leadership, was founded in 1921 to assist Russian refugees, and its remit was expanded to include Armenians in 1924 and Assyrians in 1928. In 1933, Assyrians were able to obtain so-called "Nansen passports", internationally recognized refugee travel documents issued by the League of Nations to stateless refugees.

The Paris Peace Conference, 1919

Several religious leaders and prominent Assyrian individuals were present at the peace conference, having come from Turkey, Iraq, the Caucasus, Persia and the United States to plead the cause of their Church and people, stressing the massacres and the losses suffered.[135] Among these emissaries were the following: the Chaldean patriarch Joseph Emmanuel II Thomas, the Syriac Orthodox Mor Ephrem Barsoum, the Syriac Catholic patriarch Ephrem II Rahmani and his vicar Mgr Gabriel Tappouni. Other notable individuals included Joel Warda, Lazare Georges, Shimun Gandja, Lazare Yacouboff, Rustom Nedjib, Dr Jean Zebouni, Said Namik and Major A.K. Yousuf.

As regards France, a note had been delivered to the French Consulate in Basra on 16 January 1918 by a Chaldean churchman, who requested anonymity; it was entitled "Les Victimes de la nation chaldéenne dans les massacres d'Arménie".[136] The same consulate sent on to the

French Ministry of Foreign Affairs a letter from Baghdad dated 29 January 1919 from the Chaldean patriarch Joseph-Emmanuel II Thomas, in which he claims to have provided on 28 November 1918 a report accompanied by three detailed tables of all the losses experienced by his people at the hands of the governor of Mosul. Many other such documents were to arrive on the desks of diplomats through consular channels.

In his letter to the president of France's Council of Ministers, Georges Clemenceau, Ignatius Ephrem II Rahmani (1898–1929), patriarch of the Syriac Orthodox Church appended a detailed memorandum listing the damages suffered by his nation during the war, writing:

> The Christians who live in Jezireh are partly Chaldeans, others Catholic Syrians, still more Monophysites ... Notable citizens from these three groups were arrested and imprisoned, and then the Catholic Syrian bishop, Mgr Flavianus Michael Malke, a man of outstanding virtue and zeal, was jailed with four of his priests, together with the bishop of the Chaldeans Mgr Jacque[137] and his priests. After two months in captivity, they were taken an hour's distance from the town, their hands and feet in chains, and they were massacred without pity in a place called Tcamme-Souss.[138]

Among the various memorandums produced at the time of the Peace Conference, that written by the Nestorian patriarch Mar Paulus Shimun on 21 February 1919 at Baqubah and submitted by the British authorities is particularly noteworthy. It argues for the granting of broad territorial and legal autonomy as "a unified nation, on its homeland" in a geographic area encompassing Mosul, Jezireh, Bachkale and Urmia. Other Assyrian submissions stress that their people should not be confused with Armenians, that they wish for a an independent country, that goods, pasture land and other territory forcibly seized by Turks and Kurds should be returned, and that the property of the Church and nation should enjoy the protection of the law. The Persian government is also called upon to guarantee the security of Assyrians under its jurisdiction as well as to punish Turkish and Kurdish leaders responsible for violence against Assyrians. Arnold Toynbee thought Mar Paulus Shimun's memorandum "extremely reasonable": "Assyrian territory, as defined in the Memorandum, would be kept separate from Armenia and will be under protection of Great Britain or whatever power receives mandate in northern Mesopotamia, with the exception that no change can be made in the status of districts on the Persian side of the frontier." The third point, relating to the Assyrians' rights as a *millet* (separate community) "can be granted in principle, though the exact relation of Mar Shimun and his Millet to the Mesopotamian government on the one side, and between him and the mandatory power on the other, will have to be settled."[139]

International solidarity

Russia was the first nation to distribute material aid to the Assyrians, via the Red Cross, in the form of money, clothing, food and medicines; the patriarch Mar Benyamin Shimun offered thanks: "We are indeed very grateful to the esteemed Kingdom of Russia; it has assisted our nation with funds, clothing and medical supplies."[140] In the United States, the influential American Committee for Armenian and Syrian Relief provided aid supplies from November 1915, supported by the Rockefeller Foundation; the supplies were distributed locally by the State Department. The Assyrian Relief Fund, a subsidiary body of the Committee, launched an appeal for solidarity and humanitarian assistance for Assyrian Christians in June 1916, signed by sixteen American bishops (of New York, Massachusetts, Long Island, Pennsylvania, Newark, Connecticut, Ohio, Albany, New Jersey, etc.) and by the rector of Trinity Church, Manhattan. The appeal concluded with a reference to eastern Christianity: "The Church in America should rally to the support of this ancient communion of Oriental Christians." Articles appeared in *The Churchman* (Oxford) in 1916 and in *The Living Church* (US). Three ambulances were sent by the Rockefeller Foundation in July 1916 to assist the Assyrian people.

The American Committee for Armenian and Syrian Relief published five bulletins in 1916 on the atrocities committed against the Armenians and Assyrians.[141] Before its fusion with this organization, the Persian War Relief Committee had sent aid to Assyrian refugees, while another body, Chaldean Rescue, was also active in New York. In London, the Armenian Refugees (Lord Mayor's) Fund organized a solidarity meeting for Armenians and Assyrians in Westminster's Central Hall on 4 December 1918, an event recorded by the Armenian Bureau in a pamphlet.[142] Many individuals and organizations became involved—the Friends of Armenia, the Bible Lands Aid Society, Miss Barclay, the Armenian Relief Fund; appeals for donations from prominent figures in British society were published in the press, and a debate on the subject took place in the House of Commons on 20 December 1917.

In the United States, a solemn appeal was made by bishops in support of the Assyrian cause.[143] In Britain, the Archbishop of Canterbury, Randall Davidson, who was active within the influential Assyrian Mission, launched a similar appeal in the *Times* on 10 November 1915, inviting charitable donations for the destitute Assyrians from Hakkari who had sought refuge in Salmas.[144] These religious authorities were explicit in denouncing crimes and atrocities; the Archbishop of Canterbury declared:

> The massacres of Armenian and Assyrian Christians in the Turkish empire is a crime which in scale and horror has probably no parallel in the history of the world, and the sufferings baffle description which are now being endured by the rapidly dwindling number of hunted and persecuted survivors.[145]

British parishes organized days of prayer and collected donations destined for the Armenian and Assyrian population.

The British Catholic Church was also very active. While Father Joseph Naayem was in London in 1920, as commissioned by Mgr Suleiman Sabbagh (bishop of Diyarbakir), a support group, the Chaldean Relief Committee, was established by the Catholic Lady Edith Sykes, wife of the well-known politician Mark Sykes (1879–1919), an expert in Middle Eastern politics. At a meeting at London's Mansion House in January 1929, presided over by the Lord Mayor of the City of London, Alderman Sir Edward Cooper, an appeal was launched to try to alleviate the suffering of Chaldeans in Mesopotamia. On the platform with Lady Sykes were Canon Ross (Association for the Propagation of the Faith), Canon W.H. Carnegie, M.A., the Jesuit Father Bernard Vaughan, the Very Rev. Joseph Hertz (Chief Rabbi), the Rev. Dr William Wigram, the Irish nationalist parliamentarian T.P. O'Connor, Adrian Pollock and Herbert Ward (Secretary of the Committee). On this occasion Bishop Sabbagh also sent a written appeal, while some speakers stressed that the massacres had been carried out methodically under government orders and named those responsible.

The Lord Mayor, speaking in support of humanitarian aid, reminded his audience that the Chaldeans of Mesopotamia had been Christians since apostolic days, and, notwithstanding many centuries of Arab and Turkish domination, had preserved their faith. T.P. O'Connor declared that the Chaldeans were one of the historic races of the world and that they had preferred almost to perish as a nation rather than abandon their convictions:

> We speak for the liberation of every Christian creed in Turkey. We give from this platform a strong, clear and unanimous opinion that we will not tolerate on the part of our Government the abandonment once more to the horrors of Turkish government of any of the people whom we have helped to release from their grasp during the war.

Father Naayem, who was unwell, could not join the meeting, but his speech, read by Herbert Ward, emphasized the desolation of towns and villages and the sufferings of the people. Father Bernard Vaughan's contribution was based on the idea of common brotherhood, observed the Catholic weekly *The Tablet*: "it had been thought that with the death of Abdul Hamed there would be an end of the massacres by the Turks and Kurds. It had been thought that the Young Turk was going to close the door to the chamber of horrors and never again to open it. But he has closed the door, and opened a more horrible door leading to a more ghastly picture." Rabbi Joseph Hertz remarked that: "the time had come when massacre as a method of government should be exorcised for ever. Great is justice, for it alone leads to lasting peace, he quoted from the Talmud, expressing the hope that they would help the cause of triumphant justice and thus help the cause of triumphant and lasting peace." An official appeal for aid and assistance was finally released by the Chaldean Relief

Committee, signed by Cardinal Francis Bourne and Lady Sykes, on 14 January 1920:

> We appeal to the generosity of your readers on behalf of the unfortunate Chaldeans of Upper Mesopotamia. This race, though historic, and though the victims of Turkish methods of government as much as any other of the Christian races, under Turkish rule, have not, up to the present, appreciably shared in the assistance given to their fellow Christians. Yet they have suffered in an equal degree.

This suffering was described in detail:

> The youth at the time of the war were drafted into the Turkish army, and most of them perished from ill-treatment at the hand of their Turkish commanders. Those that remained at home— men, women and children—were subjected to the same treatment as the Armenians; the men were taken the hand tied, outside their towns and villages and massacred. Just as in the case of the Armenians, women and children were driven from their home and compelled to march in convoys without rest, food or water; many of them were butchered on the way. A large number of the women and the girls were retained as slaves in the Turkish and Kurdish harems; some of the women were sold and re-sold.

Donations were to be sent to 9 Buckingham Gate, SW1.[146]

Lady Sykes was, according to *L'Action assyro-chaldéenne*, "the first heart to express all the charitable sympathy of the English for the Assyro-Chaldean nation". In an article in the *Times* she wrote:

> Their villages, houses, churches and schools are destroyed, and during the past two years famine has claimed many more victims. We cannot watch, indifferent, the extermination of this brave and valiant nation, the cause of whose sufferings inflicted by the Turks was their open sympathy for the Allies alongside whom they fought in the terrible struggle from which we are

emerging in triumph. Not only can this people count on our charity, but also, in justice, we cannot let it perish; we have contracted towards them a large debt of gratitude.[147]

Outside London, meanwhile, a public meeting presided by the Lord Mayor of Manchester was held in Manchester Town Hall on 8 June 1920, at which Father Joseph Naayem gave information concerning "the terrible plight of the Chaldeans of Mesopotamia". The speakers described that through the experience of the Chaldeans, "it appeared, the history of the Armenians massacres repeated itself". A resolution on the necessity of assistance was then adopted, moved by A. Hailwood MP, seconded by Father W. Leighton and supported by the Bishop of Salford.

Authorized by the Sacred Congregation for the Oriental Church to spend six months in the United States, Joseph Naayem formed a support committee similar to that in London. Paul Shimun, an influential figure and witness to the aid delivered to Assyrian refugees, wrote in 1916 about the various sources of solidarity and assistance:

> Measures of relief were at once begun by the American Missionaries, and the Russians have sent money and clothing. The Archbishop of Canterbury's Committee in London, as well as the Lord Mayor's Armenian Relief Fund, the Friends of Armenia, and other agencies, have sent most generous assistance. The contributions of the Rockefeller Foundation have been most liberal.

Yet he concluded with a note of bitterness: "But it is one of the saddest things in life that the majority of those who have died have perished of exposure, want, sickness and unsanitary conditions..."[148]

In France, the Lazarists were behind appeals for Catholic charity to relieve the suffering of Christians in Persia. Mgr Sontag sent Father Abel Zaya to tour French

93

dioceses in search of such support, and he carried with him a letter, dated 8 February 1916 and addressed to Cardinal Léon-Adolphe Amette, Archbishop of Paris, who was instrumental in Mgr Sontag's ordination as a bishop. Mgr Sontag's letter was also signed by Mgr Thomas Audo, Chaldean Archbishop of Urmia, and Mgr Pierre Aziz, the Chaldean Bishop of Salmas. Aimed at the generosity of the French public, it read:

> From the beginning of this year, 1915, the Chaldeans of Persia have been hunted down, looted and massacred atrociously; their villages, numbering 114, were destroyed in the space of three days, their churches ruined, their wives and daughters abused, kidnapped and forced to become Muslims, while others have been cut into pieces after suffering unspeakable torments. This innocent and defenceless nation has suffered and continues to suffer all of this for no other reason than being Christian ... Last September the Chaldeans of Turkey met the same fate. Survivors came in large numbers to seek refuge with us, in Salmas and Urmia. Hardship is thus great, very great, among these unfortunate Christians. Many are already dead and more are dying each day from cold, starvation or illnesses contracted through deprivation.[149]

Following the example of the Syriac Orthodox Church, the Chaldean Church made efforts to take in refugees, widows and orphans, in Turkey and Iraq. A Chaldean ladies' charitable association was founded in Constantinople, under the aegis of the Assyro-Chaldean National Council, presided over by Mgr Thomas Bajari, Vicar General of the Chaldean Patriarchate. In a letter of 9 July 1919, Mgr Bajari thanked Pope Benedict XV for his support:

> As a true father to all the faithful, you were so touched and saddened by the poignant misfortunes of the Chaldean nation

that despite the huge task that faces you in leading the Church, you immediately wanted to remedy the many ills that overwhelm it.

The same letter reveals that the Pope had appointed an apostolic visitor to inspect the devastated areas and to study the extent of the crisis, then suggest means to alleviate it.[150]

The national and international press: an essential intermediary

The world's press was a major intermediary not only in publishing eye-witness reports and commentary but also in alerting public opinion as to the need for urgent humanitarian aid. Above all, it exposed the massacres of Armenians and Assyrians in Persia, Hakkari, and the whole of Turkey, allowing readers to follow the acts committed by Turkish forces and sometimes Kurdish irregulars on an almost day-to-day basis.

The American press was quick to raise alarms over the abuses committed by the Turks against the Christians. In January 1915 the *New York Times* was already warning that the Christian community was in grave danger in Turkey after Talaat Pasha unambiguously declared that "there was no room for Christians in Turkey".[151] At the same time, when the tragic events of January–May 1915 were unfolding in Salmas and Urmia, the newspaper published a series of damning articles denouncing the massacres, the brutal treatment of women as slaves and the direct role of the Turkish Consul in Urmia.[152] It also covered the traumatic exodus of Christians from Persian Azerbaijan towards the Russian Caucasus, their only hope of survival.[153] Testimonies by American Presbyterian missionaries were also published, such as that by Dr W. S. Vanneman, head of the hospital at Tabriz, who wrote:

> About ten days ago the Kurds in Salmas, with the permission of the Turkish troops, gathered all the Nestorian and Armenian men remaining there, it is reported about 800. Four hundred were sent to Khosrowa and 400 to Haft Dewan under the pretense of giving them bread. They were held a few days and then all of them tortured and massacred. Many of the women and children were taken away and maltreated.[154]

Faced with such evidence, the Triple Entente had no choice but to react. On 24 May 1915, the *New York Times* revealed that the previous day Britain, France and Russia had published a shared declaration, insisting that the Sublime Porte (the central Ottoman government) take responsibility for the massacres of Armenians:

> London, May 23—A joint official statement by Great Britain, France, and Russia, issued tonight, says: "For the past month Kurds and the Turkish population of Armenia have been engaged in massacring Armenians with the connivance and help of the Ottoman authorities ... In the face of these fresh crimes committed by Turkey, the allied Governments announce publicly to the Sublime Porte that they will hold all members of the Government, as well as such of their agents as are implicated, personally responsible for such massacres.[155]

Russian troops finally reoccupied the area of Urmia, but the toll was by then terrible for the Christian population, mostly Assyrian. Dr Harry P. Packard estimated on 29 May that 12,000 people had fled towards the Caucasus, and that more than 20,000 were unaccounted for.[156] Nor had the suffering in this part of Persia come to an end; the mountain-dwelling Assyrians of Hakkari, driven from their ancestral land by Turkish and Kurdish forces, sought refuge there after taking flight in the most appalling conditions, a situation described by the *New York Times* in October 1915.[157] The *American Protestant Missionary Review of the World* (New York) also informed its readers of the perilous conditions facing Christians in Persia from 1915 to 1918.

The British press was equally keen to publicize the issue, with the *Times* (9 October 1915) printing a letter from Miss Barclay to Rev. Gabriel Alexander, outlining the Urmia massacres in which 12,000 Nestorians are calculated to have died. Other British newspapers also headlined the atrocities and the slaughter of Nestorians.[158] The *Manchester Guardian* devoted several articles to the issue from 1915 to 1920: "The Massacres in Persia" (5 November 1915, by Paul Shimun, letter to the Editor); "The Murder of a Nation (19 November 1915, letter to the Editor); "War and Massacre in North-Western Persia. The First Story of the Prolonged Reign of Terror at Urumiah" (28 October 1915); "Assyria's Call for Help. A Princess Delegate. Petition from a Homeless People (27 October 1919); "The Aims of Turkey" by Dr A. Mingana (16 June 1917); "A Martyred People. The Chaldeans' claim on the Allies" (7 June 1920); "The Chaldeans. An Appeal for Turkey's least-known Victims" (9 June 1920).

The French press, meanwhile, adopted a similar stance, with the daily *Le Gaulois* reporting the murder of the Chaldean bishop Mgr Addai Scher in January 1916; in July, Frédéric Masson of the Académie Française appealed for help: "A people small in their ruins yet immense in the glories they claim and remember, the Chaldean people have almost entirely perished without Europe being moved to indignation and without anybody taking any interest."[159] *Le Temps* reported on the massacres in Persia on 12 May 1915, while the periodical *L'Asie française* regularly provided information on the Assyro-Chaldean situation between 1913 and 1938[160] and Catholic publications such as the *Annales de la Congrégation de la mission* and *Les Missions catholiques* did the same between 1915 and 1924.

The Assyro-Chaldean press strived to focus world attention on the issue, especially the journal of the Chaldean Catholic Vicariate in Beirut, *L'Action assyro-chaldéenne*. Other influential publications were the monthly *The New Assyria*, of which Joel E. Warda was the first editor, and Naoum Fayek's *Beth-Nahrain*, also published in the United States. Nor should the Russian media be overlooked, when *Tiflisskiy Listok* and *Rousskoy Slovo* were among the earliest newspapers to report the massacres, and Russia, as stated, was the first nation to mobilize attention and humanitarian aid.[161]

Humanitarian aid

The American press emphasized the urgent need for assistance to be sent to refugees and survivors. At the height of the crisis in Urmia between January and May 1915, the *New York Times* was already claiming that US$50,000 would be needed to feed the 10,000 refugees gathered within the grounds of the American Presbyterian Mission.[162] When the plight of the Assyrian refugees from Hakkari became known, the American Committee for Armenian and Syrian Relief stepped up its activities, as did the Assyrian community, among whom Shlemon Malek Yonan was prominent in raising awareness within his adopted country.[163] Appeals for donations intensified towards the end of 1915, and later in July 1916 and January 1919, interventions by American bishops in the *New York Times* produced favourable results among donors and foundations.[164]

In Britain, both the Anglican and Roman Catholic communities actively campaigned for humanitarian donations, as in an appeal in the *Times* in November 1915 for mountain Assyrians seeking refuge in Salmas.[165] Fundraising initiatives from the Churches and western foundations as well as by Assyrian individuals such as Paul Shimun and Abraham Yohannan continued throughout 1916. Surma Khanum, sister of the Nestorian patriarch, came to England in late 1919 and was active in support of her people, launching aid appeals[166] and taking part in solidarity meetings, as in March 1920.[167]

The Vatican also came to the assistance of the beleaguered Christians, distributing significant financial aid largely through the Chaldean and Syriac Catholic Churches, both during and after the war. In a letter from Baghdad of 17 February 1919, the Chaldean Patriarch Emmanuel II Thomas wrote to Cardinal Secretary of State Pietro Gasparri: "I have the honour of informing you that only a week ago, via the delegation from Syria, I received the allowances for the Syro-Chaldean seminarians and the 10,000 Italian livres given by His Holiness to be distributed to the poor of Mosul, Catholic and nonconformist."[168] Similarly, on 9 July, the vicar general of the Chaldean Patriarchate of Constantinople, Mgr Thomas Bajari, sent his heartfelt thanks to Benedict XV: "We can confirm, Holy Father, that the Chaldean widows and orphans who will be relieved by your benefactions will not cease to bless your name and that of the Holy Catholic Church within which they were born and will die."[169]

It is evident, then, that a multiplicity of documentary sources exists to cast light on the places and events involved in the Assyrian tragedy, and that these sources allow us better to understand how these events unfolded.

2

THE SCENES AND ACTS OF THE TRAGEDY

"When you receive this order of our godhead, which is contained in the enclosure herein dispatched, you will arrest Simon, the chief of the Nazarenes. You will not release him until he has signed this document and agreed to collect the payment to us of a double-tax and a double tribute for all the people of the Nazarenes who are found in the country of our godhead and who inhabit our territory. For our godhead has only the weariness of war while they have nothing but repose and pleasure. They live in our territory [but] share the sentiments of Caesar our enemy!"

Shapur II to his lieutenants (340 AD)

"The first of these persecutions lasted forty years, and was full of every kind of horrors."

William A. Wigram (1929)

A centuries-old persecution

The Assyrians have endured persecution for centuries, and several authors writing on the 1915 massacres refer to this long and tragic history. Even in the early Christian era, Eastern writers such as Eusebius of Caesarea (265–340), Aphrahat, the third-century "Persian sage" and author of homilies, Theoderet of Cyrus (393–460) and Mar Marouta, as well as scholars such as Stefano Evodio Assemani, refer to the Assyrians as victims of persecution. This theme has been continued in more recent times by authors such as Jérôme Labourt, the Chaldean Lazarist Paul Bedjan (1838–1921),[1] William A. Wigram,[2] Addai Scher, Abraham Yohannan, Joel E. Warda, William Arsanis, Pira Sarmas, Mgr Jacques Manna, Abdelmasih Naaman Qarabachi and Albert Abouna.[3] Those covering the events of 1915 have inevitably tended to compare that year with the violent persecutions of the past, especially under Shapur II (339–379) and Tamerlane or Timur (1336–1405).

The first centuries

The earliest persecutions occurred in the first centuries AD in Roman Mesopotamia, while the second wave took place in Persian Mesopotamia, and both often in places strangely evocative of 1915: The frontier provinces where Persia and the Roman Empire met (notably the town of Nusaybin). The motives were also almost identical—geopolitical, religious and economic—as were the methods of repression. Christians living in precarious locations at the outer ends of empires in conflict were wrongly suspected of collaboration with the enemy, a foretaste of the foreign interventions to come. They were also under pressure to abjure their faith and submit to the dominant religion of the period, such as Persian Zoroastrianism, at the same time as they were crushed by punitive taxation. Among the martyrs were many women, notably nuns.

The Romans

The Church of the East was already a target for persecution when Christians in Mesopotamia were massacred under the Roman Empire[4] during the reigns of emperors such as Trajan (98–117) and Diocletian (284–305), when imperial edicts were systematically applied. Ourhai, Samosata to the north of Edessa, Amid and Mardin all felt the harsh impact of Roman rule, and after the capture of Edessa in 165 this town became the seat of government in Roman Mesopotamia. Thereafter Edessa, a Christian metropolis, was subjected to the authority and actions of the Roman civil and military governor and was a target for religious persecution, with a large number of Christians arrested, tortured and crucified. The town of Samosata fared no better. The *Acts of Sharbil, Babai and Barsamya* has survived the centuries and is today a precious document telling of the martyrdom of Sharbil, high priest of pagans converted to Christianity, in 104, of his sister Babai and of Barsamya, Bishop of Edessa, of Gouria and Schamouna in 297, and of Habib in 309.[5] Several thousand Christians were killed, while others fled.

Scarcely had the persecutions finished in Roman Mesopotamia before flaring up in Persian Mesopotamia under King Ardashir, founder of the Sassanid dynasty in 226. In 286, Zoroastrianism became the state religion, well organized and led by a structured hierarchy known for its anti-Christian zeal.

The Sassanid Persians

Four kings (shahs) were particularly vehement in their persecutions of Christians: Shapur II, Ardashir II, Bahram

V and Yazdegerd II. Shapur II, who reigned for seventy years (309–79), unleashed systematic and brutal campaigns that lasted forty years (339–79). The first accounts of atrocities against Mesopotamian Christians date from 318 and are recorded in the *Acts of the Martyrs*, a vital historical resource of eye-witness accounts in Aramaic. These texts relate how Sharpur II began destroying churches and altars, burning monasteries and attacking all Christians. Under the authority of the king, persecution, motivated by economic, religious and geopolitical aims, was particularly intense in the northern provinces and in territory adjacent to the Roman Empire. The provinces of Beth Garmai (east of the Tigris river), Beth Zabdai (a district on its right bank), Arzanene and Adiabene were the first affected, before repression spread throughout most of the country, with particular ferocity in Beth Huzaye (Khuzestan), Beth Zabdai and in the towns of Adiabene. "Around 360, Shapur took several towns in Beth Zabdai, a frontier province of the Roman Empire. Each town seized was looted, the inhabitants deported and the clergy massacred."[6] Among the martyrs in Adiabene listed by Jérôme Labourt were John, Bishop of Erbil; Abraham, his successor; Hanania; the priest John; his sister the nun Mary; five other nuns; Barhadbeshabba, Deacon of Erbil; Aithala, a priest from Erbil; and Deacon Hafsai. A priest named James and Deacon Azad were the last two martyrs in Adiabene in 373.[7]

Shapur II, absolute ruler over the valleys of the Tigris and Euphrates, had issued an imperial decree against Persia's Christians in 340. The persecutions were further motivated by the refusal of the Catholicos of Seleucia-Ctesiphon, Mar Shimun (Simon) Bar Sabbae (329–41), to collect the double taxes demanded of the Christians to subsidize Shapur's war against the Romans. The *Acts of the Martyrs*, a living testimony to the enormous suffering inflicted, was in part written by Isaiah of Arzon, son of Abad, a knight in the king's guard and an eye-witness; the author of the text on the second persecution is unknown but was also an eye-witness; the writings that cover the forty-year persecution were the work of Mar Marutha, a religious authority and skilled diplomat who was bishop of Maypherkat (Martyropolis). The texts describe how churches were entirely destroyed and hundreds of victims beheaded.[8]

Among the best-known individuals to have been martyred were the two brothers Yunan (Jonah) and Brikh Yeshu, "virtuous and dear to all Christians, from the town of Beth-Asa, killed in 327. In the second wave of persecution from 338, Shapur, "embittered by his reversals against the Romans", again attacked the Church, supported by the leaders of the Magi or priesthood. More prominent Christians were murdered: Zbayna, Lazarus, Marut, Bishop Narsi, Mahri, Elijah, Habib, Sabas and Shampita, Bishop Isaac, Abraham the Bishop of Beth Selukh and Bishop Milles of Susa (Beth Huzaye). In the third persecution, the following were executed: Mar Shimun Bar Sabbae and his companions, the priests Abdhaihla and Ananias, who were the oldest in his presbyteral council, a hundred other Christians of differing orders, Guhashtazad, Pusak and "his virgin daughter consecrated to God" and the eunuch Azad, "who had brought up the king". The Patriarch Mar Shimun Bar Sabbae was put to death on Good Friday, 14 April 341, with 133 of his companions.

The accounts of such events reveal the brutality of Mazdaist Persia, as illustrated in the following instance: after Isaac had been stoned to death, "the king ordered

Mahanes, Abraham and Shimun to appear before him, and told them they must sacrifice themselves to the sun and worship its fire. They replied: 'God preserve us from such a crime; it is Jesus whom we adore and to whom we confess.'" The king ordered that they be killed by various tortures: Mahanes was flayed alive from the top of his head to his stomach and died in agony; Abraham had his eyes gouged out with a red hot poker and died two days later; Shimun was buried up to his chest in a pit and killed with arrows. Christians secretly took their bodies for burial.[9]

Some 9,000 Christians from the fortress of Phenek in Beth Zabdai, together with their bishop Heliodorus, were deported to Beth Huzaye following a revolt. According to the historian Sozomen, a lawyer in Constantinople who closely studied the persecutions, King Shapur "inflicted martyrdom on 16,000 nobles and an unknown number of people of humble origin". He added that the Emperor Constance sent a letter to Shapur, asking him to put an end to the persecution of Christians.[10]

During the reign of Shapur II, 150 chained confessors from the town of Karka in Beth Selok (Kirkuk), along with 20,000 inhabitants, chanted, "We do not worship the sun, kill us, we are Christians".[11] Within three days, 25,000 had been tortured and sacrificed. Executions, massacres and deportations of Christians filled the reign of Shapur II until his death on 19 August 379. The historian Theodoret of Cyrus gives a graphic account of their sufferings:

> To relate the various kinds of tortures and cruelties inflicted on the saints is no easy task. In some cases the hands were flayed, in others the back; of others they stripped the heads of skin from brow to beard; others were enveloped in split reeds with the cut part turned inwards and were surrounded with tight bandages from head to foot; then each of the reeds was dragged

out by force, and, tearing away the adjacent portions of the skin, caused severe agony; pits were dug and carefully greased, in which quantities of mice were put; then they let down the martyrs, bound hand and foot, so as not to be able to protect themselves from the animals, to be food for the mice, and the mice, under stress of hunger, little by little devoured the flesh of the victims, causing them long and terrible suffering. By others sufferings were endured even more terrible than these, invented by the enemy of humanity and the opponent of the truth, but the courage of the martyrs was unbroken, and they hastened unbidden in their eagerness to win that death which ushers men into indestructible life.[12]

Other massacres: from the fourth to the seventh centuries

Ardashir II (379–99), Sharpur II's successor, was equally hostile to the Christian population, his policy—like that of his predecessors—characterized by reinforcing Persian national power, the consolidation of a centralized administration and Zoroastrianism as the state religion. During the reign of Yazdegerd I (399–420), persecutions abated and a climate of tolerance began to emerge as relations between Christians and Persians entered a new phase. The king allowed the organization of the Church of the East and its hierarchy and published a *firman* recognizing the Catholicos as head of the Church in Persia and hence as the official civil and religious spokesman of his *millet* (community). The nomination of the patriarch was to be approved in advance by the king, and this recognition allowed the Church of the East, from 410 onwards, to put an end to interference in its affairs by Zoroastrian Magi and to hold official synods. In the year XI of Yazdegerd's reign, 410, "peace and calm were re-established by the Churches":

Yazdegerd gave freedom and rest to the Congregations of Christ, and allowed the servants of God publicly to glorify Christ in their bodies, either in death or in life; he removed the tempest of persecution from all God's churches; he banished the darkness of oppression from all Christ's flocks; he had ordered that all the temples destroyed by his ancestors in his empire should now be magnificently reconstructed, that altars demolished should be carefully restored; that those who had been tested by God, who had suffered prison and torture, should be set free; that the priests, the leaders of the Holy Alliance (all the clergy including monks) should be allowed to move around in freedom and without fear.[13]

However, under his grandson, Yazdegerd II, the persecutions resumed. Mar Pethion, who had formed an apostolate in the mountains of Kurdistan, was beheaded in 447 for preaching against the Zoroastrian elites within the Persian Empire. The Chaldean scholar Paul Bedjan dedicated hundreds of pages to these martyrs in his book *Lives of Saints* (1912, pp. 242–501), as well as in his seven-volume *Acta Martyrum et Sanctorum*. From the sixth to the eight centuries, some 250,000 Assyrian Christians were massacred by the Sassanid kings.

Ottoman antecedents to the 1915 massacres

Pillaging of Christian villages by Kurds was common practice, especially in Bohtan, but the period between 1843 and 1847 was more violent, as Eugène Griselle observes:

> The Kurdish Emir of Bohtan, Badr Khan, unleashed carnage among the Assyro-Chaldeans of the province of Van. More than 10,000 men were massacred, thousands of women and girls taken away and forcibly converted to Islam, all the property of the Assyro-Chaldeans and their villages burnt.[14]

François Daoud, a Chaldean priest, wrote in 1860: "How many villages have been looted and razed, their inhabitants massacred: only the name remains, everything else is gone." The author blamed the Turkish authorities for failing to protect their subjects: "The Turkish government must be held responsible, for it never tried to put an end to the brigandage."

Badr Khan was the hereditary leader of the Kurds in the Bohtan district and had already targeted the Assyrian Tiyari tribe in 1843, who were forced to submit. In 1846 he demanded from the Assyrians a sum of money that they could not pay, then issued threats, before another massacre took place in the region of Tkhuma. Badr Khan was by now openly defying the authority of the Ottoman sultan, who was slow to react, but finally the Ottoman authorities intervened, forcing Badr Khan to surrender and then go into exile. At the same time, Turkish authority was established in Kurdistan, where local populations were soon burdened with punitive taxes as Kurdish emirs were replaced by Turkish pashas.

1895: massacres and pogroms under Sultan Abdul Hamid II

The reign of Abdul Hamid was "a violent reaction against the attempts at reform made by his predecessors".[15] This sultan governed as a despot, adopting a highly rigorous and repressive policy of pan-Islamism. The Lebanese jurist Edmond Rabbath describes his regime as follows:

> Return to Islam and religious observance, antagonism towards modernity and innovation and towards reformers such as Midhat who had tried to rejuvenate Ottoman institutions; suspension of the 1876 Constitution and suspension of elected

assemblies, centralization in the provinces and suppression of confessional privileges and local autonomy, insurrections in Crete, massacres in Armenia: these are the defining features of Abdul Hamid's personal domestic policy.[16]

Faced with various internal challenges and the threat of the disintegration of the Ottoman Empire, Abdul Hamid took a hard line, suspending the 1876 Constitution that he had just promulgated and thereby turning his rule into an autocratic and highly centralized form of power which brutally crushed any form of open opposition. The non-Muslim, and particularly the Christian, minorities were popular targets amidst general resentment.

Massacres took place in 1895 in Diyarbakir (whose *vali* was Anis Pasha), in Urfa, Mardin and in surrounding areas. In his book *Al-Qousara fi Nakabat Annasara* ("The Calamities of the Christians"), Isaac Armalet recounts these events day by day, based on a manuscript by Habib Jawé, a prominent member of the Syriac Catholic community who had kept a diary of the atrocities committed by Turks and Kurds in Diyarbakir, Mardin, Saadiye, Miapharquin,[17] Qarabach, Goulié, Benebil, Kalaat Mara, Urfa, Tal Armen, Mansuriye, Nusaybin, Tur Abdin, Veran Shehir, and Derik. In Urfa alone, Father Joseph Naayem estimated 5,000 dead:

> Alas, I had already, at the age of seven, witnessed in 1985–86 another human slaughter in which 5,000 Christians had their throats cut by the town's Turks. My poor father had been able to escape, this time at least, from the massacre, through the providential intervention of a group of Arab traders, his faithful friends.[18]

Eugène Griselle also wrote of these atrocities:

> The barbaric massacres of Sultan Abdul Hamid are not yet far removed. Almost half a million Armenians were put to the

sword or else died of deprivation without counting several thousand Assyro-Chaldeans: the property of the Christians was looted, their homes burned, their women and young girls savagely dishonoured.[19]

Western governments were alarmed by such events. On 18 December 1895, Gustave Meyrier, French Vice-Consul at Diyarbakir, produced a detailed picture of the exactions inflicted on the Christian communities, irrespective of confession, showing that the Armenians were worst affected, with more than 1,000 dead and 250 wounded in Diyarbakir alone, while the Syriacs and Chaldeans had suffered 167 dead and 21 wounded.[20] Basil Nikitin observed:

> Things worsened under Abdul Hamid, who flattered the Kurds to make them faithful servants of his throne. They were given arms and formed into several Hamidiye regiments, and as a result we saw Kurdish attacks against the 'Ashirets' [mountain Assyrians of Hakkari] increase. The Turkish revolution of 1908, while promising improvements to the different peoples of the Ottoman Empire, only served to introduce Turkish bureaucracy into Kurdistan with all its failures and exactions.[21]

The Hamidiye troops (regiments formed in 1892) attacked Van for the first time on 10 November 1895, with looting followed in 1896 by massacres of Armenians, Chaldeans, Nestorians and Syriacs. Repression was brutal and killings widespread.

1909: the Young Turk revolution and the policy of Turkification

> "When the Constitution was proclaimed in Turkey, we believed in the promises of the government who guaranteed our security, and we sold a large part of our arms, as we had been led to believe that the Kurds had also been disarmed. And so our people were left defenceless. After the declaration of

Jihad (holy war), the Turks resolved to exterminate us in the same way as the Armenians and had us attacked by their troops and by the Kurds among whom we lived."

Mar Benyamin Shimun, Nestorian patriarch, October 1915

The Young Turks' revolution of 11 July 1908 put an end to Abdul Hamid II's reign, and the Committee of Union and Progress, led by the Young Turk movement, dominated national politics. At first, the revolution was greeted with enthusiasm by many sectors, including the Assyrian minority, and with hope by Christian communities. Yet from the autumn of 1908 the Young Turks' political orientation turned towards nationalism, with Turkish becoming the sole official state language and the language of education. A policy of assimilation—one people, one language—was imposed, to the detriment of smaller nationalities. Interference in the spiritual lives of Christian communities gathered pace, while education became a tool of forced assimilation. Populism, nationalism and pan-Turkism all reinforced the ideology of the ruling party. The situation rapidly deteriorated as Talaat, Enver and Djemal, the Three Pashas, saw the national minorities as the scapegoats against whom they could direct the rage of an Ottoman power wounded by the military defeats of 1911–13. The Russian jurist André N. Mandelstam concluded:

> It must be recognized that at the beginning of their reign the Young Turks made a sincere effort to oppose the despotism of Turkish theocracy with the ideal of a tolerant and liberal Ottoman state. But this effort was short-lived ... Ottomanism gave way to a shrill nationalism, hostile not only to Christians but to all non-Turkish elements. At the same time, Young Turk power increasingly took on the terrorist aspects of the Hamid regime. From the hands of the sultan Turkey passed into those

of the Committee of Union and Progress, a Jacobin club supported by Praetorians ... To the two fundamental principles of the Ottoman state—despotism and Islamism—the Young Turks added a third: Turkish nationalism.[22]

Canon William A. Wigram, familiar with the mountain Assyrians of Hakkari, supported this view, writing: "For the Assyrians, a glimmer of hope appeared in 1907 when the 'Young Turk' party overthrew Abdul Hamid and proclaimed a policy of reform and equal rights for all Ottoman subjects."[23] He added, however, that the old functionaries were kept in place and pursued the same policies and schemes, dashing all hope among the Christians.

The year 1909 marked the beginning of a policy of repression against non-Turkish peoples by the regime and a highly centralized authoritarian system, fuelled by the rise in nationalism. That year, Christians were massacred in Adana, the provincial capital of Cilicia, followed by scenes like those of 1895 across the Ottoman Empire. Many Chaldeans died in Adana in April 1909; before the massacre there were an estimated 800, and in the aftermath of the violence only 350.[24]

The events of 1909 presaged others yet to come, but on a much greater scale.

1915: historic Mesopotamia

"Christian minorities in the Turkish Empire had a terrible ten years before them. Orthodox, Uniate, Armenian, Jacobite, and Nestorian all alike endured privation, contumely, and periodic outbursts of violence. Massacres occurred in various parts of the Turkish Empire in which hundreds of Christians were slaughtered at a time, and the total death toll must have aggregated tens of thousands."

Audrey R. Vine, 1937[25]

"History is impartial and it is its duty to record this unprecedented tragedy whose outcome was the destruction of the majority of one of the most ancient Christian peoples."

Yusuf Malek, Le drame assyrien, *1934*

In 1915, most of the Assyrian population was rural and concentrated in villages near the main towns of several *vilayets*, *sanjaks*, *kazas* and *nahiyes*—differing administrative divisions of the Ottoman Empire, redrawn and renamed on a number of occasions. There were also urban populations and some well-known individuals in towns such as Adana, Urfa, Mardin, Diyarbakir, Midyat and Urmia.

After war broke out between Russia and the Ottoman Empire, Turkish forces invaded Transcaucasia. Two months later, the Russians abruptly evacuated Urmia on 2 January 1915, Salmas on 4 and Tabriz the following day. Their departure from the region was followed by the arrival of Turkish troops. That month, sixteen villages were sacked in the Urmia district, the ensuing atrocities related by numerous testimonies including those of the missionaries Father E.T. Allen and Robert M. Labaree, an American. At Babari, a Chaldean priest was tied to a pile of dry cow dung and burnt alive. At Anhar, a priest named Hormez was shot, while in Alqaye, the Chaldean priest was seized and taken to the mosque so that he could be made to renounce his faith; refusing categorically, he was slowly stabbed to death as he knelt in prayer. In the same village, the Nestorian bishop and fifty faithful were slaughtered because they refused to repudiate their Christian beliefs. At Salmas, the skin was flayed from another priest's head before his throat was cut. The Christian villages in the districts of Baranduz, Nazlu, Targawar, Margawar, Ouchnu and Soulduz were sacked, their inhabitants killed or forced to flee.[26]

During the Ottoman occupation of the provinces of Urmia and Salmas (January–May 1915), three-quarters of the Assyrian villages were burnt and pillaged, while several thousand inhabitants were annihilated either by violence or by the epidemics that cut down the refugees crowded into the religious missions. In all, more than 10,000 people were massacred or died in squalor.

The Turkish *vilayets*

More than six Turkish provinces were involved in the Assyrian massacres. The *vilayet* of Van was divided into two *sanjaks*: Van and Hakkari. The latter had been established as a *vilayet* between 1856 and 1888, before being merged with the *vilayet* of Van. The Assyrian population of Hakkari was estimated at around 100,000 before the First World War, mainly spread out in ten *kazas*: Djulamerk, Albaq, Gavar, Shemdinan (or Naoutchia, formerly Rustaqa), Mahmudi, Norduz, Tchal, Beth Chebab, Oramar and Amadiya. In the *kaza* of Djulamerk, in the centre-west, situated at the bottom of a steep gorge, was the patriarchal village of Kotchanes, exclusively Assyrian, some thirteen kilometres north of the main town, Djulamerk. Of the *kaza*'s total population of about 33,900, almost half were Assyrian. Assyrians represented more than a third of the population of Hakkari, coming second behind the Kurds, who made up almost half.

The districts of Gavar, northern Barwar and Bachkale were subjected to looting and killings, as were all the Assyrian territories of Nordouz, Albaq, Shamsdinan, Mar Bichou and Iyl. In Mosul, the *vali* Haydar Bey took command in 1915 and, according to Father Jacques Rhétoré, "according to his own self-interest, could behave either as a reasonable man or as a barbarian". In Mosul itself, he spared the Christians, but he ordered the destruction of Achita, a village of 500 Nestorian families, while the inhabitants fled into the mountains where many died of hunger and sickness. "Haydar Bey," says Father Rhétoré, "wrote in his report to Constantinople that he had carried out extensive massacres of Nestorians. He was following the party line and he was immediately sent his appointment as Vali".[27] Joseph Naayem wrote: "all the mountain territory of Hakkari, which spreads over the Russian and Persian frontiers, peopled by 120,000 Assyrians, was ravaged. Only a few thousand managed to escape the killers and seek refuge in Persia or Russia."

The *sanjak* of Van had an Assyrian population of 3,850 and a bishopric in Van, the chief town, where a bishop had been present in the Chaldean diocese since 1610; the Anglicans were also present in Van and its sixteen nearby Assyrian villages. On his return from an expedition into Persia in May 1915, Djevdet Bey began a programme of massacres in both the town and the villages. On 15 May, the sixteen villages were attacked: Kharachique, comprising 37 families, lost 103 people; Khinno (32 families) lost 51; Armanis (22 families) was half wiped out; Sele (50 families) and Kharafsorique (20 families) were completely annihilated; Akhdadja and Rachan (30 families) had no more than two men and two women surviving. During his withdrawal, Djevdet Bey also crossed the Bhotan river and sacked more than seventy villages in that area.

The *vilayet* of Bitlis was divided into four *sanjaks*, including Bitlis, Mouch and Siirt, and into nineteen *kazas* and eleven *nahiyes*. Here, not a single Christian population was spared; the Chaldean diocese of Siirt, with more than thirty villages, was completely devastated, with its people slaughtered amidst indescribable terror, according to reports. In the town of Siirt itself the victims included the bishop, Mgr Addai Scher, twelve priests and some 4,000 faithful. Churches, convents, the bishop's residence and educational and charitable institutions were looted clean and destroyed. Those Christians who escaped death, mostly children and women, were deported from one place to another and endured appalling treatment. According to Naayem, "A few hundred surviving women and children were lined up in a convoy and driven away from their homes in order to die in the desert amidst atrocious suffering."[28]

The *vilayet* of Diyarbakir comprised three *sanjaks* (Diyarbakir, Arghan and Mardin), thirteen *kazas* and fifty-four *nahiyes*, with the *sanjak* of Mardin divided into five *kazas*: Mardin, Nusaybin, Jezireh, Midyat and Avinek. There were two Chaldean villages close to Diyarbakir itself. The population of Jezireh, situated on the right bank of the Tigris south of Mardin, and of its thirty-five villages, all Assyrian, was entirely exterminated. Naayem observed: "Not a single Armenian was to be found in this area and no pretext whatsoever existed to justify the horrible massacre of more than 10,000 Assyro-Chaldeans ... Men, women and children were put to the sword by the Turks and Kurds."[29]

The Chaldean diocese of Jezireh met the same fate as that of Siirt, with the murder of Archbishop Yacoub Abraham, ten priests and some 5,000 Christians from the town and surrounding villages. Mgr Flavianus Michael Malke, Syriac Catholic bishop, was martyred on 20 August 1915. Churches, the bishop's house, schools and homes were looted and destroyed, while those who survived, women and children, were taken away as slaves. A small number took refuge in Mosul, but they were to be devastated by the famine of 1917, the famine "that made all those who witnessesed it shudder", wrote the Chaldean Patriarch Mar Joseph-Emmanuel II Thomas on 2 December 1918.

Expelled to Mardin, where they stayed for two years, the three French Dominicans—Jacques Rhétoré, Marie-Dominique Berré and Hyacinthe Simon—were witnesses of the holocaust of 1915. Their reports were supported by those of other observers in Mardin, Diyarbakir and their dependencies: the Syriac Catholic bishop Isaac Armalet, the Syriac Orthodox bishop Ephrem Barsoum, the Syriac Catholic Patriarch Rahmani, the Chaldean bishop Israel Audo and the Chaldean priest Paul Béro.

In the Diyarbakir *vilayet*, Rhétoré put the death toll at 144,185, of whom 64,175 were Syriacs and 10,010 Chaldeans.[30] Johannes Lepsius thought this *vilayet* to be "completely outside the theatre of war" and yet he calculated that "between 10 and 30 May, 1,200 other prominent individuals among the Armenians and Syrians [*sic*] were arrested".[31] In June 1915, massacres were carried out in Nusaybin, the centre of Eastern Christianity and formerly home to the celebrated Nisibine School, and in surrounding villages. Rhétoré recorded that "the Christian villages around Nusaybin, populated by Jacobites, all endured massacres and Kurdish occupation, so that now the whole region has become Muslim".[32]

The *vilayet* of Kharput contained three *sanjaks* (Karput-Mezere, Malatia and Dersim) and eighteen *kazas*. More than twenty-four Syriac villages were destroyed, among them Mezre, Adiyaman, Malatia, Chiro, Aiwtos and Guarguar. In Kharput itself was an American missionary college, where Ashur Yousif, community leader and founder of the publication *Murshid*, taught; Yousif was arrested and killed by Turkish forces at the beginning of May 1915.

At the end of 1918, Father Naayem became acquainted in Constantinople with a trader from Kharput, Djordjis Toumas Keshishe, eye-witness to the massacres that took place in his town in May 1915. Here again, the Turkish strategy was clear: first they began by arresting prominent individuals, and above all schoolteachers, putting them in prison and searching their homes.[33] Syriacs were arrested along with Armenians and faced the same fate: "All 1,500, without distinction, were led out of the town and massacred." Besides Kharput and Mezre, Naayem mentions the little town of Adyaman (Adiyaman), where "hardly a trace of the Christians remained, all of them having been hacked to death with axes and thrown into the river which watered the locality. The priests in particular had been tortured with indescribable savagery."[34]

The *vilayet* of Aleppo was divided into three *sanjaks* (Aleppo, Marash and Urfa), twenty-three *kazas* and fourteen *nahiyes*. The German Consul General in post at Aleppo between 1908 and 1918, Dr Walter Rössler, sent a telegram dated 26 August 1915 specifying that 200 Armenians and Syriac Orthodox had been massacred at Urfa on the 19th of that month, an important date.[35] However, it was above all Jakob Künzler and Father Naayem who acted as witnesses, with the former writing how on 19 August many "Suryani" were killed, as their murderers did not differentiate between them and Armenians, both being Christians and hence *giaours* (*Ungläubigen* in German, or "infidels") to be killed.[36] Naayem wrote: "The prisons were filled with Christians; the town sunk in deep mourning. Soon came the terrible and tragically memorable day of the executions." Of the Turkish authorities, he continues:

> But the Chief of the Union and Progress Committee remained mute, saying nothing, doing nothing. We could not make out his attitude. He was probably obeying some order he had received. Everything, even one's best friends, had to be sacrificed for the Committee.

His father, he recalls, "a follower of no party, innocent of political crime, absorbed in his family and his business, loved and esteemed by all, had been taken along and slaughtered without the semblance of a trial..."[37]

Several relatively wealthy Assyrian families also lived in Trebizond (Trabzon). Naayem describes the sufferings of one Madame Habiba Turkoghlou, a senior nurse originally from Diyarbakir deported with others from Trebizond. She recounts at length her ordeal and how her brutal separation from her husband and baby, "or rather sorting out of men and women gave occasion for a thousand scenes, each more cruel than the last."[38]

Overview of the massacres

> "Make no mistake: what is being pursued is the total destruction of the Armenian people by death or by forced conversion to Islam. Then the other roots of Christianity will be attacked. The Chaldeans of the districts of Salmas and Urmia, in Azerbaijan, have been looted and massacred."
>
> *René Pinon, 1916*

> "Years of war have changed the face of the old world. We have seen dynasties and empires unravel; peoples hitherto oppressed have rediscovered their former liberty; revolutionary systems of government have come into being—But it is probable that there is no human community, in relative terms, that has suf-

fered trials and blows comparable to those endured by that small group, both Nation and Church, that bears the name of Assyrians."

League of Nations, 1935

By virtue of the Anglo-Russian Convention of 1907, Persian Azerbaijan had come under the hegemony of the Russians, who therefore occupied the town of Urmia in December 1911. The Assyrian Christians, as well as the Armenians, felt protected. Yet two months after the declaration of war between Russia and the Ottoman Empire, Russian troops rapidly withdrew, albeit temporarily, without warning the Christian population. This was the starting point of the catastrophe, as Turco-Kurdish forces flooded into the region.

The Ottoman Empire entered the war against Russia on 3 November 1914. On 29 November, Sultan-Caliph Mehmed V (1909–18) proclaimed Jihad (holy war). Living on the periphery of the Ottoman Empire in zones of conflict and contested security, the Assyrian population was perceived by rising Turkish nationalism and dominant Islamism as an obstacle to the Empire's homogeneity, and as a supposedly threatening source of separation and collaboration with the Russians and the British. The stakes were geopolitical, but articulated and exploited in religious terms; all the more so since the Turks had just lost their Balkan territories (1912–13), and the Arab *vilayets* of the Near East were showing signs of seeking independence and emancipation.

The Turks accused the Assyrians of plotting with the Russians and seeking to destabilize the Empire. It is true that since the treaty of 1774 that ended the six-year Russo-Turkish War, Russia had maintained a presence in Persian Azerbaijan and other regions inhabited by Assyrians. It was also the case that the proximity of Russia and its historic role as a Christian adversary of the Ottoman and Persian Empires gave it appeal as the protector of Eastern Christians. But if many Assyrians, isolated and cut off from the Christian world, viewed Russia with sympathy and as a source of support, they received little in the way of practical assistance. According to Colonel Ronald Semphill Stafford, in April 1915, the Russians "made further attempts to induce the Assyrians to join them. They promised arms and other material assistance."[39] Such promises seem to have been largely unfulfilled, as few arms, if any, were forthcoming.

Even before the declaration of war, in September 1914 the first symptomatic outbreaks of looting and killing began to appear on the plain of Urmia and in surrounding areas. After the official commencement of hostilities and the ensuing withdrawal of Russian forces on 2 January 1915, Turkish troops again invaded Persian Azerbaijan, beginning the carnage. This, for the Assyrians, was the start of the ordeal of Urmia-Salmas, a succession of calamities, an itinerary of blood. The exodus towards the Caucasus took place on 2 January, when around 25,000 men, women and children took to the road, following from 4 January in the Russians' footsteps. Attacks intensified on both sides of the Turco-Persian border, taking on a systematic and premeditated form. Johannes Lepsius wrote:

> The Turkish and Kurdish troops devastated all the Christian villages on Persian territory. The Assyro-Chaldean population of the Urmia region and the Armenians of the Salmas plain (around Diliman) were pitilessly massacred by the Kurds if they could not flee to Russian territory or find refuge in the American mission.[40]

According to William A. Wigram:

The first fighting took place in Persia ... Regular Ottoman troops and Kurdish irregulars swept over the border, drove the Christian clans from Tergavar, and came down towards Urmi, intending to occupy that place and call on the Shiah Musulman population to forget all feuds in Islam, and join with them in the Jehad which had been already proclaimed.[41]

For five months, Urmia was literally besieged by 20,000 Turkish regulars supported by 10,000 Kurdish auxiliaries, who attacked on the orders of Djevdet Bey, pillaging, killing, spreading terror and unleashing their hatred on Christian villages. Gripped by panic, the Assyrians took flight on foot, walking hundreds of kilometres in the middle of winter in appalling conditions. Many died on the roads, of hunger, cold and sickness, without counting those who made it to the Russian border only to die of exhaustion. Others found shelter in the American and French foreign missions. For months, about 15,000 people were confined within the American Mission, of whom a third died from epidemics or hunger. The French Lazarist Mission, much smaller, took in about 3,500 refugees.

On 24 May 1915, the Russian Cossacks returned to Urmia, and if their victory brought some relief to the Christians, their troubles were certainly not over. William A. Shedd, the doctor and missionary responsible for the American Mission, was unambivalent in apportioning responsibility for the atrocities:

There is no class of Mohammedans that can be exempted from blame. The villagers joined in the looting and shared in the crimes of violence, and Persians of the higher class acquiesced in the outrages and shared in the plunders. The Kurds were in their natural elements. The Turks not only gave occasion for all that happened, but were direct participants in the worst of the

123

crimes ... It is certainly safe to say that a part of this outrage and ruin was directly due to the Turks, and that none of it would have taken place except for them.[42]

The invasion of Hakkari by Turco-Kurdish forces

"Driven from their mountains by Turkish forces, they [the Assyrians] sought refuge in Urmia, in Persia, a town that at the time was in the hands of Russian troops."

League of Nations, 1935

During the autumn of 1914, while the Turks were preparing for war, Kurdish leaders and all the tribes of the Tigris and Great Zab regions, fanaticized by the propaganda of the Turkish authorities, gathered with the intention of sweeping through the territories occupied by Christians and spuriously known as "Little Russia".[43] In the spring of 1915, threats were already being levelled against the mountain-dwelling Assyrians of Hakkari.

At the beginning of June, Haydar Bey raised his troops against Hakkari's Christians, destroying the region from Achita to Bachkale,[44] while Lower Tyari was devastated by the Turkish army. It was then that the Assyrians began, while fighting—until their limited ammunition ran out—to flee towards the high mountains with their families and livestock. They crossed the River Zab, destroying each bridge after crossing it. The Turks and Kurds demolished the ten villages of Barwar and Lower Tyari and more than fifteen churches, stealing ancient manuscripts and liturgical books. In the district of Barwari Bala, in the south of Hakkari and next to Lower Tyari (the frontier with Iraq), several Assyrian villages came under attack: Dooreh, Kani Masi, Eqkri, Malkhtha, Baibaluk, Derishke, Maye, Hayis, Bishmeeyayeh, Jalik and so on.

In many cases, Assyrian communities put up resistance. The mountain-dwelling tribes, the Tyari and Tkhuma, were the most powerful and best-organized, the Nestorian patriarch Eliyya VIII noting in 1610 that "all are men of war and musketeers". Across the entire Assyrian territory, but especially in the rugged terrain of Hakkari, communities defended themselves as best they could. Writing of the Hakkari Assyrians, Anahit Khosroeva observes: "Their militancy and the formidability of the area's topography spared these inhabitants from the extremes of Turkish aggressions, albeit with some loss of life."[45] Yet isolated, surrounded on all sides by Turco-Kurdish forces and equipped with rudimentary weaponry, they were outnumbered and outgunned by a well-equipped military and its irregular allies. According to David Gaunt, "Many Assyrians had only their traditional flintlock weapons, while the aggressors had modern rifles, machine guns and artillery."[46]

To escape dishonour, women took part in the fighting. In Midyat, the capital of Tur Abdin, Ain Ward and Azakh, Syriac resistance has entered the collective imagination and mythology. In the Syriac village of Deir Salib in Tur Abdin, encircled by Muslim villages, the inhabitants, having taken an oath, barricaded themselves against attack and resisted the Kurds for more than two and a half months.

There were further Turkish onslaughts against the Assyrian Tkhuma tribe at the end of September, with the villages of Gundikta, Mazraya, Lower Tkhuma and others destroyed.[47] On 29 September the patriarch officiated at the funeral of his brother Ishaya, who died at Tal. The next day, 4,000 Kurds attacked the fugitives in this district which would be known as "the valley of death", with 5,000 killed and 200 women and children abducted. Escape into the mountains was perilous, and families, under siege and without hope of help, died of hunger and thirst. The Assyrians of Hakkari continued to flee towards Persia, crossing the high mountains towards Salmas on 7–8 October. Those exhausted survivors, perhaps 50,000 out of 100,000, were received by the Russian military and their own compatriots. Some stayed in Bachkale and the plain of Albaq, leaving thousands of dead behind them. Yet the local population was hostile towards them, while their fellow Assyrians were indigent; some households sheltered between twenty and thirty refugees while waiting for help.

Eastern Anatolia

Here, the horror began from 8 April 1915 under the direction of Rashid Bey, governor general (*vali*) of the Diyarbakir *vilayet* (province), with the eradication of community leaders; in May, 450 Assyrian notables were arrested. Terrible massacres ensued, followed by deportations, the seizing of young women, rape, forced conversion and looting.

The small town of Ludje, not far from Diyarbakir, experienced atrocities witnessed by Naaman Effendi, then director of the Public Debt office, who later related his story to Father Joseph Naayem in Aleppo.[48] Anisa Bey was the *kaymacam* of the town and, in the spring of 1915, "recruited a militia among the Turkish population, appointed officers and put the regiment through manoeuvres". Having dismissed all Christian public servants, he gathered together the notables of the community and imprisoned them before embarking on a widespread programme of torture among the people. The Christians in this district were Armenians and Assyrians (Syriac Orthodox); they were deported or murdered, including women and children. "Children who became exhausted from fatigue or hunger on the way were left on the roadside where they soon died"; in the convoys, "the Christians were handed over to the Turks who seized those on whom they wanted to take revenge." Young women were taken away and "the most beautiful girls were kept for a week by the Turkish officials in town and then passed on to their friends."

The chief of the Ludje militia, Ibrahim Bey, "had come to Diyarbakir, to return by favour of Rashid, Governor of Diyarbakir, with the rank of Commandant". The inhabitants of various surrounding villages were also put to the sword: Foum, Chim-Chim, Djoum, Passor, Tappa and Naghle. "The priest of Foum was arrested and dragged by the beard through the streets to prison amid the hooting of the urchins." Naaman Effendi's testimony ends by recalling that "Turkish matrons accompanied the female convoys, asking mothers to entrust their children to them. Moslem women then robbed the poor little things of their clothes and abandoned them by the roadside."

The persecutions in Diyarbakir, a multi-confessional town, affected all communities. Of the Chaldean diocese only the archbishop Mgr Suleiman Sabbagh, three priests and forty families remained in the town itself, while the villages around suffered at the hands of Rashid Bey, described as "perhaps the most hideous of the many executioners spawned by the Young Turks". All the inhabitants of Tcharokhia were exterminated, while the village of Hochine, not far from the town of Severik, was overrun by Turkish gendarmes and Kurds and all there were massacred. Mgr Sabbagh wrote in March 1919:

> The Turks, who always considered the Christians within their Empire as the friends and protégés of the Entente powers, took advantage of the state of war to unleash all their hatred upon

them and to try to wipe them out; our small Chaldean people, already so weak, was on the brink of disappearing.

The populations of the villages were killed with their priests, churches and homes were devastated, and all sorts of atrocities committed against survivors. In the towns of Diyarbakir and Mardin, a large number of the inhabitants died and many victims were looted, while the two bishops and the towns' priests lived in constant horror at the terror inflicted on the faithful. The large Syriac village of Gulie was razed in April and May 1915, and on 3 June the Turks rounded up well-known Assyrians and Armenians in Mardin, whence nearly fifty families were deported to Mosul and 500 men fled to Mount Sinjar, where they were protected by Yazidis.

As a witness to the massacre of the Chaldean faithful in his diocese, Mgr Sabbagh offers a devastating account of the abuses and deportations. All of the young Chaldean men forcibly enlisted into the Turkish army, he reported, died in the trenches, victims of privations and bad treatment. Those exempt from military service were subjected to requisitions, confiscations and excessive taxation, with the government intent on bleeding them dry. The culmination, he writes, was the massacres:

> Bolstered by the religious fanaticism of its people and its hatred of Christians, the Turkish government turned our land, as well as a large part of Mesopotamia inhabited by the Chaldean people, into an immense burial pit that our unfortunate children filled with their bones. Their hands tied like convicts, all male Chaldeans of the area, led by night out of the towns and villages by Tcherkess [Circasians] and gendarmes recruited from among the worst murderers, had their throats pitilessly cut on the road. This nameless butchery was carried out so brutally and with such cruel refinements that one might be tempted to

doubt the truth of events. Hyenas and birds of prey fed for months on the bodies of Chaldeans lying on the plains and in ravines, and for weeks the waters of the Tigris, red with their blood, swept thousands of their corpses away.[49]

Joseph Naayem's book also contains, in Chapter VIII, three important testimonies on the Diyarbakir massacres. The first, from Hanna, son of Chamounn, a Chaldean from Diyarbakir who arrived in Constantinople in the winter of 1918, tells how he had lost his brother and parents, "victims to the barbarity of the Turks". He was present at the killings in the town and related his story to Latif Bey Habib, a prominent Chaldean and member of Constantinople's Court of Appeal.

Before the notorious Rashid Bey, Hamid Bey was *vali* of Diyarbakir, and he ordered the shooting of the villagers of Qarabach near Diyarbakir, watching alongside the civil inspector Nadji Bey "with every evidence of satisfaction". In March 1915, he was replaced by Rashid Bey, whose first task was to form a militia of local notables. He then decreed that Christians should surrender any weapons they possessed within three days or face severe penalties; "the Christians were then subjected to appalling tortures to oblige them to admit that they had arms concealed in their homes. Their nails were torn out and they were shod with iron like horses."

The second act began with the roundup of Christians, supposedly to force them into the army, with 1,500 men taken away and killed a month later (Naayem's book specifies the site of the massacre and lists many Chaldean victims, murdered by the Diyarbakir police). The churches in Chaldean villages were all sacked, plundered and left in ruins, while those in town that were spared "were turned into hospitals or stables". Looting was widespread:

"Governor Rashid is said to have sent to Constantinople eighty bales of loot taken from the Christians. The remainder he gave to his friends, among whom were Deputies Feizi[50] and Zulfi."

While visiting Antoun Roumi in Aleppo, Father Naayem met a twelve-year-old Chaldean girl from Diyarbakir named Wahida, related to Mrs Roumi. "Her mother, a survivor of the massacres, had been unable to support her, her father having been killed by the Turks and her home plundered." Her father, Naoum Abid, a municipal commissioner, fearful of being killed, had hidden during the arrests, but Turkish police entered their home and took Wahida's father away to prison. She witnessed her father being killed in the prison; her mother, fearing she would meet the same fate, then made plans to flee with her children:

> Like a brave woman, she gathered all her children together, and by crossing from one terrace roof to another we finally found a safe place in which to shelter. In this way she saved us from death. When the storm had passed we returned home and found that all our furniture had been stolen. Not being able to live in an empty house, and having no money or other resources, my mother had to take service in Turkish families at Diyarbakir in order to support us. But not earning enough to feed us, she was obliged to send some of us to my uncle Petioun in Aleppo.

Tragedy in Bhotan

In parallel, towards the end of May 1915, Djevdet Bey, forced out of Van, entered Siirt with 8,000 soldiers. More than seventy villages were pillaged and their inhabitants killed in the Tigris valley around the Bhotan district: Djezire-Ibn-Omar, Bitlis, Siirt, Hassana, Mansuriye, Shakh and many others, where 10,000 Assyrians lived. Under government orders, Turkish and Kurdish troops engaged in a total and undiscriminating massacre, as confirmed by Rev. E.W. McDowell:

> There was a general massacre in the Bohtan region, and our helpers, preachers, teachers and Bible-women, with their families, fell victims to it among the rest. By order of the government, the Kurds and Turkish soldiers put the Christians of all those villages, including Jezireh, to the sword.[51]

In the locality of Jezireh, in the Diyarbakir *vilayet*, thirty-five villages were exterminated, home to Chaldeans, Syriac Orthodox and Catholics and Protestants. The bloodthirsty Rashid Bey was the chief instigator, despite the strong resistance put up by the *kaymacam* and some prominent Muslims. Among the destroyed villages were Takiann, Fechhabour, Wahsad, Hassana, Tell-Kabbin, Merga, Oz, Harbol, Guirguébadro, Mansuriye, Ischy, Baz, Haltoun, Mar-Sauricho and Shakh; Mgr Jacques Abraham, the Chaldean archbishop, was murdered along with several priests in Hassana and Mansuriye.

Formerly a patriarchal seat between 1555 and 1580, the diocese of Siirt contained thirty-seven Assyrian communities, the town of Siirt housed a Chaldean cathedral that was to be "turned into a stable".[52] In 1913, the diocese had 5,430 faithful; in 1928, only 1,600 were left. The Siirt massacres, in which nobody was spared, lasted more than a month (15 May–24 June 1915) and take up a whole chapter of Naayem's book. A Chaldean priest noted, "The Tchettas [see below] dealt with the town's Christians, the Kurds with those in the villages." Naayem recorded four testimonies in Aleppo and Constantinople from individuals present at the time: Madame Djalila, daughter of Moussa Gorguis Asam, a Chaldean from Siirt interviewed in Aleppo on 18 February 1918; Madame Halata, Hanna's daughter, a Chaldean encountered in Constantinople; Kerima, another Siirt Chaldean; and Stera and Warina, daughters of Kas Hanna Chammas of Sadagh. The latter recounted the murder of Mgr Addai Scher, the scholar and Chaldean archbishop of Siirt, and of his secretary Father Gabriel Moussa Gorguis Adamo, who was arrested, savagely beaten and killed. Before his arrest, several priests had fled from surrounding villages to the church in Siirt, but all were captured and murdered. A week beforehand, the priest of Siirt, Father Azar, who had hidden in a well, "was killed with every refinement of torture".[53]

Aged fifty-five, Madame Halata was in mourning for her only son and for many other martyred relatives and testified for several hours, telling of how the Turkish government enlisted Muslims into the infamous Tchetta corps, a sort of militia organized by the Committee of Union and Progress to carry out massacres and deportations. She explained in detail how the Christians had been arrested and held in the barracks in Siirt, while "the Mohammedan populace was jubilant at the extermination of Christians in the towns". "The Chaldean cemetery likewise had been desecrated, the tombstones had been uprooted and many of the graves profaned."[54]

Kerima, who was thirteen at the time of the genocide, saw her parents murdered. "All the objects of value which we possessed, such as watch-bracelets, gold chains and earrings, were stolen by Abdul Ferid who is now at Siirt."[55] Despite all the obstacles, three priests managed to escape from Siirt and find refuge in Russia after the retreat from Van on 18 July 1915.

After Siirt, on 25 June it was the turn of Bitlis to be surrounded by the Turks under the command of Djevdet Bey, who led a special division known as *Kassab Tabouri* (the Butchers' Battalion).[56] "Having massacred nearly all the men, they gathered the women and girls together in a vast square, where the Turks and Kurds, summoned by a town crier, came to select as many women as they wanted, then having taken their pleasures, they gave them away as gifts to one another or sold them as slaves."

A third exodus towards the Caucasus took place in July, this time from Van and Bitlis, after the tragedies there and at Azakh, Jezireh, Siirt and the Bhotan region.

The Syriacs

Besides documents in foreign languages, an important collection of texts in Aramaic and Arabic also attests to the massacres inflicted on the Syriac population. This community lived in Syria and Upper Mesopotamia; Antioch was the seat of the powerful Syriac Orthodox Church until 518, when, due to upheavals, it moved to different locations in Upper Mesopotamia before settling definitively at the Deir Zafaran monastery near Mardin in Turkey, where it remained until 1933.[57]

On the eve of the Great War, Syriacs lived mostly in the *vilayets* of Diyarbakir, Bitlis, Kharput and Urfa. Before the massacres, they numbered more than 250,000. By the time the atrocities had ended, 160 churches and convents were in ruins, 161 priests and other clergymen had been killed and 345 villages looted, with hospitals, dispensaries and schools demolished. A large number of orphans, widows and refugees made up the remaining population, while the death toll varied, according to different sources, from 100,000 to 136,000.

Documents in the British archives, presented by well-known scholar and Syriac Archbishop of Syria Mor

Ephrem Barsoum (1877–1957,)[58] are a thorough indictment of Turkish policy. An emissary of Mor Ignatius Elias III Chaker, Syriac Orthodox Patriarch of Antioch and all the East, he came to Europe in the aftermath of the First World War to plead his people's cause with governments and with the secretariat of the Paris Peace Conference. A letter of 8 March 1920, addressed to the UK's Prime Minister Lloyd George made the following six points:

1. It is to be noted that our nation, apart from the persecutions inflicted upon it in the by-gone days of the Red Sultan Abdul-Hamid in 1895, has proportionately to its number suffered more than any other nation whose fate was the cruel sword of the Turks and the dagger of their brothers in barbarism the Kurds, as it will be seen by the enclosed list, which indicates the number of our massacred people amounts to 90,000 Syrians and 90,000 Nestorians and Chaldeans.

2. We regret bitterly that this ancient and glorious race which has rendered so many valuable services to civilization should be so neglected and even ignored by the European press and diplomatic correspondence, in which all Turkish massacres are called "Armenian massacres" while the right name should have been "The Christian massacres" since all Christians have suffered in the same degree.

3. We beseech the Peace Conference in its dealing with criminal Turkey not to forget to extend its solicitude to the innocent Syro-Chaldeans ... In consequence, we demand the emancipation of the vilayets of Diyarbakir, Bitlis, Kharput and Urfa from the Turkish yoke.

4. We again contest the establishment of a Kurdish authority that a so-called delegation is attempting to

promote and which would only renew the horrible scenes of recent Kurdish barbarity.

5. We ask for indemnities in compensation of our damages.
6. We ask for guarantees concerning our national and religious future.

We are counting on the justice of the Peace Conference and that it will listen to our nation and its aspirations for a better future that will allow it to play its former role as an Assyro-Chaldean civilization.[59]

In this document, Mor Barsoum thus rejected the planned ceding of Diyarbakir, Mardin and Urfa to Turkey. He also demanded the repair of churches destroyed, as well as justice for Syriac orphans and widows, asking that these issues feature in the discussion of the Ottoman Empire's future by the British Parliament. The British archives are revealing as to the extent of the devastation suffered by the Syriacs and their resulting demands. In his February 1920 memorandum addressed to the Peace Conference, Mor Barsoum listed the damages inflicted on his community: the four *vilayets* widely devastated by the Turks, 345 villages destroyed, 13,350 families exterminated, 90,313 individuals massacred, 156 churches and monasteries ruined, 154 priests and other clergymen killed and seven bishops and patriarchal vicars martyred. The region of Midyat was the worst affected: forty-seven villages around Tur Abdin were razed,[60] 3,935 families annihilated, 25,830 people, sixty priests and other clergymen, the patriarchal vicar P. Ephrem and the Bishop of Deir el-Salib Mor Antimos Yacoub murdered, with sixty churches and monasteries destroyed.

Table 1

Vilayets, Towns and Kazas	Villages	Families	Persons killed	Churches and convents ruined	Priests and other clergy killed	Bishops and vicars killed
Vilayet of Diyabakir						
Diyarbakir and around	30	764	5379	5	7	–
Slivan		174	1195	5	1	–
Lidjet	10	658	4706	5	4	P.M.Siman
Deireket	–	50	350	1	1	–
Siverek	30	897	5725	12	12	Mgr Denha
Viranchéhir	16	303	1928	1	–	–
Mardin	8	880	5815	12	5	–
Saour	7	880	6164	2	3	–
Nusaybin	50	1000	7000	12	25	P. Stiphan
Jezireh	26	994	7510	13	8	–
Becheriet	30	718	4481	10	10	P. Gibrail
Baravat	15	282	1880	1	1	–
Midyat	47	3935	25830	60	60	P.Ephraim Mgr.Yacoub
Vilayet of Bitlis						
Bitlis	12	130	850	1	–	–
Siirt	–	100	650	1	2	P. Ibrahim
Schirwan	9	283	1870	2	4	–
Gharzan	22	744	5140	12	9	–
Vilayet of Kharput						
Kharput	24	508	3500	5	2	–
Sandzak of Urfa						
Urfa	–	50	340	–	–	–
Total	345	13350	90313	156	154	7

This memorandum, foreshadowing the March letter, also outlined the claims of the Syriacs, demanded the emancipation of Diyarbakir, Bitlis, Kharput and Urfa from Turkish control, and protested vigorously against the proposed idea of a Kurdish authority in the region on the basis of Kurdish involvement in past atrocities. It also requested both compensation and guarantees for the future of the Syriac community. A table (page 134) of damages accompanied the memorandum.

In the aftermath of the 1915 genocide, the Syriacs were forced into exile and dispersed. The haemorrhage would continue as Turkish villages were largely emptied of their Syriac population.

Syriac humanitarian action

Important humanitarian and social work was undertaken among Syriac refugee communities in the wake of their flight from Turkey. Those who had settled in Syria (in the regions of Jezireh and Aleppo) and in Lebanon (Beirut and Zahlé) established orphanages and schools under the aegis of the Assyrian National School Association, founded in New Jersey. News of the genocide had reached an earlier Syriac migrant community in the United States, and they responded by supporting thousands of orphans through the Association, known by its Aramaic initials TMS, whose origins lay in the 1895 Diyarbakir massacres and the flight of survivors to the US. Funds were collected and a first orphanage opened in Adana in 1918, a place where the presence of Allied troops had allowed Syriacs to gather in safety. Some 200 orphans were accommodated and taught Arabic, Aramaic and French, while members of the Association and their supporters reportedly fasted one day a week in order to raise funds. After the political changes brought about by the Allies in Cilicia and its takeover by Turkey, the orphanage was moved to Beirut, where land was bought in 1923 and the institution inaugurated in 1928. Thanks to its reputation, it soon attracted non-orphaned students from the rest of Lebanon, from Syria (Aleppo, Homs and Jezireh) and from Palestine, becoming an elite school.[61] Until its closure in 1956, most teachers of Aramaic graduated from this school, teaching in Syria, Lebanon and Palestine.

Other appeals for aid were launched in the United States, particularly aimed at Tur Abdin, described as "the heartland of the Syriac nation".

Extermination and deportation: the children of the Desert

The Assyrian community was also subjected to deportations into the deserts of Syria and Iraq, notably on "death marches" to Deir ez-Zor, Ras al-Ayn, Mosul and Sinjar. Father Naayem's book focuses on the experiences of two Chaldean children found alive in the desert and a twelve-year-old girl, Wahida. Before leaving Aleppo at the beginning of June 1918, Naayem learnt that his friends, the Boyadji family, had just been reunited with a grandson named Michael, aged twelve, who had been found living with desert Bedouins. He went to see the child, "very thin and suffering from a stomach ailment brought on by his privations". His younger brother, aged nine, had also been found some months earlier by his uncles. Naayem asked Michael what had happened to him and how the Bedouins had taken him with them. The child, who had almost entirely forgotten his native Aramaic, told his story in the Arabic of the Bedouins, which he spoke "perfectly".

After the roundup carried out in Diyarbakir, all men, including Michael's father, were taken to jail and then murdered and thrown in the river. Then the Turks gathered together all the women, girls and children whom they intended to deport. Michael, with his mother, sister and younger brother, was part of a convoy of 300 people. He witnessed the ensuing massacres: "the blue uniformed soldiers and turbaned Kurds who accompanied us began to sharpen their daggers before our eyes. Then they rolled up their sleeves and commenced." The women and girls were placed in groups of ten, then killed and thrown into a well, and even the elderly were not spared. When there were only young girls and children left, it was decided not to kill them but to hand them over to the local Arabs and Kurds, who came and made their choice.

Michael was given to a Bedouin Arab named Ahmed who took him to his village, where he stayed for three years, looking after Ahmed's camels. When he left the convoy, the child had taken some small belongings with him, including a prayer book and a crucifix. The Bedouin's daughter took the prayer book and tore it up, keeping the other objects. His wife, on the other hand, was kind, but Michael tried unsuccessfully to escape. His master eventually seemed to change his mind and one day, when delivering goods to Nusaybin, by chance recognized two of the boy's uncles, Elias and Joseph Boyadji. He told them that he had their nephew at his house and asked them to go and take him away with them. The testimony ends: "I was saved. My uncle kept me for a while at Nusaybin until he found a chance to send me back to Aleppo."

Father Naayem provides other accounts of the deportations into the desert, such as that of Louis Ganima, an employee of the Baghdad Railway Company whom he met in Aleppo in May 1918. He told of the convoys of 10,000 women, girls and children which arrived in Mohamadi Khan, "an almost desert spot between Waren-Chehir, Urfa and Ras al-Ayn", in the autumn of 1915. He described an "awful holocaust" with victims killed by Kurds and Turkish police in "visions of horror".

Habiba's story

Father Naayem introduces Habiba Turkoghlou's testimony, both revealing and atrocious, as a record of her "deportation and long wanderings and sufferings".[62] He met her in Aleppo in May 1918 after she had left Caesarea (Keysarya), and they travelled together to Constantinople, where Naayem recorded her account. Working as a senior nurse at the Red Crescent hospital in Trebizond, she learnt on Saturday 18 June 1915 that the Turks had ordered all Christians to leave the city within four days. A large number of families attempted to take their sons and daughters to the safety of the American College, while other young women were taken in under the guise of being teachers. Habiba describes the atmosphere of fear. "The Christians were in tears, and their cries resounded everywhere. Trebizond was a city of mourning. A crowd of breathless women was running about the streets, pursued by soldiers deaf to their prayers." After the men were arrested and several hundred Russian citizens taken out in boats and drowned at sea, the terror grew among the Christians: "In their desperation some burnt their houses; others threw themselves into wells, and many committed suicide by jumping from roofs and windows. Not a few, some among them women, lost their reason." To save her baby, Dico, Habiba was forced to hand him over to the American Mission. In the meantime, the order had been given for all Christians to leave their homes; men and women were brutally separated, and a large convoy was formed.

She tells in detail of the privations endured, the bestial scenes witnessed, the rapes and murders; "we were physical wrecks and our whole nervous systems broke down. The separation of the men from the women was the last straw. We plodded along like cattle, brainless, stoically waiting to be finished, or begging God to end our sad existence by death."

After fifteen days' marching from Trebizond to Kemah, ten women including Habiba begged the leader of the convoy to leave them in the town so that they could work at sewing in return for bread. Finally, they were handed over to a rich Turk, Halil Bey, Deputy of Erzindjan, who had become chief of the local Tchettas; he gave them a room in his house, where they slept four nights on the floor without bed or blankets.

Three days after their arrival in Kemah, a convoy of a thousand young children and some women appeared; it had numbered 5,000, she reports, aged between three and ten, when it left Trebizond. These were the children who had been left in the care of the American Mission, now "ill and in a pitiable state". Over the next forty days, she and her companions saw convoys of the deported arrive daily.

Habiba remained in Kemah for eleven months, in a state of misery, "perpetually seeking a relation among the people who formed the convoys passing through the town". Despite all her sufferings, the memory of her child whom she had left in Trebizond never left her. She learnt that a Turkish doctor, Mehmed Aouni, had taken Dico from the American Mission and adopted him. He had then left for Constantinople with the child; she wrote repeatedly, but received no reply.

On 16 February, a fortuitous turn of events occurred when Erzurum fell into Russian hands. The panic-stricken inhabitants of Kemah began leaving town, while the Red Crescent arrived to set up a hospital. Habiba decided to apply for a post as a nurse, hoping that she would one day be able to reach the Red Crescent headquarters in Constantinople and see her son again. Her application was successful and she left Kemah with the other medical staff when the mission was transferred to Caesarea, a sixteen-day journey. She began work in the nearby village of Zindjirdere. Still determined to find her son, she was also indignant at the abuses inflicted on the hospital's young nurses and resigned. Thrown in prison for twenty-three days on the pretext of belonging to a secret society, she writes: "There I remained, without money and helpless, despairing of seeing my child again; for I did not expect to live. I became seriously ill."

Leaving prison, she returned to Caesarea, where she made the acquaintance of a Lebanese priest, Antoun Hadji Boutros, who assisted her and her Christian companions. Aiming to go to Constantinople, she applied to the Ministry of the Interior for permission to travel to Aleppo to visit relatives. "Being a Chaldean, the necessary permit was eventually sent to me by the ministry, and I left Caesarea on 17 April 1918." Arriving at Aleppo, she met Father Naayem and left with him for Constantinople, where on 17 June she was reunited with her son Dico, three years after she had left him. Her testimony concludes:

THE SCENES AND ACTS OF THE TRAGEDY

My martyrdom had been long and hard. In the deportations I lost many most dear to me. God had willed that I should be spared for the supreme task of saving my child from the hands of his kidnapper. Henceforward, I have but one object in life, and that is to bring up my son.

3

STRATEGY AND METHODOLOGY
OF ERADICATION

"We are shut off from the world, and thousands are held in this bondage by a few hundred Osmanli troops and a few wandering Kurds."

Mary Schauffler Platt, during the siege of Urmia,
12 February 1915

"The driving force was not in the mountains but in the capital. I would sooner deny the existence of the sun than the truth of this axiom: 'The Young Turks of Constantinople massacred the Christians of Turkey'.

Hyacinthe Simon, 1919

All observers and witnesses confirm that the conduct of the Turkish authorities was motivated by a premeditated, defined and criminal objective. Here was the physical, cultural, religious and territorial genocide, geopolitical in nature and deliberately planned, of an ethnic and religious group. As can be seen through contemporary documents, reports and testimonies, orders came from on high, conceived by a central authority; their implementation was methodically planned and systematically executed.

In his work *Mardin: la ville héroïque*, the Dominican missionary Hyacinthe Simon (1867–1922) alerts the reader that his book consists of notes gathered "between two silences like thunder", then committed to paper "between two agonies of the soul". From March to November 1915, he writes in his prologue, something monstrous, beyond definition and bloody happened in Turkey:

> The young Ottoman fatherland decimated, or rather extermi-nated with its own hands, its own sons—most of them under its banners—and emptied their homes, raped their daughters, took away their wives, dispersed their families, set fire to their villages, deported the survivors and burnt the dead.[1]

In his first chapter, "Premières révélations lugubres" ("First Dark Revelations"), Simon insists that the massa-cres, a term that he emphasizes and describes as general, were the result of a strategy adopted in January 1915 at the very top of the Ottoman state hierarchy, adding that he received information to this effect from a high-ranking military officer. His view was supported by an article in the *New York Times* (13 January 1915) entitled "Christians in Great Peril", whose subtitle, a quotation attributed to Talaat Bey, left little doubt as to the ideological intentions of those in power and their desire to homogenize and Turkify the country: "Talaat Bey declares that there is room only for Turks in Turkey."[2]

Father Jacques Rhétoré, who was also at Mardin, placed responsibility for the atrocities with "those ministers in Constantinople who decreed the massacres and those highly placed functionaries who accepted the assignment to carry them out". Surma Khanum and Mgr Manna, both eye-witnesses, equally accused the Turkish authorities, with the latter particularly singling out Djevdet Bey, the *vali* of Van, as an instigator. Surma Khanum alleged that the Turks had armed the Kurds of Hakkari, writing in a letter of 9 October 1915 to Rev. Heazell, "The Kurds were helped by the artillery of the Turkish government".[3] Mgr Israel Audo, Chaldean Archbishop of Mardin, identified the brutal police commissioner Mamdouh Bey as a ringleader.

Recalling events in Jezireh, Hassana, Mansuriye, Shakh and Siirt, situated in the Tigris valley not far from the ruins of Nineveh, Professor Abraham Yohannan spoke in *The Death of a Nation* of a general, state-approved massacre: "We are told that by order of the government the Kurds and Turkish soldiers put the Christians of those villages to the sword."[4] The men of Shakh were killed by Turkish soldiers who were billeted in the village by order of the government, while the women and children who survived were reduced to a state of captivity. After the first killings, Kurds attempted to intervene to save the Christians, but the Turkish government stopped them; the decree, writes Yohannan, was to finish the job or face punishment. In his conclusion, he remarks that his account is not exhaustive, the list of atrocities being too long:

> I have not told the whole story—the whole story is too gruesome and horrible—but have confined myself in these statements to the usual course of the crime. I have not mentioned the extravagance of wickedness, the barbarity of tortures, and the details of the outrages against the women, that would make a shameful and terrible page of modern history which is unfolding in Persia and Turkey.[5]

In the massacres at Diyarbakir, Urfa. Kharput, Mardin and Midyat, the population faced a "literal deluge of blood" and villages were totally destroyed. Joel E. Warda lays the prime responsibility with the regular Turkish troops who slaughtered the Assyrians.[6] Eighty-six Syriac Orthodox churches and fourteen monasteries were razed to the ground and 186 priests killed.[7] Jacques Rhétoré dedicates a chapter to the Siirt massacres which began in June 1915, emphasizing the role of Djevdet Bey:

> In Siirt itself, during the day of 5 June, according to reliable sources, the massacres were conducted by Djevdet Bey, *vali* of Van, after his expulsion from that city. He had put himself at the head of a troop of soldiers as fervent as him and whom he had named the Butchers' Battalion (*Qassab Tabouri*) towards the end of May 1915.[8]

This same Djevdet Bey was chillingly to boast, after killings in Urmia and Salmas from January to May, that "we have made tabula rasa of the Armenians and Syrians [Syriacs] in Azerbaijan"—words recorded by Mgr Manna, Johannes Lepsius and Fridtjof Nansen.

Dr William A. Shedd describes how the Turkish forces operated during their occupation of Persian Urmia between the beginning of January and 20 May 1915:

> The Turks collected large Kurdish forces from the Soujboulak region and from districts in Eastern Turkey; these, together with smaller forces, moved through Urmia and Salmas against Khoy, joining Turkish forces from Van under Djevdet Bey. During the months of Turkish occupation there was never a time of real safety for the Christians ... During this period the Turks were guilty not only of failure to protect the Christians effectively, but also of direct massacre committed under their orders.[9]

Turkish troops in Urmia committed many other acts of violence, notably against the American and French Missions, where Assyrians had taken refuge. The *New York Times* of 27 March ("Turks continue Urumiah Slaying") described how soldiers forced their way into the mission compounds and murdered Christians. It reported that the American consul at Tabriz, Gordon Paddock, had sent on a message from Robert M. Labaree, an American missionary in Urmia. Labaree stated that the Turkish consul there had forcibly entered the American Mission with a number of regular Turkish troops and taken Assyrian refugees outside to be killed. The Turkish forces had also beaten and insulted the American missionaries, with similar occurrences at the French Lazarist Mission.

At Salmas, before his retreat, Djevdet Bey gathered together the 800 people who had been unable to escape, mostly the old, indigent and some girls, and had them murdered. According to Shedd, the villages around Salmas were in the same state as those near Urmia. At Bohtan—Jezireh, Mansuriye, Shakh, Hassana, etc.—it was "a general massacre", claimed Rev. E.W. McDowell in the "Blue Book", adding that the murder of Christian villagers by Turkish and Kurdish soldiers was "on government orders". Among the victims he lists Kasha Mattai, pastor in the village of Hassana, Kasha Elia, an elderly pastor, Kasha Sarguis, retired, Muallem Moussa, pastor at the church at Jezireh, and his sixteen-year-old son, Philip. Many of the women of Mansuriye, he writes, threw themselves into the Tigris rather than fall into the hands of the Kurds, while others were taken away and enslaved.[10]

The "secret committee"

Most observers concur that the massacres were ordered by the central Turkish government. A name was given to the organization in charge of the process, wrote Hyacinthe Simon: the "secret committee"; to give it a semblance of "legality", it operated as a quasi-business with its own regulations.

Simon lists those responsible at the top of the state apparatus; the supremo was Talaat Pasha, Minister of the

Interior, followed by his chief lieutenant Dr Rashid Bey, *vali* of Diyarbakir, "the citadel of blood". The latter had succeeded Hamid Bey, himself a mass murderer of Christians, notably the people of Qarabach, near Diyarbakir. These names and those of other executioners appear repeatedly in documents of the period. Jacques Rhétoré refers to a "committee of execution" in charge of the massacres, and Isaac Armalet describes its members as "enemies of humanity".[11]

In the preface to the English edition of Joseph Naayem's book, *Shall This Nation Die?*, Viscount James Bryce states explicitly that the massacres were "organised and carried out with every circumstance of cruelty by Enver and Talaat, chiefs of the ruffianly gang who were then in power in Constantinople".[12] *The Treatment of Armenians in the Ottoman Empire* (the "Blue Book") concluded:

> The exact quantitative scale of the crime thus remains uncertain, but there is no uncertainty as to the responsibility for its perpetration ... In one way or another, the Central Government enforced and controlled the execution of the scheme, as it alone had originated the conception of it; and the Young Turkish Ministers and their associates at Constantinople are directly and personally responsible, from beginning to end, for the gigantic crime that devastated the Near East in 1915.[13]

In the second part of *The Death of a Nation*, "A Chapter of Horrors", Yohannan focuses on the atrocities that took place in Urmia-Salmas in northern Persia and the tragic exodus to the Caucasus after the invasion begun on 2 January 1915 by Djevdet Bey, supported by the Kurds. Rumours were circulating over the withdrawal of the Russians and the imminent arrival of the Turks: "The Turks are coming, the Russians are withdrawing, flee for your life." Three pages are given over to what he calls the "red horror", the worst of the massacres which occurred in March 1915 in Salmas district, to the north of Urmia. This area was inhabited by Assyrians, Armenians and Muslims. In the Armenian village of Haftvan, an unusually savage killing spree resulted in all men over the age of twelve being murdered and some cut into pieces. Such acts, Yohannan adds, were committed on the orders of "Jevdet Pasha [Djevdet Bey], son of Takis Pasha".[14] These "barbarian" forces, reminiscent of Tamerlane's conquest, were all the more incited to commit atrocities against unarmed civilians by the call to Jihad, which was followed by pillage, murder, rape and torture.[15] Even if these acts were committed by Kurds, observes Yohannan, the Turks, who gave the orders, can in no sense be exonerated. Persian Muslims joined with the Kurds in attacking their Christian neighbours. Yohannan concludes his list of horrors on the plain of Urmia-Salmas with a vision that, in hindsight, remains chilling:

> To visualize the villages in that beautiful plain of Urmiah, lying in ruins, the homes burned, the men massacred, the girls taken captive, the women, even children, outraged, is so horrible that one recoils, it makes the flesh creep.[16]

Wide-scale massacres, premeditated acts intended to destroy a group, a committee of execution—these facts confirm that, as defined in Article II of the United Nations' Convention on the Prevention and Punishment of the Crime of Genocide, genocide took place.

The executioners

Isaac Armalet considered Rashid Bey, governor of the Diyarbakir *vilayet*, whom he described as "the tyrant of Diyarbakir", to have been the vector of the massacres: "the microbe of hypocrisies and corruption, the instigator of tensions and violence, the apologist for bloodletting and atrocities". In a strategy of collusion, he claims, the Committee of Union and Progress installed him as *vali* of Diyarbakir, handed him many privileges and unlimited authority and supplied him with a band of killers such as Rushdi Beg, Khalil Beg, the notorious Mamdouh and many others. Also named is Khalil Edib, representative of the Committee of Union and Progress, "who roamed through Nusaybin, Midyat and other towns, calling on the Aghas to shed blood".[17]

Paul Béro likens Rashid Bey to a "Nero", while Jacques Rhétoré calls him "the Great Chief of the exterminators", claiming that he "made himself the blind instrument of the sultan and his ministers, Talaat and Enver, for the massacre of the Christians, anticipating in this operation the huge profits that he indeed made".[18] In the same vein, Joseph Naayem reports that when installed in the governorship of Diyarbakir, Rashid Bey created a bodyguard "of forty or so 'Tchettas', true bandits, all Circassians like him".[19] His first concern was to organize a militia of local notables, among whom were the feared police commissioner Mamdouh, "author of thousands of crimes", Attar Zade Hakki Efendi of the Committee of Union and Progress, the Circassian (Tcherkesse) Rashid, commander of the deportation convoys, and Deputy Feizi Bey, "one of the committee's most influential members, the principal provocateur of the massacres" and "one of the most bloodthirsty of individuals".

Drawing on the testimony of a Chaldean, Hanna, who had arrived in Constantinople from Diyarbakir at the beginning of the winter of 1918 having lost his brother and parents, Naayem relates how Feizi Bey, "determined that all the Christians should be slaughtered, went with Rashid Bey to the telegraph office and sent a wire to the Central Office of the Committee for Union and Progress, demanding the extermination of the poor wretches". He managed to obtain "the necessary order by pretending that if the Christians were not punished the Turks, who had taken fright and barricaded themselves in the mosques, would not dare to return to their homes".[20]

When Rashid Bey had finished his dirty work at Diyarbakir, adds Isaac Armalet, he went to Constantinople to stay with his close friend Talaat Pasha, who complimented him on a job well done, obtained honours for him from the sultan and appointed him *vali* of Ankara.

From June to October 1915, massacres took place continuously in the Christian villages around Mardin. The Turks, wrote the Syriac Catholic patriarch Rahmani in 1919, had all Christians sacked from their jobs on the false pretext that they were "traitors", and then "the Turkish government gave the order for the military to pounce on the villages".[21]

The month of June 1915 saw the atrocities reach their most intense, inspired and carried out by the killers mentioned above. According to Rhétoré, the Chaldean priest Hanna Chouha of Nusaybin was "one of the first to fall victim to Mesopotamia's Christian bloodbath".[22] His account is supported by that of Isaac Armalet, a day-by-day report of the atrocities perpetrated in and around Mardin, in which he rebuffs the allegations that Christians were concealing weapons, were agents of foreign states and enemies of Turkey and were in possession of secret documents. Most of these Christians, he argues, could scarcely read or write and spoke no foreign languages. This, however, did not prevent the searches and pillaging of houses that ensued. At the outset of the war, wrote Armalet, the Turks burnt down the souk at Diyarbakir, where most stores belonged to Christians; their property was confiscated and their homes occupied, with 1,578 Christian-owned shops razed to the ground during the nights of 19 and 21 August. The victims' claims for reparations went unheeded.

Massacres spread across other regions. In Kharput, the Turks began by arresting prominent personalities and above all, according to Naayem, schoolteachers like Ashur Yousif, a well-known member of the Syriac Orthodox community and editor of the Turkish-language *Murshid* newspaper. In the small town of Adiyaman, Christians were "hacked to death with axes and thrown into the river which watered the locality. The priests in particular had been tortured with indescribable savagery."[23]

Methodology of murder

Once the "secret committee" established by Turkey's rulers had revealed its objectives and strategy, a methodology for implementing its aims was devised. Three main points were agreed upon in the first instance: (1) to remove suspects from their communities; (2) to exile and send to forced labour on the roads any individual who possessed arms, even if they had not used them against the state; (3) to put to death anyone whose actions were deemed to constitute a threat to the Empire's security. A more detailed *modus operandi*, according to Hyacinthe Simon, was to be applied in all areas:

1) Make mass arrests of men and, above all, notables;
2) Send them away to an unknown destination;
3) On the road to the destination, divide the convoy into groups of between 50 and 100;

4) Where executions are to take place, force the victims to remove their clothes before massacring them and throwing their bodies into wells;

5) As sworn on the Koran, nothing should be told to the Christians of the town about the acts committed by the executioners or the fate of those executed.[24]

In terms of implementation, local functionaries were active participants: "each functionary in his district would have to carry out the orders of the said Committee under pain of dismissal or death," said Simon. This extermination programme was to involve Armenians as well as Assyrians, since "it was soon appreciated that the Armenian nation would encompass all the Christian elements of the six *vilayets* of Erzurum and Van, Bitlis and Sivas, Kharput and Diyarbakir: witnesses of the blows to be dealt to Catholics of all rites and schismatics of all sects."[25] According to a senior Muslim, the persecution was, claims Simon, to target both sexes: men between seven and seventy, and women between ten and sixty.

All means to the end, he observed, were good. To encourage efficiency, the Ottoman government would attach its gendarmes to the police, its militias to the gendarmes and its ammunition to the militiamen. It would also "unleash the Kurds", who were "pre-warned", while local magistrates were complicit in the crimes. Commenting on the method of extermination, Simon remarks that the town or village where the massacre was taking place "would neither be disturbed by the cries of the victims nor stained by their blood"; it would also ensure that "one would be more aware of the Government's work".

Jacques Rhétoré supports this analysis of the methods: first the high-ranking Christians were arrested *en masse* and disposed of, then the common people were attacked. These attacks everywhere followed "an order established in advance" with which the protagonists "were familiar" and which they "followed". He adds:

> All the men had first to be taken away and, after them, the women with their children. The men were doomed to death, while the women, in principle, were to be merely deported, but were no less destined to die on the roads from exhaustion, hunger and poverty; and then those in charge of them had been given complete freedom to kill them or to hand them over to the Muslims for their use.[26]

Returning to the methodology of extermination in Chapter XIV of his book, "Les dessous d'un mystère d'iniquité" (The Underside of an Evil Mystery), Simon states that the same implacable system was applied everywhere "in accordance with a scrupulously worked out and identical programme":

> Each prisoner is captured and tied up, then a convoy of several hundred men is sent several hours away from the town to a place suitable as a killing field. There, the victims are stripped and are offered apostasy, and whether they accept or refuse, they are anyway killed by any means. With saving the State's ammunition in mind, they are slashed at the neck and stomach with sabres, then thrown, often wounded and still alive, into deep wells.[27] Sometimes hands and arms are cut off, and the half-executed are left like that, exposed to the sun ... One Kurd said: "Our soil is too pure to act as a tomb for Christian dogs."[28]

His macabre description continues:

> According to the general system of execution, the corpses of the men are left lying on their stomachs, the women on their backs ... Often children were seized by the feet, quartered and then thrown into the ditch ... Gendarmes would even sometimes rape young women who were dying.[29]

Who undertook this repugnant work? "At the beginning," writes Simon, "it was the soldiers and the Kurds. At the end the task was given only to the militias in charge of the convoys. The Kurds and the soldiers, however, were only instruments receiving orders from outside." Blaming the central authority in Constantinople, he claims: "The driving force was not in the mountains but in the capital. I would sooner deny the existence of the sun than the truth of this axiom: 'The Young Turks of Constantinople massacred the Christians of Turkey.'"[30]

Simon finds further proof in the composition of the militiamen whom he describes as a "bunch of good-for-nothings, all too happy to parade their fifty years and evil instincts under military colours and to go and enrich themselves from the spoils".[31] He also cites the testimonies of the Kurds themselves: "'What?' said an agha, 'has the Empire gone mad? First it commands us to kill: then, when we've killed, it punishes us...'" Another, a policeman, confessed: "What do you expect? We were forced."[32]

Finally, Simon also finds evidence of government complicity in the *firman* (edict or order from the Ottoman sovereign) that was read out to victims before their execution in order to provide a veneer of legality. The convoy would be stopped and an officer would unfold a letter decorated with a red seal: "You are all condemned to death..." "But," Simon points out, "this letter could only have come from the government's offices."[33] Describing the massacres as a bloodbath and a holocaust, Simon concludes his observations on the role of Constantinople and the extermination methods as follows: "And so you encounter everywhere and always, in the smallest place and at any time, those common characteristics of extermination, the same procedure and the same factors: convoys and militiamen followed by Kurds—and the whole thing authorized and at the behest of the imperial government."[34] He wonders what motivates all such death sentences: politics, religion or bloodlust? He asked many people, and some had replied politics, others religion, still more despair... but all agreed that it was "madness".[35]

Rape

Witnesses reported a great many sexual attacks on women and young girls. The Presbyterian William A. Shedd confirmed that hundreds of women from as young as eight had been raped during the 1915 Turco-Kurdish occupation of the Urmia region. In the official British "Blue Book", he denounced "the outraging of hundreds of women and girls of every age from eight or nine years to old age".[36] In two pages dealing with rape, Abraham Yohannan considered these crimes more revolting than the murders, pillage and torture inflicted on the Assyrians, because they were attacks on the honour of women. When the men had been taken away from their village, women and girls were not killed but kept alive for a more humiliating fate, sent to harems and destined "to a fate worse than death": "We weep for them because they were not killed by the butcher's knife."[37]

Similarly, the American Medical Department in Urmia mentioned the cases of women and girls, including two children of eight and ten:

> One of the most terrible things that came to the notice of the Medical Department was the treatment of Syrian women and girls by the Turks, Kurds and local Mohammedans. After the massacre in the village of ......, almost all the women and girls were outraged, and two little girls, aged eight and ten, died in

the hands of Moslem villains. A mother said that not a woman or girl above twelve (and some younger) in the village of ......, escaped violation.[38]

Joseph Naayem reproduces one testimony revealing that officers kept young Christian girls, stolen from the convoys, in their tents; this witness "spoke in particular of one very beautiful Chaldean girl from Diarbekir, kept as a prostitute, and passed from one Turk to another. By a miracle the girl survived and is living today in Urfa."[39]

Here are clearly evidenced serious violations of the physical and psychological wellbeing of the Assyrian national group.

Islamization as a means of suppression

Many observers attested to frequent instances of forced conversion to Islam, as a means of destroying a group by eradicating a fundamental feature of its identity. The German pastor Johannes Lepsius reported in 1916:

> The number of Armenian and [Syriac] Christians who were converted to Islam in the course of the deportations will not be established, even approximately, before the war is over. We can assume that it is very considerable, since all the girls, women and children stolen by the Turks were treated by them as Mahometans.[40]

Abraham Yohannan also refers to several cases in which young girls and women, faced with forced Islamization, preferred to refuse at the risk of their lives or throw themselves into a river. He also describes instances of extortion and theft, another form of abuse, with property seized under threats of death.

The Presbyterian E.W. McDowell gives the example of the kidnapped and Islamized women of Mansuriye village in Bhotan, whom he had known, he says, as if they were his own children and whose names he recalls with sadness: Sarah, Hatoun, Priskilla, little Nellie and other young girls. "What is their condition?" he wonders anxiously.[41]

The example of Hakkari

"The [Assyrian] mountain dwellers must also, at this very moment, be surrounded by Turkish troops. On 30 September [1915], a great many Nestorian refugees from Djoulamerk in the upper Zab valley arrived in Salmas. These Syrians told us that 30,000 other Nestorians, among whom the Nestorian Patriarch Mar Shimun, were in flight, and that he would follow them. They had been attacked and driven away by Turkish troops. They reported that more than 25,000 Syrians from the mountains had been encircled by Turkish troops and that it would be difficult to escape extermination."

Johannes Lepsius, 1916

The Assyrians of Hakkari suffered as much as those in other regions, with sources referring to "combined" and "concerted" attacks by Turco-Kurdish troops. The border country of Hakkari is a mountainous zone, difficult to access, blessed with a wild beauty of steep valleys, and highly strategically valuable for its position in the extreme south-east of Turkey; here, Assyrians had been living in a compact and homogenous community since Antiquity, surrounded by their immediate neighbours, the Kurds. The Ottoman authorities and military had never been able to take control there, at least until 1880, and then only partially and precariously.

The entirely Assyrian village of Kotchanes, in the upper Zab valley, perched at over 1,700 metres in altitude, had been the seat of the patriarch of the Nestorian Church of the East since 1662 and contained a library rich in documents and manuscripts. Thus this was historically an Assyrian territory, shared in some areas with the Kurds, who were in the majority, and with several minorities: Jews, Armenians, Yezidis—and Turks. Hakkari formed a *sanjak* within the *vilayet* of Van. The Christian presence in this mountain region dated from the first centuries AD, but "came to a tragic end in 1915 under the onslaught of the Ottomans and the Kurds..."[42] The hereditary patriarch lived in Kotchanes, north of Djulamerk, the base of the local governor. The earliest churches dated back to the fourth century: Mar Zaya at Jilu, Mar Bishu at Iil, Mar Shalita at Kotchanes, Mar Mamo at Oramar, Mar Saba at Ashita.[43] The Chaldean Catholic diocese at Van was also extremely ancient, with bishops in place since 1610.

In a tragic turn of history, a large part of the Assyrian population was exterminated by Turks and Kurds during the war, while those in convoys died of thirst, exhaustion and sickness on the roads towards exile in the direction of Salmas and Urmia. Those who escaped took refuge in Iraq, Syria and Lebanon and in the Caucasus (notably Armenia). Today their descendants live in the cities of the United States, Canada, Australia, New Zealand and Europe, in large part defined by the memory of Hakkari, their home-land, stolen from them and which they still celebrate.

Writing of these events, Surma d'Bait Mar Shimun observed that it must be fully understood that such hor-rors could not have occurred without the knowledge of officials; every detail was sent in writing to the *vali* of Van and to the relevant local authorities. Yet, she said, it was impossible to obtain either justice or mercy for the Christians, or even the slightest reaction of sympathy from those in command. She concluded that as long as she lived, she would never forget the days of terror and deprivation, the secret meetings at night in the patriarchal residence.[44]

The Turkish state had a pre-planned policy for strategically important Hakkari, as for the rest of the country, and nothing was left to chance. Talaat Pasha, Minister of the Interior and later Grand Vizir, wanted an end to the Armenian question and to the Assyrians, obstacles to his policies of domination and expansion. As such, he had adopted a strategy of elimination that was both physical in nature and aimed at destroying identity. He aimed to deport the Assyrian mountain population in order to disperse and scatter it, diluting it in the Turkish melting pot and hence destroying it. He sought to unbalance its social organization by demolishing its tribal, clan and religious structures, in which *maliks* (chieftains) at the head of each tribe played an important role, with Mar Shimun, the patriarch, exercising above them the supreme function of arbitrator, watching over the general interest and maintaining religious authority.

Basil Nikitin, the Russian consul at Urmia, insisted that it was the deliberate intention of the Ottoman authorities to massacre Hakkari's Assyrians from the beginning: "In the month of November [1914] war was officially declared, the order was given to the Kurds, Holy War was proclaimed and the massacres and plundering were started, notably at Albaq, near Bachkale."[45] William A. Wigram confirmed that the Bachkale killings took place "with the open approval of the local Ottoman authorities", adding: "It must be owned that the fact that the Turks had provided the Kurds with bombs for the mountain fighting opens a disquieting possibility."[46]

The war in this mountain redoubt started with the call to Jihad. The Tkhuma, the Tyari, the Jilu and the Baz were pitilessly slaughtered. Kotchanes was attacked and pillaged by the Kurds, the books and manuscripts hidden at the time of the exodus found and destroyed. Wigram wrote: "Houses were burned, water-channels ... were broken down, churches by the score were desecrated and plundered. Some forty churches in Jilu alone met this fate..."[47]

At the outbreak of war, the Assyrian areas of Albaq and Gavar were also attacked, pillaged, with their populations widely massacred.

Another tragic event was to occur when the *vali* of Mosul, Haydar Bey, resorted to treachery in order to intimidate the Assyrians and force them to capitulate. Hormizd d'Mar Shimun, brother of the patriarch Mar Benyamin Shimun, had been studying in Constantinople since 1912. When Turkey entered the war, he was arrested and imprisoned as a hostage without charge, then taken to Mosul. Haydar then threatened the patriarch and his community that the hostage would be executed if they resisted Turkish authority. Remaining steadfast in the face of blackmail, the patriarch defended his people to the end and his brother was duly killed, a black chapter in the history of Ottoman Turkey.

Another alarming sign in October 1914 was the change of leadership in the *vilayet* of Van. Djevdet Bey replaced Tahsin Bey—considered insufficiently harsh—not only as *vali* but as commander of the troops stationed on the frontier with Persia. At that moment, several acts of violence and mass killings were perpetrated against the Assyrians on the order of Turkish officials. About fifty men from the district of Gavar, to the north of Hakkari, were sent to Bachkale and murdered. In the region of northern Barwar, Turks looted the homes of Assyrian peasants, carrying off even the children's socks. A deacon

163

was brutally assaulted and women were abducted, two of whom were deemed beautiful enough to satisfy the desires of their Kurdish kidnappers. All this was done, wrote Surma d'Bait Mar Shimun, "on the direct orders of the functionary in charge".[48] Indeed, every Assyrian district in Hakkari with the status of *rayet* (no tribal communities, subject to Ottoman or Kurdish rule) would be subject to these atrocities.

On 23 June 1915, the Lower Tiari tribe was attacked by Turkish troops from Mosul and Kurdish irregulars commanded by the *vali* Haydar Bey. At the same time, the *kaymacam* of Djulemerk, together with Artosh Kurds, launched an assault on the Upper Tyari district. During that summer, the Assyrians were forced to abandon their mountain valleys for the higher mountains and then refuge in Persia, where many died en route. Among those who exhibited particular violence against them were Rashid Bey of Barwari Bala, who devastated Lower Tyari and murdered Malik Yosip, father of Malik Khoshaba, national leader between 1915 and 1920; Suto Agha Oramarli (from Oramar), who massacred women and children from Koversin to Diz; Haydar Bey; and Agha Tahir Doski.

Holy war against the Assyrian Christians

Holy war was proclaimed in Kurdistan and Kurdish tribes responded enthusiastically under the planned and concerted direction of the Turkish authorities, as the following Kurdish declarations, published by Basil Nikitin, confirm.[49] Tahir, chief of the Kurdish Doski tribe, issued a call to Jihad during the war, announcing to the renowned Suto Agha, chief of the Oramar tribe (a district in Hakkari), and to Abdul-Rahim that he and other Turco-Kurdish leaders including the *kaymacam* had sworn to wage holy war:

> O you, Suto Agha and Abd-ul-Rahim, who are highly placed and with power and courage, with the will of Allah, be in good health. Know after receiving our compliments that I and the Kaymakam and Rustem Bey and Omar Agha have together sworn an oath and made an agreement that we are firmly in favour of a great Jihad, and that we believe it would be good if you joined with 200 or 300 men of war ... The costs of food as well as clothing and arms will be met by the government. In any case, you need not worry. We await your reply.

In a second letter to Suto Agha, Tahir Doski tells him that he is keen to meet Haydar Bey, *vali* of Mosul,[50] and that he is ready to attack the Christian villages of Hakkari:

> You write to me that Haydar Bey has arrived to reprimand the non-Muslims, and that we must also be ready: that is very good. Let us know when he is returning to Amadiya so that we can all go there. But if His Excellency the *vali*'s return there is delayed, it is imperative that all of us, together with the people of Oramar, attack those of the Christian villages that are still intact in the region of Diz[51] and, God willing, sack them.

He concludes: "Send us your news."

A letter from Suto Agha to Haydar Bey reminds the *vali* of the spring 1915 Turkish invasion of the Assyrian territories of Tyari and Tkhuma, and asks for relief from taxation:

> I had the honour of presenting myself to Your Excellency last spring at the time of the Great Jihad when the *askers*[52] were going towards Tiari and Tkhuma[53] and you gave me the order that my Oramar tribe[54] should not stay, and that is why the flocks were driven to the kaza of Dehok, while I and my men stayed in Oramar. Nonetheless, the fiscal authorities are now

demanding a tax on the livestock of our poor in Dehok. I beseech Your Excellency not to impose taxes on refugees and I hope that you will not do so.

This time, the Assyrians left their ancestral lands definitively and against their will.

This is how events were reported by Abraham Shlemon from Barwar.[55] The troubles began very rapidly, some months before the Armenian massacres in April 1915. In the previous autumn, as the Turks were entering the war against Russia and the Allies, all the Sheikhs, *aghas* and different Kurdish chieftains from Neri and Rawanduz to the east, and from the south from Jezireh to Mosul, including all the tribes from the Tigris and the Great Zab, planned the next spring "to combine and sweep over the lands of the Christians and to exterminate them". At the beginning of June 1915:

> the Vali of Mosul began to get ready and collect a big army against the Nestorians. He had some 7,000 Turkish troops with regular artillery and some 15,000 Kurds from all these regions. In twelve days they reached Berwar and Amadia, on the banks of the Great Zab, a tributary of the Tigris ... On 18 June the Vali of Mosul, Rashid Pasha, reached Berwar and after a few days' rest attacked Tyari, from Asheta the largest village to Lezan of Malick Khoshaba.[56]

The villages of Sarispedo and Ashita, the latter with 500 families, were devastated, as were Geramon, Arosh, Halmon, Zawita, Minyanish, Margi, Leza and Zarni, and ten villages of Barwar.[57] "They destroyed over fifteen churches and took off all their old manuscripts and service books, kept for generations."

In the Turkish attack on the whole of Hakkari, the territories of the Assyrian tribes were reduced to blood and ashes; more than sixty churches were destroyed. "From one church they carried off booty, over 180 loads, the property of the church and what the people had deposited there as being the safest place."[58]

The plight of the refugees arriving in Bachkale was described by an eye-witness, Yoel B. Rustem, a graduate of the American College in Urmia, in an account published in Aramaic in 1916 and then translated by Paul Shimun, revised by William Walker Rockwell and included in the latter's book.[59] The author claimed that a third of the refugees died from exhaustion in the winter of 1916.

Genocide and ethnocide

Physical genocide was accompanied by cultural genocide, or ethnocide, which saw the culture of this people, represented by its language, religion and institutions, completely ruined and obliterated. Historic monuments were wrecked and left derelict, churches profaned and manuscripts stolen. Libraries, rare books and manuscripts, churches, bishops' residences, various institutions, properties and legacies of all sorts disappeared.

Christianity had been present in Mardin since the third century, a region which, according to V. Minorsky and C.E. Bosworth, "played an exceptionally important role in the development of Eastern Christianity".[60] A third of its population, reported eighteenth-century travellers, was Christian. According to Joseph Naayem, the town of Diyarbakir (formerly Amid) features in the annals of the first centuries of Christianity in the East. The monastery of Deir Zafaran in Tur Abdin (mountain of the servants of God) was the patriarchal seat of the Syriac Orthodox Church from 1293 to 1923, the date of its move to Syria.

There are many traces of Christian history in Hakkari; Oramar was an early Christian stronghold, and Mar Pethion, martyred in 447 by the Persian Sassanids, was a missionary in the region, as was Mar Saba (St Sabbas the Sanctified) in the same century. Two centuries later, the patriarch of the Church of the East Mar Gewargis (661–80) came from Roustaka (later known as the Chemdinan/Naoutchia district).

In Hakkari, the Turks operated a scorched earth policy, seizing property and demolishing churches. The Chaldean episcopal palace in Van and its chapel were looted and razed, along with the valuable library of the diocese of Siirt and its priceless manuscripts, carefully conserved by the Orientalist scholar Mgr Addai Scher, himself murdered. (The manuscript third volume of his magisterial work in Arabic, *History of Chaldea and Assyria*, was also stolen; despite searches, it has never been found).[61] Sixteen villages around Van suffered the same atrocities as Van itself. The village of Ashita in Hakkari was attacked and partly burned by Turks and Kurds, while its inhabitants fled into the mountains. Paul Shimun wrote of Kotchanes, seat of the Nestorian patriarch in Hakkari, "The Patriarchal house, the English mission, and the larger part of the place were plundered and burned. Even the tombs of former Patriarchs were violated." The Assyrians thus witnessed the dispossession of a great many of their sites of memory and culture.

In all, more than 250 churches and monasteries were left in ruins, and cemeteries were defiled—in Siirt the cemetery was completely "desecrated, the tombstones had been uprooted and many of the graves profaned," wrote Madame Halata to Joseph Naayem.[62] All the dioceses of the Syriac Catholic Church were devastated. In Jezireh,

Bishop Flavianus Michael Malke was martyred, as were the Syriacs of Nusaybin and its dependencies. In Mardin, the Turks took from the Syriac Catholic monastery of St Ephrem "all precious objects and things of value that were kept there".[63] In Tur Abdin, 156 Syriac Orthodox churches and monasteries were destroyed.

Some churches were turned into mosques. In the district of Nazlu, villages were plundered and their inhabitants killed. Gulpashan, Sopurghan and Goetapa suffered the same fate, and the Nestorian Bishop of Gulpashan was martyred. Fifty-six villages in the region were systematically pillaged. In Hakkari, the religious hierarchy was completely dismantled and prelates executed. The Nestorian patriarchal library in Kotchanes and the library of the Anglican missionary William Henry Browne were ransacked, with hidden books discovered and destroyed. Basil Nikitin wrote of one such vandalized church: "The famous church of Mar Zaia in Jilu, dating from the fourth century, was desecrated for the first time in its history. Chinese vases brought back long ago by missionaries vanished."[64] William A. Wigram confirmed the facts: "It was at this time that the famous church of Mar Zaia in Jilu was plundered for the first time in its history, and a collection of votive curios that was absolutely unique was scattered with the wind ... Seventh-century jars, brought from China by Nestorian missionaries in the old days, were smashed by savages..."[65] Nikitin, visiting the region in September 1917, told how, after the sacking of Mar Zaia, a young Kurdish chieftain who was standing at the door and watching his men carrying off loot shouted: "May all Christian churches in the land perish in the same way!"[66]

Table 2

Dioceses	Churches	Districts	Churches
Mar Oraham of Gondok	13	Elki	1
Mar Ishou of Barwar	20	Khergel	1
Mar Shimun the		Matta de Oumra	1
Patriarch	75		
Mar Sarguis, Jilu	37	Nevgweezan	1
Mar Sliwa of Gawar	34	Khandekki	1
Rustaka	30	Deira Zengel	1
		Marwanan	1
		Oulama	1
		Tell Géri	1
		Beit-ul-Shabab	5
Total	209		14

Before 1915, this area contained a total of 223 churches divided into six dioceses and ten districts (see Table 2), all under the jurisdiction of the Nestorian patriarch Mar Shimun. The oldest dated from the fourth century.

What remains of these 223 churches and of Hakkari today? Now, there is nothing but ruins, traces of devastation, deserted villages, empty and abandoned places of worship.

Lamenting a tragedy

This tragic history is related in compelling form through laments (*dourekta*), poems written by eye-witnesses. Passed down orally, recited and sometimes sung, these poems, in Arabic or Aramaic (Western and Eastern) name those responsible, and perpetuate the memory of events and misfortunes. Such is the case of *Dourekta d'firman* (on the 1915 genocide) by the priest Kasha Yonan Bidawid from the village of Bedare, written down in 1916 and today sung by the Chaldean Father Aziz Yalap, and a team comprising Andraos Yaqo, Warda Gulan, Behnan Zayto and Nemroud Hanna, in Father Yalap's parish of Sarcelles, near Paris.[67] Father Yalap had previously composed a historical text on the genocide in 2003, read by his son Antoni Yalap.[68] Mgr Israel Audo, Archbishop of Mardin, concluded his written report on the 1915 massacres with a poem on the Year of the Sword (*Seyfo*).[69]

There exist numerous poems in Western Aramaic on the subject of the *Seyfo*, among which are works by Gallo Shabo, Naaman Aydin, Kashisho Ephrem Safar from Midyat, the *Dayroyo* (monk) Yohanna Kefry and Yousef Chahine, as well as the songs of Isa Ishler. Originally from the village of Kfarze in Tur Abdin, Ishler, who wrote poems based on what he had heard from family and friends, recited them in 1990 in Belgium, to keep alive the memory of 1915's painful events and prevent future generations from forgetting. Tuma Nahroyo (1936–2002), also a native of Kfarze and the composer of many melodies, wrote poetry about the *Seyfo*. In September 1999, he recorded a CD of fifteen poems entitled *Sahdo* (Martyr) in the Brussels studio of Radio Panik, during the programme *La Voix des Assyriens* (Assyrian Voices) hosted by Nahro Beth-Kinne; among the poems were "Seyfo", "Tour Abdin" and "Goloutho".[70] Isaac Armalet cites other poems, in Arabic, in *The Calamities of the Christians*.[71]

Some contemporary poems on the *Seyfo* called for resistance against Turkish attacks, as was the case in Hakkari, in Ain Ward in Tur Abdin and in Azakh in the district of Jezireh. In Hakkari, *Shamasha* (Deacon) Aprem de Sarai wrote a poem in Aramaic that was sung from village to village in the mountains, urging a rising against the Turkish oppressors, centred on the patriarchal family:

> From Tyari to Jilu, from Tkhuma to Baz, all the tribes and clans, united, must march in tight formation and go to battle around Mar Shimun. Over the mountains we must advance, our hearts full of tenderness, towards the fertile Mosul valley. On the banks of the Tigris sits the holy city of Nineveh whose walls will be our crown. Listen to the cries of our Nation, she calls, our Assyrian grandmother. Then and there the Assyrians will be able to settle...

The poem ends: "Let us go then into battle in the name of Mar Shimun."[72] Responding to the call to arms, many of the mountain-dwelling Assyrians defended themselves village by village, despite rudimentary weaponry, and a large part of the community was lost in the process.

The massacres and the United Nations

On reading the United Nations' Convention on the Prevention and Punishment of the Crime of Genocide, unanimously adopted on 9 December 1948, it is hard to escape the conclusion that it applies entirely to the massacres perpetrated against the Assyrians. These atrocities had religious and national motives, with all commentators and witnesses agreeing that the Armenians and Assyrians were massacred simply because they were Christians and of non-Turkish ethnicity. They were a group who faced elimination on the sole basis of their collective identity.

The General Assembly of the United Nations began to address the concept of genocide from 11 December 1946 (resolution no. 96), defining it as a "crime under international law which the civilized world condemns". The preamble to the 1948 Convention, adopted at the Palais de

Chaillot in Paris in the presence of Raphael Lemkin, recognizes "that at all periods of history" genocide "has inflicted great losses on humanity" and that "in order to liberate mankind from such an odious scourge, international co-operation is required".

Listing the forms that it can take, the Convention specifies that genocide may be defined as "acts committed with intent to destroy, in whole or in part, a national, ethnical, racial or religious group". These terms—intent, destroy, national, religious—are wholly congruent with the Assyrian experience in 1915.

The Convention goes on to raise other questions relevant to the Assyrian case, concerning motives and responsibilities. Was there "conspiracy to commit genocide", "direct and public incitement to commit genocide" and "complicity in genocide"—all punishable acts under Article III? Were the instigators "constitutionally responsible rulers, public officials or private individuals?" Before answering these questions, it is worth recalling that Professor Lemkin explicitly listed "Christian Assyrians" among genocide victims in the text of a talk of 1948, held in UNESCO's archives:

> Whether the victims were called Huguenots, Waldenses, early Christians, Jews, Christian Assyrians, Armenians, Poles, Gypsies, Slavs of different nationalities, whether the attack was directed in the dark Middle Ages or in our enlightened times, there have always been two tragic questions. Are these people crying for help entitled to international protection, and, if such protection comes, does it interfere with the right of a state to do whatever it pleases with its own citizens?[73]

The Assyrian group, known under its different names—Assyrian, Chaldean, Syriac, Nestorian—is, as we have seen, a historically recognized people, moreover acknowledged by the Ottoman Empire, albeit with limits and imprecise structure, as a *millet* (nation and Church). This much is confirmed in an international diplomatic document, the Treaty of Sèvres (10 August 1922) and in the documents of the League of Nations, notably in 1935:

> It must be counted as a proof of uncommon courage and tenacity that the Assyrian community succeeded in holding together through long centuries of neglect and contempt, preserving something of its ancient traditions both as a Church and as a people.[74]

Another paragraph traces the long history of this people:

> Small, remote and insignificant as they were—so remote and insignificant that their very existence was forgotten in the West until the nineteenth century—they have never, it seems, enjoyed that happiness which falls to "the people whose annals are empty". Their poverty has not saved them from invasion and aggression: their small numbers have not saved them from internal disunion. They have existed for centuries on the margin of history, bearing its burdens, excluded from its glories and rewards. Yet this people, poor, disunited, unshepherded, has handed down from generation to generation its strange ancestral titles—the shadowy heritage of the ancient name of Assyrian, the substantial succession of a once mighty Church.[75]

The Assyrian people thus has all the characteristics of a nation: geographic, ethnic, cultural and religious. Additionally, because it was aware of its own collective identity, it has always rejected, at the risk of being persecuted, policies aimed as its dispersal or at its aggressive assimilation into the dominant societies, Turkish or Arab, and has wanted to live as a compact and homogenous group under the authority of its patriarchs.

174

The acts listed in Article II of the Convention, all specifically considered genocidal, cover the different types of violence inflicted on the Assyrians in 1915:

(a) Killing members of the group;
(b) Causing serious bodily or mental harm to members of the group;
(c) Deliberately inflicting on the group conditions of life calculated to bring about its physical destruction in whole or in part;
(d) Imposing measures intended to prevent births within the group;
(e) Forcibly transferring children of the group to another group.

From the various accounts and reports we have studied, it has been amply demonstrated that the Turkish authorities, in a deliberate and systematic policy, committed lethal acts against the Assyrian people on a massive scale, as well as intentional attacks on their physical and mental wellbeing: deportations, attacks on women, rapes, abductions, forced Islamization—exposing them to conditions of life aimed at leading to their physical and psychological destruction. To this can be added the kidnapping of women, of whom some were pregnant, the use of mass imprisonment, the abduction of children and young girls and their subsequent forced conversions and sexual abuse: all forms of trauma directed at women and children, resulting in depopulation and a dramatic decline in the birthrate.

Article III specifies which acts shall be punishable under the Convention:

(a) Genocide;
(b) Conspiracy to commit genocide;

(c) Direct and public incitement to commit genocide;
(d) Attempt to commit genocide;
(e) Complicity in genocide.

Here again, sufficient evidence has been presented to conclude that the events of 1915 constitute a genocide, that there was a conspiracy and complicity, accompanied by public incitement. Article IV stipulates that those guilty of genocide or of any of the above acts will be punished, "whether constitutionally responsible rulers, public officials or private individuals". On this point, too, the evidence is unambiguous.

4

AFTER 1915

THE TRAGEDY CONTINUES

"The law of Turkish amnesty did not apply to the Assyrians who, in no circumstances, should be allowed to enter Turkey; any Assyrian attempting to enter Turkey is to be punished."

General Consul of Turkey in Baghdad, 25 June 1928[1]

"It must be borne in mind that the principle of nationality as understood in the West is almost unknown in the Near and Middle East."

Dr Alphonse Mingana, The Manchester Guardian, *4 June 1919*

1918: from Salmas and Urmia towards Hamadan and Iraq

"Moving 300 miles south-eastward in disordered retreat with their families, live-stock and possessions, the Assyrians finally arrived at Hamadan, decimated from perpetual attacks on all sides from the Turks, Kurds and Persians alike. Scorched in the burning summer heat and ridden with typhus, dysentery, small-pox and cholera, old people and children exhausted with fatigue and fever were left to die by the wayside, marking the path of

retreat with the dead and the dying. At length, 20,000 fewer in number, the survivors made contact with the British troops."

League of Nations, 1935

The Assyrian tragedy did not end in 1915, but continues to this day. Its second stage took place on the Urmia front in July 1918. Bolshevik Russia had signed a peace treaty on 3 March at Brest-Litovsk with the Central Powers: Germany, Austria-Hungary, Bulgaria and the Ottoman Empire. It was a crucial moment leading to political turmoil in Europe and dramatic consequences for the Assyrians. Persian Azerbaijan suddenly found itself in a situation where order and security were non-existent, due to the structural weakness of the state.

In December 1917, following the Bolshevik Revolution, the Russians withdrew definitively, and in hurried and chaotic fashion, from the Turco-Persian front. This retreat alarmed Christians but encouraged the Turks in their quest to occupy Persian Azerbaijan. An Assyrian delegation immediately set out for Tiflis (Tbilisi in Georgia) to express its fears for the future and to demand Russian protection. It was composed of three prelates: Mar Thomas Audo, Chaldean Catholic Bishop of Urmia, Mar Elia, an Orthodox bishop, and the Protestant pastor Rev. Isaac Malek Yonan.

Shortly afterwards, Basil Nikitin, then Russian consul at Urmia, received a telegram from General Lebedinsky, commander-in-chief of the Russian Army of the Caucasus, who was anti-Bolshevik and organizing resistance against the Turks. Lebedinsky announced that he was planning to form and train Christian troops in Urmia with the cooperation of Allied military attachés such as the French Colonel Chardigny and British officers. On 3 December 1917, Patriarch Mar Benyamin Shimun met General

Simonoff at Urmia with a view to incorporating the Assyrian community into a force that would defend its own threatened existence and assist the Allied cause.

The Allies were also attempting to organize themselves following the Russian capitulation. The French lieutenant Nicolas Gasfield arrived with orders from Colonel Chardigny to establish Assyrian and Armenian battalions. To bring those Assyrians settled in Persia under the banner of the Allies, Gasfield was counting on the assistance of Paul Caujole (1878–1961), medical chief of the "Alpine French Ambulance", sent from France as a gesture of solidarity with Russia and based in Urmia. The British also dispatched an officer to Urmia, Captain George Gracey, to organize the training of troops. The Assyrians eventually formed a corps, composed of several units and four battalions, determined to resist the Turkish advance and to hold the front abandoned by the Russians, which they did until the end of July 1918.

Assyrians at arms

The Assyrian forces numbered some 6,000 men and were under the command of General Agha Petros and the tribal leader Malik Khoshaba, flanked by Allied (mainly Russian) troops. Their task was to hold the front against the Turks, who wanted to advance on the city of Baku. For seven months (January–July) they achieved this aim while surrounded on all sides by enemy forces and hostile populations. The Assyrian battalions were, in reality, commanded by the Russian Colonel Kuzmin and were equipped by Russia's General Vadbolski with artillery, machine guns, ammunition, supplies and medical and communications equipment. Yet their organization met with several technical and logistical difficulties, in particular material and senior staff shortages. Besides three Frenchmen including Nicolas Gasfield, Colonel Kuzmin had only thirty Russian officers and NCOs of variable quality to lead the 6,000 Assyrians.

Paul Caujole, who was to write an acclaimed book on the mission,[2] had time to study and familiarize himself with the Assyrian population, and particularly the mountain dwellers of Turkey, a "race of tough farmers, honest workers and skilled artisans, intelligent and courageous". On 10 June 1922, he published an article on "The Situation of the Assyro-Chaldeans", seeking to draw the French public's attention to "the cries of despair reaching Europe from the distant banks of the Tigris and the Great Zab". As an eye-witness, he recalled:

> When, in December 1917, the disintegration of the Russian army left the German-Turkish front in Urmia defenceless, the Assyro-Chaldeans did not hesitate to take up arms and continue the Allied cause, the struggle abandoned by the Bolsheviks. For eight months they fought with the greatest bravery, immobilizing with their six thousand men six German-Turkish divisions and effectively covering the Kermanshah-Hamadan-Kasvin-Enzeli communication line that the British had established from Baghdad towards Baku.[3]

The Persian authorities in Tabriz reacted negatively to the Assyrian units, considering them illegal, and demanded, unsuccessfully, that they be disarmed. There was even an uprising on 24 February 1918, and on 18 March the patriarch Mar Shimun was murdered, having been ambushed by the Kurdish leader Ismail Simko in Kohne Shehr. This assassination unleashed passions, and in reprisal a punitive Assyro-Syrian expedition took over Simko's residence, but he managed to escape. In April, Turkish forces advanced, and at the beginning of May, as a new battle with the Turks began near Khoy, the order came for Caujole's ambulance unit to withdraw. From that moment, the Assyrians were on their own.

In early June the Turks went on the offensive to the north, forcing the Christians to evacuate Salmas and retreat to Urmia. The withdrawal caused disarray within their ranks, and on 23 July, under pressure from the Turkish troops, the military units and those of the entire Christian population (Assyrian and Armenian) fit to do so left Urmia for Hamadan to join with the British forces in Mesopotamia. In his memoirs, Basil Nikitin wrote, attributing responsibility to the Turks: "Beginning in the streets of Urmia, the conflict spread and spilled into the field of military operations against the enemy. It is in any case probable that the battle of Urmia was provoked by Turkish agents."[4] At the end of the month, waiting in vain for the promised military aid from the British, the Assyrian forces had no choice but to abandon the region. It then fell into the hands of the Turks, Kurds and Persians, who wasted no time in perpetrating fresh massacres against the remaining Assyrians; among the victims were many priests from Urmia, including the French Alsatian Mgr Sontag, head of the Lazarist Mission, and the scholar Mgr Thomas Audo, Chaldean Bishop of Urmia. The Lazarist Aristide Châtelet described events:

> In July 1918 came the terrible disaster of a final invasion, spreading death and fire everywhere. Our leader, Mgr Sontag, died gloriously on Charity's field of honour; a Chaldean bishop, three of our brothers, forty priests and hundreds of Christians, pitilessly massacred, shed their blood in our missions at Khosrova and Urmia ... The entire Chaldean people, chased from their homes, are fleeing frantically through an enemy land, leaving corpses and captives in their wake.[5]

Paul Caujole observed:

> The Turkish and Persian governments have always practised a
> policy of persecution against the Assyro-Chaldean population.
> That implemented by the Turks has been particularly odious,
> and if the East is indelibly stained with Armenian blood, it
> should not be forgotten that the blood of Chaldeans flowed
> like water for the same reasons at Jezireh, Diyarbakir and
> Adana during the massacres of 1850, 1895 and 1909.[6]

The rest of the population sought sanctuary in the
south of Persia, close to the British in Hamadan, reaching
their destination in mid-August. The British then sent
them on to modern-day Iraq, putting them in two spe-
cially constructed camps, at Baqubah to the north of
Baghdad and Mindan, north of Mosul. The British, when
later in control of Iraq, would recruit troops from among
these refugees, known as the Assyrian Levies (see below).

Lieutenant Gasfield, based in Urmia, described the
exodus from Urmia-Salmas towards Hamadan:[7]

> For days and days on end these unfortunates arrived, exhausted,
> starving and terrorized by the Kurds who repeatedly attacked
> them on their long and dismal road. It was a tragic exodus,
> provoked by the sudden appearance of Kurdish gangs at Urmia.
> The sick and the old, who could not undertake the long march
> in the tropical heat, fled to the Catholic Mission, where as soon
> as they entered they were killed by the Kurds.

Thousands "died on the road from Urmia to Hamadan,
some from exhaustion, others massacred by the Kurds;
their debilitated livestock, deprived of fodder and water in
this desert land, dropped alongside their masters..."

> Shortly after this exodus, I was sent by the British forces staff
> from Hamadan to Bijar; all along the main road taken by the
> poor wretches lay a terrifying number of bodies, men, women
> and children, who had been stripped by the Kurds; flocks of

crows covered the corpses; next to them lay horses and buffaloes; the horror was all the more unbearable as the blazing sun of Persia had decomposed the cadavers and filled the air with an appalling and nauseating stench.

"Suffice to say," concludes Gasfield, "that of the 80,000 Christians who left Urmia, only half reached Hamadan". The mullahs, he notes, "incited the faithful to take up arms against the Christians. The Persian Democratic Party, supported by German emissaries, encouraged Muslims to revolt." These observations are corroborated in the League of Nations document *The Settlement of the Assyrians: A Work of Humanity and Appeasement*.

Humanitarian aid was again organized. The *New York Times* of 26 January 1919 carried an article entitled "For aid to Assyrians", reporting that fifty-four bishops of the Protestant Episcopal Church in the United States of America and fourteen from Canada had sent a petition to the Archbishops of Canterbury and York, asking them to use their influence and to ask of the Paris Peace Conference that the demands of Christian Assyrians in Mesopotamia, Kurdistan and Persia be recognized. This request was supported by Professor William Walker Rockwell and the American Committee for Relief in the near East.

Yet what Gasfield called the "tragic exodus" did not necessarily mean the end of the Assyrian drama. Ten months after the armistice, in June and July 1919, the districts of Zakho and Amadiya, to the north of Mosul, were invaded by Kurds who "put the men to death, and, after pillaging and sacking everything, rode off with the women and girls".[8]

The Assyrian Levies

As we have seen, the refugees from Hakkari and the plateau of Urmia were sent on by the British to Baquba, several kilometres north of Baghdad, under the command of Brigadier-General Herbert Henry Austin, who was to write a book on his experiences.[9] A total of 12,000 Assyrian men left for modern-day Iraq. Commanded by British officers, the first Assyrian troops were enrolled in the Baquba concentration camp, reinforced in 1922, with the support of the patriarchal family. For eight years they were led by Brigadier Gilbert John Browne, whose detailed account gives an important insight into their role;[10] Major A.D.W. Bentinck also commanded a battalion of Assyrians for twelve months in 1922 and 1923. The Assyrians formed an important part of the Levies force (sometimes known also as the Iraq Levies), which fought with the British during their post-war Mandate in Iraq.[11]

In 1922, the Assyrian Levies comprised two infantry battalions, two companies of cavalry and an artillery platoon. They were used against the Kurds (1919–24), to suppress the Iraqi insurrection of 1920, against the Turks in Hakkari (see below) and to protect the Iraqi border around Mosul (1921–24). They guarded the Royal Air Force bases at Hinaidi and Habbaniya. All British observers attested to their loyalty and bravery in combat. In a June 1923 article in the *Royal Central Asian Journal*, entitled "The Assyro-Chaldeans", Major F.F. Rynd praised them: "The Assyrian mountaineers were perhaps the smallest nation to be drawn into the vortex of the Great War. They have considerable claim to our interest and sympathy by virtue of their ancient origin and the part they took on our side against the Turco-German forces in the Middle East during the war."

In August 1924, Turkey invaded Hakkari, two years after some Assyrians had attempted to resettle the area. Turkish troops looted and burnt Christian villages, forcing an estimated 8,000 Assyrians to flee into Iraqi territory. The Turks pursued them, hoping to retake Mosul, but were stopped by the Assyrian Levies, charged with protecting the still disputed Turco-Iraqi frontier. In January 1925, the British air vice-marshal in Iraq expressed his sincere thanks to Lady Surma for her invaluable help in organizing the counter-offensive, sentiments echoed in the report of Colonel Herbert Thomas Dobbin: "I wish to make special mention of the great help given to me by Lady Surma d'Bait Mar Shimun after the formation of the irregular units. The large number of them who came to my aid after their initial retreat was above all due to her efforts and orders, and during the whole period covered by this report she offered inestimable assistance and was by counsellor in all matters related to these troops."[12]

Even so, the Assyrians' attitude towards the Levies and towards the British presence in Iraq was to change over time; the initial attraction of working with the British gradually faded, to be replaced by harsh criticism when the mandatory authorities decided to grant Iraq independence in 1932 and thus, as they saw it, to abandon the Assyrians. In a book of 1935 entitled *The British Betrayal of the Assyrians*, written after the 1933 Simele massacre (see below), the Assyrian leader Yusuf Malek (1899–1959), hardened by experience, evoked the tragic consequences of Mandatory Iraq and accused the British of using the Assyrians before leaving them to their own fate:

It is true that at the Baqubah Refugee Camp, the British authorities treated the Assyrians well but that was because they were in need of their services in the stormy years that were to follow. The British were in hostile Arab country and had wide experience of Arab treachery during the days of the war and knew that they could not have found more loyal people than the Assyrians to maintain a balance of power in the country.[13]

Malek believed, correctly, that the Assyrians' involvement in the Levies would make them yet more vulnerable to reprisals from their neighbours. William A. Wigram asked:

> Can it be said that we have 'played the game' by those to whom we gave promises and who served us because they trusted those promises? We have left them to the revenge of those who hated them because they served us, and the official whose blunders brought the disaster about has himself had to own that the moral responsibility is on us.[14]

The Turkey–Iraq frontier (1925)

After 1918 and 1919, the woes of the Assyrian people continued under Kemalist (Atatürk's) Turkey, particularly in Hakkari between 1923 and 1925, when efforts were made to delineate the frontier between Turkey and Iraq, and in Tur Abdin, the Syriac heartland, in 1925–26.[15] At the Lausanne Conference (1922–23) it had been impossible to settle the border question and to persuade Turkey to relinquish the *vilayet* of Mosul. Article 3 of the Treaty of Lausanne thus stipulated that the Turkey-Iraq frontier would be definitively drawn up in the following nine months, through friendly negotiations between the two governments (and Britain in the case of Iraq), failing which the dispute would be brought before the Council of the League of Nations. The text added: "pending the decision to be reached on the subject of the frontier, no military or other movement shall take place which might modify in any way the present state of the territories of which the final fate will depend upon that decision". Turkey was determined to keep control of Hakkari for strategic reasons, and took steps to maintain the territory and prevent the mountain-dwelling Assyrian refugees, who had been forced to flee to modern-day Iraq in July–August 1918, from returning to their homeland.

The 29 October 1924 meeting of the League of Nations Council (session XXXI), held in Brussels, adopted the recommendation of the Swedish *rapporteur* Branting, establishing a provisional demarcation line, the so-called "Brussels line", which maintained the status quo and practically coincided with that drawn under the Treaty of Lausanne. A neutral zone was also established between the Turkish and British armies, to avoid any fresh clashes. Yet this provisional ruling did not prejudice a definitive resolution, and as the question was still contested, an international commission of inquiry was set up by the League of Nations. The commission, comprising three members, was to report to the Council, having considered submissions from the Turkish and British authorities and inspected conditions in Mosul itself.

The three commissioners—Einar af Wirsén, Swedish Ambassador to Bucharest, Count Teleki, former Hungarian prime minister, and Colonel Albert Paulis of the Belgian army—visited the Mosul *vilayet* between January and March 1925 before presenting their report in Geneva on 16 July. Among its important findings, the report raised the problem of the Assyrian population and its need for protection, but did not rule on a definitive demarcation of the border. Rather, by granting Hakkari to Turkey and at the same time criticizing the conduct of the Assyrians ("who are of a warlike temper and have somewhat rough manners"), the commission effectively buried the Assyrian question.

In the context of a future Turkish-controlled Hakkari, the commission recognized that the Assyrians should enjoy a significant degree of autonomy and control as a *millet*:

> It is not within our competence to enumerate all the conditions which would have to be imposed on the sovereign State for the protection of these minorities. We feel it is the re-establishment of the ancient privileges which they possessed in practice, if not officially, before the war. Whichever may be the sovereign State, it ought to grant these Assyrians a certain local autonomy, recognising their right to appoint their own officials and contenting itself with a tribute from them, paid through the agency of their Patriarch ... The status of minorities would necessarily have to be adapted to the special conditions of the country; we think, however, that the arrangements made for the benefit of minorities might remain a dead letter if no effective supervision were exercised locally. The League of Nations representative on the spot might be entrusted with this supervision.[16]

The second section of Chapter V, Part Three in the report is entirely dedicated to the Assyrians, under the title "The Assyrian Problem".[17]

On the issue of the Assyrians' rights, the Turkish Foreign Minister Tewfik Roushdy Bey declared that it was "a question completely extraneous to the debate" and that "the number of Assyrians is far from being enough to exercise any influence on the question in dispute".[18] After several debates, the League of Nations commission opted that Hakkari should remain under Turkish sovereignty and suggested that the Mosul *vilayet* should be given to Iraq under the following conditions: "(1) The territory must remain under the effective mandate of the League of Nations for a period which may be put at twenty-five years; (2) Regard must be paid to the desires expressed by the Kurds..."[19]

In parallel, the Council commissioned the Estonian general Johan Laidoner to look into the situation of those populations living in the frontier region. His report was submitted on 14 December 1925, with an attached memorandum that constituted an indictment of Turkey's actions. Obstructed in his research mission and only allowed to operate in the British-controlled Iraqi sector, General Laidoner noted that some 3,500 deported Christians in Zakho had come from the villages situated between the "Brussels line" and the area further north claimed by the British government. He reported that the population was unarmed, that mass deportations had taken place and that troops from the Turkish 62nd Regiment had "subjected the inhabitants to atrocious acts of violence, going as far as to massacre".[20] The report described the pitiful state of the refugees, adding that "in order to define the real reasons for the deportation, it would firstly be necessary to hear the explanations of the Turkish authorities and then to undertake an inquiry in the localities where the evacuated villages are situated, which it was not possible to do".[21]

In his memorandum, dated 23 November 1925, General Laidoner gives a full account, supported by testimonies, of the deportations: the refugees who had managed to escape at the time of the deportations carried out by the Turks were divided between the town of Zakho and the village of Berseve. The villages that the refugees had left behind were Billo, Baijo, Alto and Marga, with those from the first three settled by the Iraqi authorities in Zakho, and those from Marga in Berseve. Living conditions, he wrote, were rudimentary in the extreme: a simple military tent or a mud-built shelter. The refugees were in considerable physical and emotional distress; a complete lack of hygiene resulted in devastating epidemics of malaria and dysentery. On 1 November 1925, the total number of refugees numbered around 2,800; now, he wrote, that number had passed 3,000 as each day groups of fugitives continued to arrive in Iraq. The total Assyrian population of the affected villages was approximately 8,000. Their principal economic activities were agriculture and livestock, and all were subject to the feudal authority of an *agha* who was generally owner of the village and absolute master of the lives and properties of the Christians living under him.

The information submitted by General Laidoner was supported by other sources, notably: a British government letter to the League of Nations secretary general (19 September 1925);[22] a telegram to the secretary general from the British high commissioner in Baghdad (24 September);[23] a report from the Commission for the Protection of Women and Children in the Near East, presented to the Council of the League of Nations by Austen Chamberlain on 25 September in the name of the British government;[24] and a letter to the secretary general from Leo Amery, British Colonial Secretary (24 September).[25]

Also of note is the long deposition of the Chaldean priest and well-known writer and poet, Father Paulus Bédaré of Zakho (1887–1974), partly composed of letters sent to him by Assyrians who had stayed in their ancestral district; according to Professor Louis Le Fur, it made "a significant impression on one of the most influential members of the Commission and was not without playing a part in his decision".[26] The report was submitted to the League of Nations' commission by the Union Catholique d'Études Internationales and again focused on the disputed frontier area between Iraq and Turkey and, in particular, on twenty villages near Goyan, close to Zakho. Since 1924, Turkish troops, earmarked for an invasion of Iraq, had been encamped in the neighbourhood:

> And suddenly, in September 1925, these troops went into action, cutting off the Christian villages, surrounding them and deporting their inhabitants en masse towards Anatolia. Some European newspapers reported these events, but sceptically; the Turks formally denied involvement with a disconcerting degree of impudence, but the well-informed British press covered developments accurately. We were awaiting confirmation or denial of the news from local sources and then two letters arrived from Zakho itself fully corroborating the disaster and describing it in its brutal reality.[27]

On 16 December 1925, the Council of the League of Nations, on the commission's recommendation, adopted a final resolution granting the *vilayet* of Mosul to Mandatory Iraq and confirming the "Brussels line" as the definitive border between Iraq and Turkey. With demands for the frontier to be revised in the Hakkari region rejected, Leo Amery commented:

> His Majesty's Government regrets that the Council was unable to accept its proposal to revise the frontier, which would have been preferable from a strategic and administrative point of view, and which would have guaranteed security in their homes to the Assyrian refugees as well as to the Chaldeans of Goyan, whose unfortunate fate has been brought to our attention in reports by the commission of General Laidoner. Nonetheless, His Majesty's Government, in his name and in the name of Iraq, accepts the Council's decision and will abide by it loyally.[28]

Considering the Council's decision, the Dominican Thomas-Joseph Delos, a professor of law at Lille Catholic University, observed with some bitterness:

The Assyrians had dreamt of assuring their independence and preserving their individuality by grouping their tribes together in a homogenous territory. The realization of their dream, encouraged by the Powers who had used them as soldiers and allies against the Turks, became impossible. There was talk of a "mistake" on the part of the commission and the League of Nations' Council. Subsequent events have shown that this is the most convenient judgement. The original homeland of the Assyrians was definitively shared out between the new Turkey and Iraq under British mandate.[29]

After the proclamation of the Kemalist Turkish Republic in October 1923, it was as if nothing had changed in eastern Anatolia. From early 1926, renewed massacres took place, this time in certain villages around Jezireh, where the Christians were forced into a repetition of the 1915 exodus. Literature in Syriac written by eye-witnesses such as Khoury Yousef Chahine, who wrote a poem on events in 1926, recalls what happened. Louis Le Fur also wrote in that same year:

> In this region the Christians had managed to protect their villages against Turkish attacks during the war; in one Turkish assault they had even captured a piece of artillery. In January and February 1926, the Turkish government imposed heavy taxation and demanded the total disarmament of the Christians. Under pressure from Jacobite bishops, they agreed to relinquish their weapons subject to a formal assurance from the Turkish government that it would guarantee their safety. No sooner were the arms handed over than villages, notably Azakh and Esfes, were plundered, the men massacred in the course of a so-called deportation towards Diyarbakir and Jezireh, and the women and children left at the mercy of the soldiers.[30]

After 1920, the resettlement in Iraq of the mountain-dwelling Assyrian refugees from Hakkari encountered many difficulties, above all in the matter of conserving their autonomy as a discrete group and keeping the traditional status to which they owe their existence. Their presence in Iraq provoked incomprehension and, fuelled by nationalism, the newly independent Iraqi state saw in this minority a threat to its stability, not least because of the role of the Assyrian Levies under the British mandate. The response of the Iraqi government was brutal when unrest broke out around Simele in the north of the country in July–August 1933. Further killings took place, as described by Colonel Ronald Semphill Stafford:

> Machine gunners set up their guns outside the windows of the houses in which the Assyrians had taken refuge, and having trained them on the terror stricken wretches in the crowded rooms, fired among them until not a man was left standing in the shambles. In some other instance the blood lust of the troops took a slightly more active form, and men were dragged out and shot or bludgeoned to death and their bodies thrown on a pile of dead."[31]

He added: "When I visited Simmel [sic] myself with Major Thomson on 17 August few traces could be seen of what had occurred, but the sight of the women and children is one which I shall never forget and I spent more than three years in the trenches in France!" He concludes the chapter "The August Massacres" as follows: "Up to 4 August the Iraqi Government had an excellent case, but this case was completely destroyed by what happened in Simmel and elsewhere. The massacres have blackened the good name of Iraq for many years to come."[32] The *Journal de Genève* estimated the dead at 2,000, while the Assyrians themselves claimed 3,000 victims with several villages ransacked and burnt.

Survivors again took the road into exile, this time towards the River Khabur in north-eastern Syria, and became de facto Syrian citizens. Since then, the situation has constantly vacillated between mistrust and repression, with no real recognition of the Assyrians' status.

Other massacres occurred in Turkey, in Tur Abdin in 1964 and in Beit Zabde, accelerating the exodus towards the countries of the West. The situation has worsened ever since; caught between the Turkish military and Kurdish guerrillas, much of the remaining Assyrian population has fled to various countries in Europe, abandoning their troubled homeland.

Fleeing Turkey

There were no more than 20,000 Assyrians in Turkey by 1995. Following continued depopulation since the genocide, only 450 remained in Hakkari in 1985, in the southwestern Beth Chebab *kaza* between the villages of Meer and Gaznakh, and since then the outflow has not ceased. In June 1994, the village of Meer was finally abandoned, and was no more. Not only has the Turkish state obstructed all efforts by Assyrians to return to their former homes, but it has also manifested contempt for this minority by allowing it to be persecuted and massacred without intervening. For those who survived the Year of the Sword in 1915, or who succeeded in returning home despite the obstacles, their tragedy persists to this day.

Another mass departure took place in the 1970s and 1980s following Turkish intolerance and repression, harsh living conditions, the situation in Iran since 1978, oppression by Kurdish *aghas* and turmoil in the wake of the Kurdistan Workers' Party (PKK) rebellion, which began in 1984. Murders, abductions and military raids followed one after the other without any government response;

Table 3

Assyrian name	Turkified name
Harbol	Aksu
Betspen	Gurumlu
Bazyan	Dogan
Ischy	Ombudak
Gaznakh	Cevizagaci
Meer	Kovankaya
Oz	Ayirim

many crimes went unpunished and unsolved by those in power. Widespread emigration thus began in 1975, with large and significant numbers leaving Hakkari, Bohtan, Urfa and the districts of Silopi, Siirt, Diyarbakir, Mardin, Tur Abdin and Midyat.[33]

The Assyrians of the Hakkari district[34] were now concentrated in five villages: Bazyan, Ischy, Gaznakh, Meer and Oz, names that were Turkified by the authorities, as above in Table 3.

In May 1986, the Turkish Ministry of the Interior ordered a new process of Turkifying village names, and 12,861 out of 24,957 were re-baptized, with 80 per cent of villages in south-east Anatolia receiving Turkish names. At the same time, the traditional patronymic names of Assyrian families had been undergoing a similar process of linguistic transformation since the 1930s.

Over a six-month period in 1984, a process of mass emigration emptied the village of Bazyan of its population as most of the 550 families sought refuge in France, with the others going to Istanbul. The future of the community's church, Mart Maryam, remains uncertain. In 1986, in the Paris suburb of Clichy-sous-Bois, I was able to collect testimonies. In 1957, Abdul Ahad was assassinated by a Kurd—his son fled to France in 1984 with his family. In June 1972, Jimmi Ziro was murdered by Kurds, while Daniel Doman was killed on 16 April 1983 by a Kurd who wanted to expropriate his land; his widow sought asylum in Clichy-sous-Bois with her three children and the victim's brother. On the same day, Hanna Doman, his cousin and mayor of Bazyan, was murdered, again by a Kurd, in the presence of his brother Yonan, who narrowly escaped death and took refuge in France.

Ischy met the same fate as Bazyan. Today, its inhabitants have settled near the French capital in the Val d'Oise and in Seine-Saint-Denis, where this testimony was given in 1986: a fourteen-year-old girl named Farida Petrus Hanna was abducted in October 1979 by Kurdish neighbours. Her parents attempted the impossible to find their daughter, paying more than a million Turkish *lire* to civil and military authorities, as well as to the local Kurdish *aghas*, in the hope of recovering Farida. All such moves were in vain, and eventually her parents took refuge in Sarcelles.

It was the same story in Gaznakh, where two-thirds of the inhabitants moved to France, Belgium, Germany and the United States; the final third followed them after 1990. Nor has the village of Meer escaped the phenomenon of mass migration. In June 1994, the village was destroyed by Turkish forces who burned the poplars, the pasture land and the bee hives. Meer's last seven families then moved to the village of Cevizagaci, fifteen kilometres away. As he was travelling to Beth Chebab to meet the prosecutor, the mayor, Hürmus Diril was arrested and jailed for alleged complicity with the Kurdish PKK.[35] More than 700 people from this village have moved to

Sarcelles, 500 to Clichy-sous-Bois and 100 to Montluçon. Before the exodus, more than 1,000 people lived in Meer, which had two Chaldean churches and a monastery dating back to 320 AD, Marta Shmuni, which once housed 600 monks. The 500 inhabitants of Oz, meanwhile, fled to France and Belgium. In all these villages, many abuses were inflicted on Assyrians, from murder and abduction to corporal punishment and pressure to convert to Islam.

The district of Silopi and Bohtan contained ten Assyrian villages: Harbol, Betspen, Hassana, Upper Deran, Lower Deran, Cenet, Azakh, Shakh, Mansuriye and Berhinci. In 1918, there were still around 3,000 Assyrians in Bohtan: 420 at Hassana, 360 at Mansuriye, 60 at Mar Youkhanna, 180 at Shakh, 360 at Tikuba, 960 at Jazirat-ibn-Umar, 180 at Mar Akha, 140 at Azakh, 300 at Harbol and 160 in various other villages.

Harbol, situated between two mountains rich in coal mines, was exclusively inhabited by Assyrians, but, at eight kilometres from the Iraqi border, was targeted several times during the Turkish army's incursions into Iraq in pursuit of Kurdish militants. From 1980 onwards, 1,500 inhabitants left for Europe, of whom 437 arrived in France. The other villages of Bohtan did not escape from the implacable law of forced emigration; out of 544 Assyrians at Betspen, 500 were forced to abandon their lands, homes and property, and the same was true of Hassana, Azakh and Mansuriye, already victims of the general massacre of 1915. Their history is littered with rapes and abductions, with abuses of all sorts, with persecution and pillage. Many from this region have consequently come to form communities in France, Belgium, the Netherlands, Sweden and Germany.

The region of Siirt is now deserted, whereas in 1913 the town of Siirt alone counted 5,480 Assyrians. Three villages—Dentas, Piroze and Hartvin—survived until 1968, but their inhabitants took refuge in Midyat (1968–72) and then Istanbul (1972–79) and finally France in 1980. Other families remained in Turkey, in Mersin on the Mediterranean, far from their villages in the south-west.

Other Turkish regions inhabited by Syriacs witnessed the same mass departures, with Tur Abdin deserted in the space of several years. Between 1970 and 1976, all the inhabitants of Kerboran found refuge in Sweden, Germany and Belgium. An Austrian delegation led by Mgr Florian Küntner, Auxiliary Bishop of Vienna, visited the region in 1992 to see the remaining Christians, who received Western priests for the first time in decades. According to Mgr Küntner, Tur Abdin in 1992 was at the heart of the conflict between the Kurdish liberation movements and the Turkish military, leaving the Christians "between a rock and a hard place". For the region and for the survival of the Christian minority, respect for human rights was thus "the fundamental problem".[36]

The turn of the twenty-first century has seen continued emigration, following the 1991 Kurdish uprising in northern Iraq, the two Gulf Wars (1990 and 2003) and their aftermaths, and above all the conflict in Iraq after 2003.

The diaspora in the US and Britain

The US diaspora is by far the largest of the world's Assyrian migrant populations, the oldest and the most important in politico-cultural, economic and financial terms. The United States is the main magnet for migration, and some 500,000 people—Nestorians, Chaldeans,

Syriacs and Protestants—are settled in the US. There are no fewer than thirteen Chaldean churches and a multiplicity of community organizations. Assyrians are to be found all over the country, concentrated in the Great Lakes region (Detroit, Chicago), on the East Coast (New Jersey, Connecticut, Pennsylvania, New York), in Arizona (Phoenix) and in California (Los Angeles, San Jose, San Diego, Turlock, Modesto, Ceres).

The first migrants arrived from Persia after 1880, originally from Urmia, Salmas and Tabriz and under the influence of American Protestant missionaries then active in Persian Azerbaijan. Some came to study, others in search of work. Others came after the First World War, forming a significant community in Modesto, Turlock and Ceres[37] and then in Michigan (Flint), Indiana (Gary) and Philadelphia in the industrial sector. Today the main population centres are in and around Chicago (100,000), Detroit (100,000) and California (50,000). There are many organizations representing these communities, including the Assyrian American Association of Chicago (dating from 1917), the Assyrian Foundation of America, San Francisco (1954), which promotes education, the Assyrian American National Federation (AANF), founded in 1933, which brings together many organizations, and the Assyrian National Council of Illinois in Chicago.

Certain churches in the US are already centennial, with the first Chaldean parish, Mar Aphrem in Chicago, dating from 1913 and the first Assyrian church, the Mar Sargis Assyrian Church of the East, also in Chicago, from 1914 (one of five in the area). Adherents to the Church of the East (Old Calendarists) have a church in Chicago, Mar Audisho. Assyrian Protestants are also well represented,

199

with various churches in Turlock and Chicago dating back to the 1920s.[38]

Between 1915 and 1924, a number of publications, some of an Assyrian nationalist tendency, appeared in the US: *The New Assyria* (founded by Joel E. Warda), the *Assyrian American Courier* (*Izgadda*)[39] and the *Assyrian American Herald*. There are also several academic reviews, such as the important *Journal of Assyrian Academic Studies* (JAAS), published by the Assyrian Academic Society (AAS), documentation centres like Chicago's Ashurbanipal Library and many diverse religious and political newsletters. Also present are radio stations, a television channel (ANB Sat) and news organizations such as the influential Assyrian International News Agency (AINA).

Though with a much smaller diaspora than the US, Britain has also attracted Assyrian migrants, especially from Iraq. As we have seen, links between the Church of England and the Assyrian Churches were important, and several personalities such as Paul Shimun, representative of the patriarch, worked in Britain to win support for the Assyrian cause. A Chaldean scholar, Dr Alphonse Mingana (1878–1937), was Keeper of the Oriental Manuscripts at Manchester's John Rylands Library and a strong critic of Turkish policy in a series of articles in the *Manchester Guardian* (1919–20).

It was in the aftermath of the 1915 massacres that a number of refugees of all religious confessions found refuge in Britain. The Chaldean patriarch Joseph Emmanuel II Thomas visited in 1920, as did Joseph Naayem, author of *Shall This Nation Die?* After the British withdrawal from Iraq, a number of Assyrians opted to follow in their wake. But it was after 1950 that their number grew steadily, particularly in the 1980s under Baathist persecution in Iraq, and there are currently an estimated 2,000 families originating not only from Iraq, but from Syria, Lebanon and the Gulf States. They are mostly located in London (Ealing), Surrey, Leeds, Cardiff, Manchester and Scotland. All the religious communities are present in Britain, sustained by regular visits from their ecclesiastical representatives, and all have their places of worship and cultural centres.

From Hakkari to Sarcelles

The first Assyrians from this region arrived in France on 4 February 1974 as immigrant workers from Bazyan, and the first to successfully apply for political asylum received this status in 1978. At the time, political asylum was hard to obtain, as almost nothing was known about this community.[40] Since then, the situation has evolved and the community has been welcomed by France and the French, and assimilated. It also enjoys a high profile thanks to the important positions occupied by many of its members.

Following the military coup d'état in Turkey on 12 September 1980, another mass movement of Assyrians towards the West took place. Today, the largest numbers are to be found in and around Paris in the *départements* of Val d'Oise and Seine-Saint-Denis. Their civil and religious leaders have worked to achieve integration into French society without losing the community's spiritual and ethnic identity in the dominant culture. They have sought to preserve a cultural individuality and maintain a linguistic and religious heritage. Much has been achieved in a short space of time: a Chaldean church opened its doors in Sarcelles on 7 February 2004, built in the Babylonian architectural style, and another was consecrated at Arnouville on Sunday 6 March 2016. Organizations such as the Association des Assyro-

Chaldéens de France (AACF) and the Union des Assyro-Chaldéens de France (UACF) offer courses in Aramaic and other educational and sporting activities, with the AACF aiming to "ensure the continued existence and the development of Assyro-Chaldean culture at the heart of the community and to support its cultural identity at the same time as integrating its members in French social life". From 1995 to 2004, the AACF published the periodical *Hammurabi*, a rich source of information and opinion; from 2001 to 2004, the AACF youth section, Jeunesse assyro-chaldéenne (JAC), published a monthly bulletin, *Les Lions de Babylone* (Aryé d'Babel).[41]

The UACF is also very active, offering among its many services social and administrative support, a women's section, school and job-seeking support, organized trips for youth and trips for older people to religious sites in France and abroad, sporting activities, Chaldean language lessons, literacy courses and cultural events and conferences. The UACF also maintains links with other Assyrian associations in Europe. For a short period (2001–02), it published a cultural and social magazine, *Huyada* (Union), in French, Aramaic, Arabic and Turkish, aiming to perpetuate the traditions and history of Mesopotamia and Assyrian culture.

Monuments commemorating the 1915 genocide have been erected, such as the Place des Martyrs Assyro-Chaldéens, inaugurated in Sarcelles on 29 June by Deputy Mayor François Pupponi. Young members of the community have become involved in local politics and civil society, and several have been elected to positions of responsibility. Today, as of the March 2014 local elections, fourteen councillors are in place, thirteen elected in Val d'Oise and one at Chelles in the Oise; the communes in question in Val d'Oise are Sarcelles, Arnouville, Villiers-le-Bel, Gonesse, Saint-Brice-sous-Forêt, Piscop, Ezanville, Montmorency and Groslay, with three deputy mayors— Georges Oclin, Mathieu Doman and Daniel Auguste— representing Sarcelles, Arnouville and Villiers-le-Bel. Thus diaspora activities of many types have intensified over the last thirty years in the vicinity of Paris, as well as in other cities such as Lyon, Marseille, Toulouse and Bordeaux.[42]

From Tur Abdin to Sweden, Germany and Belgium

Assyrians form a sizeable community in Sweden, well integrated, and carrying some weight in society. Swedish researchers—sociologists and anthropologists—were quick to take an interest in this group, and the Commission on Immigration Research (EIFO) and Stockholm University's Department of Social Anthropology have undertaken various projects, looking particularly at Syriac migrants from Turkey in a sociological context.[43] Sweden is also home to the important monthly *Hujådå* (Union), published since 1978 in eastern and western Aramaic, Arabic, Turkish and Swedish by the Assyriska Riksforbundet I Sverige (Federation of Assyrian Associations); its impact is considerable thanks to its extensive global distribution. The monthly *Bahro Suryoyo* (Syriac Light), representing the Syrianska Riksförbundet I Sverige (Federation of Syriac Associations) is also worthy of mention. Recognized as intermediaries and partners by the Swedish state, these associations contribute to integration while maintaining the Assyrian population's expressions of identity, necessary for its wellbeing and survival. All Churches of the Syriac tradition are active and well attended, structured around numerous parishes and dioceses.

In Germany, the Gesellschaft für bedrohte Völker (Society for Threatened People) has for more than thirty years attempted to alert public opinion to the dangers confronting ethnic minorities in the Middle East. Its journal *Pogrom* has featured many articles on the massacres of 1915–18 and on subsequent forms of repression. In 1978, Gabriele Yonan, an academic and activist, published a well-researched book, *Assyrer Heute*, on the contemporary history of the Assyrians.[44] Communities and churches are also very active in Germany.

Assyrians in Belgium are concentrated in the Brussels area (Saint-Gilles, Saint-Josse, Schaarbeck, Molenbeck, Brussels) and in Malines/Mechelen, Louvain-la-Neuve, Namur, Liège and Anvers/Antwerp and its surroundings. Supported by dynamic NGOs, where the Churches are prominent, their plight has frequently drawn the attention of the government, civil society, the Belgian press and European institutions. Particularly influential is the work of Droits de l'Homme sans Frontières (Human Rights Without Borders), under the direction of Willy Fautré,[45] and that of prominent Assyrians such as Nahro Beth-Kinne, president of the Belgian Institut Assyrien and a specialist in photography and filmmaking. There is also an influential Institut Syriaque de Belgique.

In the Netherlands, refugee communities are active and many in Amsterdam and in the province of Overijsselm, especially in Enschede and Hengelo.

Towards Iraq and Syria: the continuing tragedy

Iraq, Syria and Lebanon have been the main destinations of the mass exodus after 1915. Syrian Jezireh—Hassakeh, Qamishli, Amouda, the villages of the Khabur—and the city of Aleppo have received a large number of refugees.

Today, Iraq and Syria are being torn apart by war and are threatened with disintegration, a situation that once again carries dramatic consequences for this scarred community. A massive exodus is also once again under way, and nothing, it seems, can halt it. News in July–September 2014 from the north of Iraq was particularly alarming. Ultra-radical jihadist groups were spreading horror while engaged in a genocidal policy of ethnic and religious cleansing in Mosul province and Mount Sinjar against Christians and Yazidis, reminiscent of the atrocities of 1915. Anna Bachir, a Christian from Mosul who sought refuge north in Karakosh, described her community's plight to a journalist from *Le Monde* in simple terms: "Our life is an exodus."[46] Karakosh itself has now been emptied of its Christian population.

Since then, the situation has further deteriorated, leading to an intense mobilization by the international community on humanitarian and political fronts.[47] In both Iraq and Syria, the very existence of Christian communities is under threat from the so-called Islamic State, or Daesh, and forced migration continues towards the West as well as neighbouring countries. Two regions in particular have been affected—Nineveh province in Iraq and the Khabur district in Syria—with criminal attacks, the kidnapping of innocent civilians and mass flight in the wake of terrorist atrocities. Entire villages have been looted and depopulated. Fuelled by an ideology of hatred, the radical Islamists have infiltrated Mosul, Nineveh province and the Khabur area with a pre-planned strategy of driving out the Christian communities through the spread of terror.

In Mosul, conditions worsened dramatically after June 2014, when Daesh demanded that Christians convert to Islam, pay an "infidel" tax or leave their homes. Since then, the symbolically named Nineveh province (Ninawa in Aramaic) has undergone systematic repression and an unprecedented level of emigration that has seen the villages of Karakosh (or Bakhdida), Tall Kayf, Tel Esqof, Alqosh, Bartella, Karamlish, Baachika and Bahzan abandoned by their Christian inhabitants. In the ensuing humanitarian catastrophe, some 120,000 people have been made homeless, living in poverty in Iraqi Kurdistan, followed by thousands of Yazidis forced to leave Mount Sinjar.

Following the destruction of historic and "un-Islamic" monuments in Iraq, starting with the sacking of Mosul's museum in February 2015, attacks on the ancient Assyrian sites of Nimrud and Hatra in March and the demolition of churches and holy sites by obscurantist forces, an attempt is under way to wipe out the memory of a people and the traces of a civilization—of Mesopotamia, one of the cradles of humanity. These acts of vandalism have been vigorously denounced by UN Secretary General Ban-ki Moon, and by Irina Bokova, Director-General of UNESCO, who condemned them as "war crimes".

In February 2015, Daesh began its assault on the Assyrian Christian villages of Syria's Khabur region, having previously demanded that inhabitants remove the crosses from their churches. Several villages such as Tall Tamr, Tal Shamiram and Tal Hermuz were attacked by Jihadists with heavy artillery, while inhabitants of other villages fled to the towns of Hassakeh and Qamishli. An irony of fate has it that these pacific yet persecuted Assyrian communities in Syria are the descendants of those who escaped the 1933 massacres in Iraq, themselves children of the Ottoman Empire's victims in 1915.

CONCLUSION

RETURNING TO THE STAGE OF HISTORY

"Could men still exist in a corner of mysterious Asia who are the sons of the famous 'Pastors of Chaldea', the first astronomers? Men who, through the mists of four millennia of legend, still remember that the glory of Semiramis and Nebuchadnezzar was that of their kings, and that the splendour of Nineveh and Babylon was that of their capitals?

How many among us know enough history to be able to return through the centuries to the origins of a people who were great among the great and who, consigned to the grave, now raise their tombstone to let the world hear their appeal to be resurrected?"

Dr Paul Caujole, La situation des Assyro-Chaldeens,
10 June 1922

Supporting the death toll figure given in this book's introduction, Father Joseph Naayem wrote in 1919, "There is not the slightest doubt that no less than 250,000 Assyro-Chaldeans, perhaps rather more than a third of the race, perished through Turkish fanaticism during the Great War, and immediately after the signing of the Armistice."[1]

We have seen that individuals from many different vantage points were witnesses to the massacres. We have also shown, through many documents, that Ottoman Turkey acted according to a carefully prepared plan. The killings took place on a huge scale. Mgr Pierre Aziz, the Chaldean Bishop of Salmas who miraculously escaped death, wrote on 14 April 1919: "If I had to compile the history of all the evils that this sad war has caused us ... from the tragic events of a first and fatal flight to Russia on 4 January 1915, I would require a whole book."[2]

After years of waiting, while preserving as best they could their collective memory, the Assyrians have, since 1980, experienced profound changes in their sense of belonging and in their reading of their contemporary history. In the gradual strengthening of national awareness underlying their sense of renewal, they have once again begun to explore and analyse the events of 1915, which the 1933 massacres in Iraq had partly obscured from view.

The first signs of this national, cultural and political reawakening began in the cradle of the Middle East, where Iran and Syrian Jezireh were important centres of rebirth. The years 1952–70 were fruitful in Iran, where important work in western Aramaic[3] was published by Nemrod Simono (1908–2004), Benyamin Arsanis, Kourech Benyamin, Pira Sarmas and William Sarmas. The community had two private schools, Chouchon and Behnam, and a rich tradition of publishing that included the magazine *Gilgamesh* (April 1952–December 1961) and the literary output of the Assyrian Youth Cultural Society.

Tur Abdin in Turkey and Syrian Jezireh were also instrumental in producing writing in western Syriac on the genocide. The manuscript *Maktabzabno* (Stories) by Khoury Numan Aydin de Bath-Kashisho Gorguis, completed in 1975, contains material on the events of 1915. The Syriac-language teaching materials by Malphono Abrohom Nuro from Aleppo are of major importance, in particular his two books *Suloko* (1989), a new approach to teaching the language, and *Tawldotho* (1997), on Syriac neologisms, principles, criteria and original examples.

The impact of the diaspora

Today, thanks to the greater profile of the diaspora in the West and its place in the social landscape, we are witnessing the revitalization of the Assyrian community and its emergent new spring of culture and memory. Through its dynamism, the community has succeeded in attracting attention and interest, while the Assyrian question has also become a field of scientific investigation that appeals to students and researchers, historians and sociologists, linguists and anthropologists. At the same time, there is a profusion of books, documentaries, internet sites and press articles, such that increasing numbers of researchers and activists are engaging with the topic of the genocide. This upsurge in research, particularly on the genocide, became particularly evident in the 1980s (see Appendix).

In the diaspora, work is under way to transmit the history of the homeland to new generations. In France, members of the community, without necessarily being specialists, are tackling the recording and narration of stories, memories and testimonies relating to those of their village of origin or close family circles. Several villages have been studied in this way.

In 1993, a booklet entitled *Un village chaldéen: Ischy* was published in Sarcelles, produced by Toma Mikho[4] and with the support of various contributors originally from the village whose names appear within. Dedicated to the former inhabitants of Ischy, the booklet tells the story of a "millennial" village, placed under the protection of the celebrated mystic and ascetic monk Joseph Hazzaya (Joseph the Seer) because of his goodness and holiness. Among the aims set out by the authors was to "raise awareness among the young, in order to awaken their desire to know their origins, to love their community and to discover and preserve their social, religious, linguistic, ethnic and cultural heritage".[5] The conclusion insists that, even though the village has been physically destroyed, its memory must not be forgotten: "Now it is the task of the young to preserve this inheritance and to perpetuate those traditions that were once so hard to safeguard among a population persecuted, downtrodden and deprived of freedom. Is this not a moral duty?"[6] The book closes:

> Aucun terrien n'existe sans racine,
> Alors, n'oubliez point vos origines,
> Soyez fiers d'être Assyro-Chaldéens.[7]

> (No child of the soil exists without roots,
> So do not forget your origins,
> Be proud to be Assyro-Chaldeans.)

In 2010, Zackarie Yaramis wrote a succinct history of certain aspects—social and cultural life, traditions and customs—of his family village, Gaznakh:[8] Describing it as a "nest of civilizations", the author writes briefly about the repression, massacres and genocide of 1915 and their impact on this Hakkari village.[9] Its inhabitants have since been dispersed to nine separate countries—Russia, Iraq, France, Germany, Belgium, Denmark, Sweden, the United States and Australia. In his conclusion, Yaramis explains that he wanted to pay homage to his parents and ancestors, and that the aim was "to cast light on some of the injustices and sufferings (genocides, massacres, repression, looting) endured by the Assyro-Chaldean people over the course of the last centuries". Despite the sufferings, he adds, "our ancestors succeeded in safeguarding their identity. Better still, they managed to pass on to us all those inestimable riches."[10]

A DVD in Aramaic about the village of Meer appeared in 2012.[11] Following research undertaken in the village, "lost in the mountains of Hakkari", Risko Hanna Kas, who was ten in 1990 when his family emigrated, directed and provided the commentary for this documentary. Meer had been destroyed several times during its history, notably during the 1915 genocide, "which left terrible scars on the villagers". In 1980, there were still an estimated 570 inhabitants, but they began to leave their "ancestral" lands in 1990 due to growing conflicts, and as a result the village was completely deserted. The families emigrated to Europe, the large majority to France, which is now home to more than 1,300 *Meeryayé*. An unpublished typescript also exists of a sort of Assyrian autobiography, written by Nisan Doman, founder and first president of the Union des Assyro-Chaldéens de France, and Frédéric Praud. Mixing ancient and modern history with life in the diaspora, it is entitled *Les Origines du peuple assyro-chaldéen. Un aller sans retour* ("Origins of the Assyro-Chaldean People: A One-Way Journey").

Preserving memory

Memorials to the victims of the genocide have been erected around the world, in Australia, the United States (Chicago), France, Belgium, Sweden, Ukraine, Greece and Armenia, by the descendants of those who died or escaped, with the support of local or sometimes national authorities. In France, four such memorials exist—in

Sarcelles, Gonesse, Arnouville and Saint-Brice-sous-Fôret—with another planned at Villers-le-Bel. The monument at Sarcelles is evidence of the dynamism of the two local associations, the AACF and the UACF, and is the centrepiece of annual commemorations on 24 April. In Belgium, a Seyfo memorial was unveiled on 4 August 2013 at the spiritual centre in Banneux on the initiative of the Institut Syriaque de Belgique and the Seyfo Center; representing a dead dove and Assyrian religious symbols, the monument was carved from a twelve-tonne slab of granite by the well-known Assyrian artist Moussa Malki.

Progress has also been made in persuading politicians and governments to acknowledge the reality of what occurred in 1915. In 2010, the Swedish parliament adopted a motion stipulating that Sweden should recognize that a genocide was perpetrated against Armenians, Nestorians, Syriacs, Chaldeans and Pontic Greeks. In Yerevan, the Armenian capital, a monument was inaugurated on 25 April 2012, dedicated to "the Memory of the innocent Assyrian victims of 1915". A ceremony in Moscow on 9 June 2014, presided by Mar Dinkha IV, the Nestorian patriarch, saw the unveiling of a bust in memory of Mar Benyamin Shimun, murdered by the Kurdish chieftain Simko in Salmas on 4 March 1918. In Australia, where great steps have been taken to raise awareness of the genocide, a monument was inaugurated in Bonnyrigg on 7 August 2010 in memory of the Assyrian victims, while on 1 May 2013 the Parliament of New South Wales Legislative Council unanimously approved a motion recognizing the Assyrian, Armenian and Greek genocides.

In Britain, Baroness Cox spoke in the House of Lords in June 2015, asking the British Government "whether they have any plans to recognise the killings of Armenians,

Greeks and Assyrians in 1915 as genocide". She pointed out that "over 20 states have recognised the genocide, including France, Canada, Poland, Chile and Austria, as well as the European Parliament and the Welsh Assembly", and highlighted the "irrefutable evidence of the systematic slaughter of 1.5 million Armenians, Greeks and Assyrians". The government whip Viscount Stopford replied that the Government recognizes "the terrible suffering inflicted on the Armenian people and other groups living in the Ottoman Empire in the early 20th century", yet believes that it is possible to "help the peoples and Governments of Turkey and Armenia to face their joint history together" without acknowledging this as genocide. Baroness Cox reminded the Minister that Pope Francis recently "emphasised the necessity of genocide recognition for healing, reconciliation and moving forward".

This process of recognition and awareness is gathering pace at a global level, and now it is an international movement that supports the principal demand made by the Assyrians—that their genocide be recognized as such. In Turkey itself, a movement in this direction fuelled by civil society has come into being. The south-east of the country is showing signs of renewed dynamism, almost as if new life has been breathed into these formerly moribund districts. In Diyarbakir, Mardin, Midyat, Tur Abdin and Bohtan, developments are taking place, with Kurdish support, as reconstruction projects funded by the diaspora and visits in search of old communities show the continuing strength of attachment to the ancestral birthplace. A few villages in Tur Abdin and Bohtan district have benefited from these initiatives, and even a few Assyrians were reported to have returned, at least temporarily.

Moreover, cooperating with the Kurdish People's Democratic Party (HDP), the Assyrians have a member of the Turkish parliament, Erol Dora, re-elected in November 2015 and the first ever ethnic Assyrian Turkish MP. The Syriac community is also—significantly—represented by a joint mayor, Februniye Akyol, who shares power in the city of Mardin with a Kurdish mayor. As such, this community, estimated at 20,000 in Turkey, is gradually gathering momentum despite the obstacles of instability and hostilities between Turkey and the Kurds. Under the influence of extreme nationalism and again in conflict with the Kurds, Turkey is once more victim to internal repression and attacks on freedom of expression.

In Hakkari, the land of Surma Khanum, who was driven out with her family in 1915 by Turks and Kurds, there was for many years nothing but the echo of death and destruction. The Assyrian community's houses were destroyed, their property confiscated and those homes left standing occupied by Kurds. Now Hakkari is almost exclusively Kurdish. Yet this region, abandoned by its Assyrian population a century ago, has still figured large in the collective memory, evoked by poetry and songs. It was Surma, of course, who had accused Kurdish forces of using Russian artillery against Assyrian villages, and it was her brother who had been murdered by the Kurdish warlord Simko. It is no small historical irony, then, that the majority-Kurdish population of the city of Hakkari chose in 2014 to name a new park after Surma Khanum.

Iraq: homeland or safe haven?

On 9 April 2003, Baghdad fell and Saddam Hussein was overthrown by coalition forces led by the United States.

Since then, the country has been confronted by interminable conflicts and rivalries of a political, ethnic, religious and sectarian nature, worsened by the presence of so-called Islamic State or Daesh. Particularly vulnerable have been the remaining Assyrian communities, among whom an unprecedented exodus has taken place.[12] In 2003, there were perhaps a million in Iraq; now that figure has fallen to some 400,000.

The Iraqi parliament approved a draft constitution in August 2005, adopted in October by referendum. It recognized the Iraqi state as federal (Article 1), democratic and parliamentary in strong contradistinction to the presidential and dictatorial *ancien régime*. Federalism was adopted without extensive debate, and the resulting imprecisions can be traced to the absence of a federalist culture. Iraq defines itself as composed of various ethnic groups, religions and languages (Article 3), with Arabic and Kurdish the two official languages of the state (Article 4). At the same time, the Constitution guarantees the rights of speakers of Turkmen, Syriac and Aramaic in public and private spheres (Article 4.1), and "The Turkmen language and the Syriac language are two other official languages in the administrative units in which they constitute density of population" (Article 4.4). Moreover, Article 125 specifies: "This Constitution shall guarantee the administrative, political, cultural, and educational rights of the various nationalities, such as Turkomen, Chaldeans, Assyrians, and all other constituents, and this shall be regulated by law." In the province or governate of Ninevch, ravaged by Daesh-inspired violence since July 2014, Assyrians have lived in "density of population" around the capital Mosul, itself with a strongly Sunni majority, since time immemorial. Desperate for protection and supported by the diaspora, notably in the United States, this remaining community has argued for a "homeland", a geographical and administrative area of its own where security and cultural and religious rights can be guaranteed within a relatively homogenous zone—a safe haven. This idea, backed by Assyrian political groups,[13] was approved in a non-binding resolution by the European Union's parliament in March 2015.

If, according to Article 125 of the Iraqi Constitution, the political rights of the Assyrians, like other minorities, are guaranteed by law, it is regrettable that this principle has not been put into action. It is also the case that the experiences of Kurds and Assyrians have been very different. Articles 116–121 grant a large degree of decentralization to regions (*iqlim*) and provinces (*mohafazat*).[14] The Kurds have three provinces in the north, grouped into the Iqlim Kurdistan, the Kurdish autonomous region recognized both since 1992 in an earlier constitution and in that of 2005 (Article 117). Yet the Assyrians have no province of their own, let alone a region of their own. While Nineveh province remains the area where the demographic presence is most marked, the rest of the population is largely to be found in autonomous Kurdistan, with others scattered in neighbourhoods of Baghdad and, to a lesser extent, Kirkuk and Basra.

The notion of an autonomous territory for the Assyrians has antecedents, dating back to the 1919 Paris Peace Conference and then recurrently in 1930, 1935, 1937 and 1945. Such a project would not, *a priori*, be incompatible with the Iraqi Constitution, but the small numbers of Assyrians and the politics of demography (large Arab and Kurdish populations) make its realization unlikely. The Kurds enjoy a degree of autonomy, while the Arab population of Iraq is in its majority opposed to minority autonomy and wary of political initiatives that may be seen as secessionist. The history of such projects is painful, reminding us that each time the Assyrians have demanded autonomy they have faced refusal and repression, only mitigated in 1933 when the international community intervened. If it seems clear that they are determined to create a "homeland", it is less certain that they have the means and the support to make this dream a reality.

Although the Iraqi government is obliged to protect its minority citizens and the Constitution guarantees a wide range of political and cultural rights, the prospect of a settlement to the autonomy question seems distant. Since independence, no policy in favour of ethnic or religious minorities has been seriously considered by Arab countries, by Turkey or by Iran. The potential human and cultural wealth of these countries has been outweighed by dominant nationalism and by a pervasive lack of democracy.

Turkey, meanwhile, consistently refuses to acknowledge either the Assyrian or the Armenian genocide. The Turkish Prime Minister Recep Tayyip Erdoğan addressed the Armenian issue on 23 April 2014, without mentioning either genocide or the Assyrian experience:

> It is indisputable that the last years of the Ottoman Empire were a difficult period, full of suffering for Turkish, Kurdish, Arab, Armenian and millions of other Ottoman citizens, regardless of their religion or ethnic origin.
>
> Any conscientious, fair and humanistic approach to these issues requires an understanding of all the sufferings endured in this period, without discriminating as to religion or ethnicity.
>
> Certainly, neither constructing hierarchies of pain nor comparing and contrasting suffering carries any meaning for those who experienced this pain themselves.

The task is not to construct "hierarchies of pain", but to identify clearly the aggressor and the aggressed, the perpetrator and the victim of genocide. Only then will it be possible to allot responsibility without diluting it.

Are we witnessing a historic turning-point? As the exodus from historic Mesopotamia continues, the strength and self-confidence of the Western diaspora is conversely growing. The Assyrian cause is gaining support among politicians and sections of civil society, while memory of the events of 1915 is strengthening rather than fading. Such developments give grounds for hope, and encourage the belief that this people may yet finally return to the stage of history.

NOTES

* Abraham Yohannan, *The Death of a Nation or the Ever-Persecuted Nestorians or Assyrian Christians*. New York & London: G. P. Putnam, 1916, preface p. 5.

PREFACE

1. See *L'Osservatore Romano*, Rome, 16 April 2015, p. 10 (also available in French). Page 13 of this edition also contains the article "Un ouvrage de Joseph Yacoub. La tragédie assyro-chaldéenne-syriaque".

INTRODUCTION

1. See Joseph Yacoub, "Assiro-Caldei. Un Olocausto Cristiano", *Avvenire*, trans. Anna Maria Brogi, Milan, 22 June 2014.
2. Certain documents, as we shall see, erroneously refer to them as Syrians (because of resemblances with the term Syriac), risking confusion with the inhabitants of Syria. Wherever documents refer in this context to Syrians, they are, in fact, designating Assyrians. As early as 1918, the Lebanese historian Philip Hitti, professor at Columbia University in the US, was distinguishing between the two terms in order to avoid such errors. His letter to the *New York Times*, 17 August 1918, was titled "Assyrians not Syrians", in which he wrote, "Failure to keep clear the distinction between Assyrians and Syrians has often led to great confusion."
3. Joseph Yacoub, *Babylone chrétienne. Géopolitique de l'Église de Mésopotamie*, Paris: DDB, 1996; *Menaces sur les chrétiens d'Irak*, Chambray-lès-Tours: CLD, 2003; updated Italian translation, *I Cristiani d'Iraq*, Milan: Jaca Book, 2006.
4. See Rev. John Stewart, *Nestorian Missionary Enterprise: The Story of a Church on Fire*, Edinburgh: T. & T. Clark, 1928.

5. See Jean-Maurice Fiey, "Proto-histoire chrétienne du Hakkari turc", *L'Orient syrien*, 9, 1964, pp. 469–470.

6. Vital Cuinet, *La Turquie d'Asie. Les divisions administratives de la Turquie et de l'Empire ottoman*, Paris: Ernest Leroux, 1891, vol. II, pp. 719–720.

7. Michel Chevalier, *Les montagnards chrétiens du Hakkari et du Kurdistan septentrional*, Paris: Publications du Département de Géographie de l'Université de Paris-Sorbonne, 1985, pp. 61 & 196.

8. Surma d'Bait Mar Shimun, *Assyrian Church Customs and the Murder of Mar Shimun*, London: Faith Press, 1920, republished by the Mar Shimun Memorial Foundation, Turlock, CA, 1983, pp. 57–58.

9. Arthur John Maclean and William Henry Browne, *The Catholics of the East and His People*, London: SPCK, 1892, p. 25.

10. Mar Shimun, op. cit., pp. 58–59.

11. *Ibid.*, p. 68.

12. Maclean and Browne, *op. cit.*, p. 25.

13. Asahel Grant, *The Nestorians, or the Lost Tribes*, London: John Murray, 1843, p. 54.

14. See Edgar T. A. Wigram, "The Ashiret Highlands of Hakkari (Mesopotamia)", *Journal of The Royal Central Asian Society*, III, 1916, pp. 40–59.

15. An Arabic term: *Nakabate* is the plural of *Nakbat*, meaning painful event, tragedy or calamity.

16. Habib Jarwe's text on the 1895 *Nakabate* appears in Isaac Armalet's book, *Al-Qousara fi Nakabat Annasara* ("The Calamities of the Christians"), Beirut, 1919, pp. 42–66.

17. "Une conférence sur les souffrances des Assyro-Chaldéens", *L'Asie française*, August–November 1919, pp. 238–242.

18. Miss Mary Schauffler Platt, *The War Journal of a Missionary in Persia*, Chicago: Woman's Presbyterian Board of Missions of the Northwest, 1915.

19. The preface is by William Ambrose Shedd, an American missionary and witness to the events. The diary would be attributed to Miss Mary E. Lewis, an American Presbyterian missionary and future wife of William A. Shedd. In his preface, dated November 1915, the latter writes: "The following journal gives a vivid account of the months of distress and peril that the native Christians and missionaries at Urmia, Persia, passed through last winter and spring. To one who went through it, every incident mentioned and every harrowing detail brings before the mind the panorama of terror, privation and disease

that passed before our eyes day by day. No history can ever exaggerate the horror of it all as a whole." Platt, op. cit., p. 3.

20. This book was translated into English in 1921, into Turkish in 1999 and into Arabic, in Baghdad, in 2006.

21. Just as the noun "genocide" was coined in 1944 by Raphael Lemkin (see his book *Axis Rule in Occupied Europe*), who also instigated the 9 December 1948 UN Convention on the Prevention of Genocide), the neologism "ethnocide" was invented in 1970. On ethnocide, see Robert Jaulin, *La Paix blanche. Introduction à l'ethnocide*, Paris: Éd. du Seuil, 1970.

22. Gorek de Kerboran, "Les Assyro-Chaldéens", *La Croix*, 28 March 1923.

23. "Une conférence sur les souffrances des Assyro-Chaldéens", op. cit., p. 239.

24. *Annales de la Congrégation de la Mission*, 84, 1919, pp. 509–514.

25. Cited in William Henry Taylor, *Antioch and Canterbury: The Syrian Orthodox Church and the Church of England 1874–1928*, New Jersey: Gorgias Press, 2005, pp. 104–105.

26. *L'Action assyro-chaldéenne* wrote in 1921: "Father J. Naayem is accomplishing a fine patriotic mission across Europe. Sent by order of his bishop, Mgr Suleiman Sabbagh, he is relating to all charitable and generous hearts the sorrows of his massacred nation. He tells of the sufferings of starving survivors, naked, homeless, held as slaves, sold like beasts of burden. In his mission he is inspired by the martyrdom of those he saw die disembowelled, beheaded, hanged, drowned." Beirut, p. 19.

27. James H. Tashjian, *Turkey: Author of Genocide. The Centenary Record of Turkey 1822–1922, A Publication of the Commemorative Committee on the 50th Anniversary of the Turkish Massacres of the Armenians*, Boston, 1965, reproduced in *Armenian Review*.

28. Published by the Comité Européen pour la Défense des Réfugiés et Immigrés (CEDRI), Forcalquier, September 1986.

29. See "Préserver un Irak multiforme et multireligieux", *La Croix*, 30 July 2014; Guillaume Lamy, "Chrétiens d'Irak: extinction humaine et civilisationelle", *Lyon capitale*, 30 July 2014; Jérôme Cordelier, "En Irak, les chrétiens sont menacés d'extinction", *Le Point*, 31 July 2014, pp. 28–31; "In Iraq quasi condannati all'estinzione", *Avvenire*, trans. Anna Maria Brogi, 12 August 2014.

30. Louis Le Fur, "L'affaire de Mossoul", *Revue générale de droit international public* (*RGDIP*), Paris: Pédone, 1927, p. 82.

31. "Il y a un demi-siècle, les massacre occulté des Assyriens d'Irak", *Le Monde*, 1–2 January 1984.

1. WITNESSES TO GENOCIDE

1. E. Smith and H.G.O. Dwight, *Researches of the Rev. E. Smith and Rev. H.G.O. Dwight in Armenia, including a Journey through Asia Minor, and into Georgia and Persia, with a Visit to the Nestorian, and Chaldean Christians of Oormiah and Salma*s, 2 vols, Boston, Crocker & Brewster, 1833.
2. On the links between the Anglicans and the Church of the East, see J.F. Coakley, *The Church of the East and Church of England: A History of the Archbishop of Canterbury's Assyrian Mission*, New York: Clarendon Press, 1992.
3. *The Colonial Church Chronicle*, London, 1868, pp. 134–137. See also Audrey R. Vine, *The Nestorian Churches: A Concise History of Nestorian Christianity in Asia from the Persian Schism to the Modern Assyrians*, London: Independent Press, 1937.
4. *Ibid.*, pp. 55–56
5. William Henry Taylor, *Antioch and Canterbury: The Syrian Orthodox Church and the Church of England, 1874–1928*, Piscataway, NJ: Gorgias Press, 2005, pp. 102–103.
6. See Coakley, *op. cit.*, pp. 18–54.
7. See Taylor, *op. cit.*, pp. 15–47.
8. William A. Wigram, *Our Smallest Ally: A Brief Account of the Assyrian Nation in the Great War*, London: Society for Promoting Christian Knowledge (SPCK), 1920, pp. 7–8.
9. *Annales de la Congrégation de la Mission ou Recueil de lettres édifiantes écrites par les prêtres de cette Congrégation (Lazaristes) et par les Filles de la Charité*, Paris: Adrien Le Clere & Cie, vol. 81, 1916, pp. 240–263.
10. The Persian governor.
11. Noury Bey succeeded Raghel Bey in March, mid-conflict; the latter, a former student at the Saint-Benoît college in Constantinople, was considered more sympathetic towards France and towards the Christians.
12. Eugène Griselle, *Syriens et Chaldéens, leurs martyres, leurs espérances, 1914–1917*, Paris: Ed. Bloud & Gay, 1918, pp. 40–59.
13. This American doctor attached to the Presbyterian mission at Urmia was himself the author of a report sent to Pope Benedict XV (*Annales de la Congrégation de la Mission*, 84, 1919, pp. 509–514).

14. See "Les événements de Perse. Lettre de M. Abel Zaya, prêtre chaldéen de la Congrégation de la Mission", *Les Missions catholiques*, 48, 1916, pp. 234–236.

15. By Abel Zaya. See also *"La Chaldée martyre.* Lettre à Mgr F. Charmettan", *Bulletin de l'œuvre des écoles d'Orient*, May–June 1916, pp. 41–46. In the same issue is a letter from the Chaldean Patriarch Emmanuel II Thomas, pp. 46–48.

16. The German Lutheran mission at Urmia began in 1881. Two Nestorian priests, one of whom had travelled to Germany, organized branches of the German Lutheran Church that year in two villages near Urmia. The United Lutheran Church of America also supported several pastors and sent a missionary to Urmia in 1905. The German Evangelical Association for the Advancement of the Nestorian Church was founded in 1906 in Urmia by a priest who had received his Lutheran training in Berlin. The German Orient Mission opened an orphanage outside Urmia for mountain-dwelling Assyrian refugees from Hakkari.

17. Johannes Lepsius, *Le Rapport secret du Dr Johannès Lepsius, président de la Deutsche Orient Mission et de la Société germano arménienne sur les Massacres d'Arménie*, Paris: Payot & Cie, 1919, pp. 121–123.

18. Joseph Naayem, *Les Assyro-Chaldéens et les Arméniens massacrés par les Turcs*, Paris: Bloud & Gay, 1920, p. 220.

19. Joseph Naayem, *Shall This Nation Die?*, New York: Chaldean Rescue, 1921, p. xi. James (Viscount) Bryce was the author of several works of history including *The Holy Roman Empire*. He was translated into French: see *L'attitude de la Grande Bretagne dans la guerre actuelle*, London: Darling and Son, 1916; *Réflexions d'un historien sur la guerre. Dans le passé et dans l'avenir*, trans. Lucien Herr, Paris: Armand Colin, 1918.

20. *Ibid.*, pp. xi-xiii.

21. The English-language version of Naayem's book was translated into Arabic by Ramsen Racho in Chicago in 2001 (195 pages) and by Nafi Toussa (175 pages) and revised by Dr Yousif Thomas, director of the magazine *Al-Fikr al-Masihi* (Christian Thought), in Baghdad in 2006; it was republished in 2011. The French version was translated into Turkish in 1999 in Södertälje, Sweden, and published by Mezopotamya Enstitüsü.

22. Mgr Ignace Maloyan (1869–1915) was arrested on 5 June 1915 and martyred on 11 June. On the occasion of his beatification, Father

Salim Rizkallah, OFM, dedicated a booklet to him, published in Bzommar (Lebanon) in 2001, entitled "Le Bienheureux Ignace Maloyan, archevêque arménien catholique. Martyr de la foi à Mardin 1869–1915", Couvent Notre-Dame de Bzommar. In the booklet (Chapter IX, pp. 35–37) he reproduces the account of Maloyan's martyrdom that features in Isaac Armalet's book.

23. Isaac Armalet, *Al-Qousara fi Nahabat Annasara*, Beirut, 1919 (in Arabic).

24. Letter from Isaac Armalet to Cardinal Gasparri, Beirut, 17 July 1923, Archivio Segreto Vaticano, AA.EE.SS, Affari Ecclesiastici Straordinari Stati Ecclesiastici, anno 1923, rubrica 134, fasc. 1, p. 54.

25. Archivio della Segreteria di Stato, anno 1923, rubrica 134, "Siria", no. 20915.

26. The Ottoman Constitution was introduced in 1876 and restored, albeit unsuccessfully, at the beginning of the Young Turk Revolution in 1908.

27. Lepsius, *op. cit.*, pp. 125–126.

28. On Surma Khanum, see Claire Weibel Yacoub, *Surma l'Assyro-Chaldéenne (1883–1975). Dans la Tourmente de Mésopotamie*, Paris: L'Harmattan, 2007.

29. Surma d'Bait Mar Shimun, *Assyrian Church Customs and the Murder of Mar Shimun*, London: Faith Press, 1920, republished New York: Vehicle Editions, 1983. See in particular the chapter "The Great War", pp. 65–93.

30. Jacques-Eugène Manna's text is included in Griselle, *op. cit.*, p. 25.

31. *Ibid.*, pp. 22–28.

32. George Lamsa and William Chauncey Emhardt, *The Oldest Christian People: A Brief Account of the History and Traditions of the Assyrian People and of the Fateful History of the Nestorian Church*, New York: Macmillan, 1926; republished in 1970.

33. Paul Shimun, *Massacres of Syrian Christians in N.W. Persia and Kurdistan*, New York: Columbia University Press, 1916.

34. Kasha Samuel Nweeya, *Persia and the Moslems, A Historical and Descriptive Account of Persia from the Earliest Age to the Present Times; with a Detailed View of its People, their Manners, Customs, Matrimony and Home Life, Religion, Education and Literature, Textile and Contemporary Arts and Industries, the King, his Court, and Form of Punishment, Including the Moslems in Arabia, Turkey, India, Egypt and Palestine*, St. Louis: Press of Von Hoffmann, 1924.

35. Many of the documents in western Aramaic quoted in this book were

sent to the author by Nahro Beth-Kinne, originally from the town of Midyat in Tur Abdin and president of the Institut Assyrien de Belgique. We express our sincere thanks.

36. Israel Audo, *Histoire des persécutions des chrétiens de Mardin, de Amid, de Séert, de Djéziré et de Nisibine en 1915*. Translated into western Aramaic on the occasion of the ninetieth commemoration of the 1915 genocide (Jönköping, Sweden: Assyriska Riksförbundet I Sverige/Ashurbanipal bokförlag, 2004).

37. *Ibid.*, pp. 47–48. Chief Commissar Mamdouh was sent to Mardin by the Governor of Diyarbakir, Rashid Bey, invested with unlimited powers.

38. See Théophilos Georges Saliba (Syriac Orthodox Metropolitan in Lebanon), "Malphono Abdelmassih Carabachi" (in Arabic), *La Revue Patriarcale*, April–May–June 1990, Damascus, pp. 180–185.

39. Republished 1986–89 (Glane/Losser, Holland: Bar Hebraeus Verlag).

40. *Dmo Zliho. Gunhe w sharbe mshihoye d shato 1915–18* ("Spilled Blood. The Massacre and Suffering of the Christians in the Years 1915–18"), Jönköping, Sweden: Ashurbanipal bokförlag, 1997. It has been translated into English, German, Swedish, Arabic and Polish.

41. A village near the town of Diyarbakir; the governor of the *vilayet* of the same name had the Syriac villagers shot. *Ibid.*, pp. 46–47.

42. *Seyfe. Das Christen Massaker in der Turkei, 1714–1914*, Diocese of the Syriac Orthodox Church of Central Europe, Glane/Losser, Holland: Bar Hebraeus Verlag, 1981.

43. H. Numan Aydin, "Maktabzabno", Midyat, 1975.

44. See particularly pp. 86–108

45. Suleyman Henno, *Gounhé d'Souryoyé d'Tour Abdin*, Syriac Orthodox Monastery of St Ephrem, Glane/Losser, Holland: Bar Hebraeus Verlag, 1987.

46. *Ibid.*, pp. 161–173.

47. *Ibid.*, pp. 178–181.

48. Translated into Arabic by Subhi Yonan and published by the Syriac League in Lebanon, April 1986.

49. Preface by Mor Yohanna Ibrahim, Syriac Orthodox Metropolitan of Aleppo, published by Dar Urhai, founded by the same Metropolitan, 1993.

50. Malik Loko Shlimon d'bit-Badawi, *Assyrian Struggle for National Survival in the 20th and 31st Centuries*, Chicago, 2012.

51. Jacques Rhétoré, *"Les Chrétiens aux bêtes": Souvenirs de la guerre sainte proclamée par les Turcs contre les Chrétiens en 1915*, Paris: Cerf, 2005, pp. 9–10.

52. Quoted in Fernando Filoni, *L'Eglise dans la terre d'Abraham. Du diocèse de Babylone des Latins à la nonciature apostolique en Irak*, Paris: Cerf, 2009, pp. 132–133. Mgr Filoni, who was apostolic nuncio in Iraq from 2001 to 2006, refers to the archive of the Nunciature of Iraq, which contains the document by Marie-Dominique Berré, "Massacres de Mardin", dated 15 January 1919.

53. *Annales de la Congrégation de la Mission*, vols. 79 to 89, 1914–24.

54. *Ibid.*, 80, 1915, p. 524. See also Joseph Eyler, *Monseigneur Sontag, Martyr en Perse*, Mutzig: Imprimerie Girold, 1996, p. 94.

55. *Ibid.*, 83, 1918, p. 1094.

56. *Ibid.*, 80, 1915, p. 528.

57. *Ibid.*, 83, 1918, p. 1095.

58. Eyler, *op. cit.*, pp. 98 & 105. Most of the report is reproduced in this book (pp. 96–106) and extracts in *Annales*, 83, 1918, p. 1094. Mgr Sontag was martyred on 31 July 1918 at Urmia. See Joseph Yacoub, "Un Alsacien martyr pour les Assyro-Chaldéens", *Dernières Nouvelles d'Alsace*, Strasbourg, 18 May 2001.

59. *Annales*, 80, 1915, pp. 530–531; 84, 1919, pp. 239–265.

60. *Les Missions catholiques*, 47, 1915; 48, 1916; 49, 1917; 55, 1923; 56, 1924; and 59, 1927.

61. See the website www.leonardmelki.org.

62. *Rapport du Père Bonaventure de Baabdath O. M. C. sur la résidence d'Orfa (Mission d'Arménie) pendant la guerre 1914–1918*, Doc. 43, pp. 192–214. See also *Récit des massacres d'Arménie et Mésopotamie—en 1919—"Journal d'exil"*, by one of the first women missionaries, Religieuses franciscaines, Lons-Le-Saunier: Archives of the Sœurs franciscaines de l'Immaculée-Conception,

63. *Ibid.*, pp. 193–194.

64. Mary Lewis Shedd, *The Measure of a Man*, New York: George H. Doran Company, 1922.

65. *The Treatment of Armenians in the Ottoman Empire, 1915–16, Documents presented to Viscount Grey of Fallodon, Secretary of State for Foreign Affairs by Viscount Bryce, With a Preface by Viscount Bryce*, London: HM Stationery Office, 1916, p. xxviii.

66. Printed under the authority of His Majesty's Stationery Office, by Sir Joseph Causton and Sons, London, 1916.

67. Published by Hodder and Stoughton, 1916. Before the commercial edition, the documents were held in British diplomatic archives under the heading, "Arnold Toynbee papers and documents on the Treatment of Armenians and Assyrian Christians by the Turks, 1915–1916, in the Ottoman Empire and North-West Persia", Public Record Office (PRO), Kew, Richmond, 3 Class 96, Miscellaneous, Series II.

68. *Le Traitement des Arméniens dans l'Empire ottoman (1915–1916). Extraits du Livre Bleu du Gouvernement britannique, Documents présentés au Vicomte Grey of Fallandon, Secrétaire d'Etat aux affaires étrangères par le Vicomte Bryce, avec une préface du Vicomte Bryce,* Laval: G. Kavanagh & Cie, 1917. It is surprising that the only chapter from the original not to be translated was precisely the one devoted to the Assyro-Chaldeans: Chapter IV, "Azerbaijan and Hakkari". The reason given was as follows: "As this French translation is only concerned with the massacres and deportations in Turkey, no translation has been made of the twenty documents dealing exclusively with Azerbaijan, which is in Persia, and the Sandzak of Hakkari, which is part of Kurdistan. These documents, moreover, are cited in neither the preface nor in the historical résumé." Yet the translators omit to mention that the massacres perpetrated in Persian Azerbaijan were also attributable to the Turks, who took part in them. As for those in the Sandzak of Hakkari, they did in fact take place in Turkey, as that territory was part of the *vilayet* of Van and its inhabitants were Turkish subjects.

69. *Ibid.,* p. 16.

70. Arnold J. Toynbee, *Les massacres arméniens,* preface by Lord Bryce, Lausanne & Paris: Payot, 1916, pp. 10–11.

71. *The Treatment of Armenians in the Ottoman Empire, op. cit.,* p. 201 & 216.

72. This committee, comments the Blue Book, is composed of "citizens of high standing in a neutral country and gentlemen of unimpeachable good faith".

73. See Joseph Yacoub, *The Assyrian Question,* Chicago; Alpha Graphic, 1986 (reprinted 1993), pp. 49–136.

74. See his study, "The Syrians of Persia and Eastern Turkey", *Bulletin of the American Geographical Society,* 35, 1, 1903, pp. 1–7.

75. See his study, "The Ancient Nestorian Church and its Present Influence in Kurdistan", *The Journal of Race Development,* 2, 1, 1911, pp. 67–88.

76. *The Treatment of Armenians in the Ottoman Empire, op. cit.,* p. xxix.

77. *Ibid.*, p. xxix.
78. *Ibid.*, p. xxix.
79. *Ibid.*, p. xxxi.
80. *Ibid.*, p. xxxii.
81. *Ibid.*, p. xxxii.
82. *Ibid.*, p. xxxvi.
83. Joseph Yacoub, "À propos de *The Treatment of Armenians in the Ottoman Empire*, Arnold Toynbee et les Assyro-Chaldéens", *Gamk* (Armenian-language newspaper), Paris, 10 May 1985, pp. 5–7.
84. *The Treatment of Armenians in the Ottoman Empire*, *op. cit.*, p. 102.
85. *Ibid.*, pp. 110 and 113.
86. *Ibid.*, pp. 162–163.
87. *Ibid.*, p. 161.
88. *Ibid.*, pp. 585–586.
89. *Ibid.*, pp. 116–117.
90. *Ibid.*, p. 103.
91. *Ibid.*, p. 131.
92. *Ibid.*, p. 134.
93. *Ibid.*, p. 136.
94. *Ibid.*, p. 158.
95. See Claire Weibel Yacoub, *Le rêve brisé des Assyro-Chaldéens. L'introuvable autonomie*. Paris: Cerf, 2011, pp. 123–124.
96. Paul Caujole, *Les Tribulations d'une ambulance française en Perse*, Paris: Les Gémeaux, 1921.
97. Nicolas Gasfield, "Au front de Perse pendant la Grande Guerre. Souvenir d'un officier français", *Revue d'histoire de la Guerre mondiale*, 3, July 1924, Paris: Alfred Costes, pp. 120–151.
98. Herbert Henry Austin, *The Baqubah Refugee Camp: An Account of Work on Behalf of the Persecuted Assyrian Christians*, London: Faith Press, 1920.
99. Abbé Griselle was secretary general of the Catholic Committee on French Propaganda Abroad.
100. Eugène Griselle, *op. cit.*, p. 23.
101. *Ibid.*, p. 29.
102. André N. Mandelstam, *Le Sort de l'Empire ottoman*, Lausanne & Paris: Payot, 1917, p. 335.
103. André N. Mandelstam, *La Société des Nations et les Puissances devant le problème arménien*, Paris: Pédone, 1926, p. 23.
104. *Ibid.*, note 3, p. 23. Mandelstam was also the author of *La protection des minorités* (1923) and *La protection internationale des droits*

de l'homme (1931), on minorities in international law and, among other things, assistance to refugees.

105. Georges Dubois, *La question assyro-chaldéenne*, Paris: Imprimerie Henri Maillet, 1921.

106. "La situation des chrétiens assyriens", *L'Asie française*, Paris, May–September 1918, p. 95; "Les chrétiens nestoriens", *ibid.*, October 1918–January 1919, p. 158; "Une Conférence sur les souffrances des Assyro-Chaldéens", *ibid.*, August–November 1919, pp. 238–242.

107. *L'Asie française*, October 1918–January1919, p. 158.

108. *Bulletin de l'Oeuvre des Ecoles d'Orient*, Paris, July–August 1915, p. 420. The article first appeared in Italian in *Il Messaggero*, 25 August 1915.

109. "Le calvaire des Assyro-Chaldéens (1915–1935)", *L'Unité de l'Eglise*, 1935, pp. 417–421 & 449–452.

110. Between 1896 and 1899, Lepsius opened seven missions in the Ottoman Empire and north-west Persia. The Urmia "Dilguscha" orphanage for Assyrian girls was founded in 1899.

111. Lepsius, *op. cit.*

112. *Ibid.*, pp. 88–89.

113. *Ibid.*, p. 124.

114. *Ibid.*, pp. 125–126.

115. Johannes Lepsius, *Deutschland und Armenien 1914–1918. Sammlung diplomatischer Aktenstücke*, Potsdam: Der Tempelverlag, 1919.

116. *Archive du génocide des Arméniens. Recueil de documents diplomatiques allemands extraits de "Deutschland und Armenien 1914–1918", par le Dr Johannès Lepsius*, preface by Alfred Grosser, Paris: Fayard, 1986.

117. *Ibid.*, pp. 33–34.

118. *Ibid.*, p. 111.

119. *Ibid.*, pp. 107–108, no. 110, Holstein to the German Ambassador in Constantinople, 10 July 1915.

120. *Ibid.*, pp. 129–130.

121. Jakob Künzler, *Im Lande des Blutes und der Tränen. Erlebnisse in Mesopotamien während des Weltkrieges*, Potsdam: Tempel, 1921. See also Tessa Hofmann, "Rapports de témoins oculaires allemands sur le génocide des Arméniens 1915/1916", in *Le crime du silence. Le génocide des Arméniens*, Paris: Flammarion, 1984.

122. Künzler, *op. cit.*, p. 32.

123. Abraham Yohannan, *The Death of a Nation*, New York & London; G.P. Putnam's Sons, 1916, pp. 115–116.

124. William Walker Rockwell, *The Pitiful Plight of the Assyrian Christians in Persia and Kurdistan, Described from the Reports of Eye-witnesses*, New York: The American Committee for Armenian and Syrian Relief, 1916.

125. Joel E. Warda, *The Flickering Light of Asia or the Assyrian Nation and Church*, New Jersey: published by the author, 1924. Dr Warda was also the first editor of the monthly bulletin *The New Assyria*, the first edition of which appeared on 1 September 1916. This journal, which ceased publication in 1921, was an invaluable source of information and historic documents. At the same time, Warda published a periodical in Assyrian, *Azguedda*, and a weekly, *Assyrian American Courier*, in New York City.

126. Henry Morgenthau, *Ambassador Morgenthau's Story*, New York: Doubleday, Page and Company, 1918; republished Detroit: Wayne State University Press, 2003.

127. James L. Barton, *The Story of Near East Relief (1915–1930), An Interpretation*, New York: The Macmillan Company, 1930, p. 63.

128. |Yacoub, *The Assyrian Question, op. cit.*, pp. 127–129.

129. National Archives and Record Service, "Records of the American Commission to Negotiate Peace (1919), Inquiry Documents", no. 363, Washington DC, 1974, typed.

130. National Archives and Record Service, "Records of the American Commission to Negotiate Peace. Inventory of Record Group 256", edited by Sandra K. Rangel, Washington DC, 1918. See "Assyria", p. 90; "Report on the Assyrian Christians" by David Magie (doc. 629); "Assyrians" by Abraham Yohannan, 20 February 1918; "Armenia", pp. 88–90.

131. Leslie A. Davis, *La Province de la mort. Archives américaines concernant le génocide des Arméniens (1915)*, Brussels: Complexe, 1994.

132. F.N. Heazell, *The Woes of a Distressed Nation: Being an Account of the Assyrian People from 1914 to 1934*, London: Faith Press, 1934.

133. "Urmia, Salamas and Hakkari: Statement by Mr Paul Shimun, November 1915, Second Exodus from Urmia: Narrative of a Nestorian Victim, the Wife of the Rev. David Jacob of Urmia", *Ararat: A Searchlight on Armenia*, London, January 1916. *Ararat* had appeared since July 1913.

134. Fridtjof Nansen, *L'Arménie et le Proche-Orient*, Paris: Librairie Orientaliste Paul Geuthner, 1928, p. 335.

135. See Weibel Yacoub, *op. cit.*

136. Arthur Beylerian, *Les Grandes Puissances, l'Empire ottoman et les Arméniens dans les archives françaises (1914–1918)*, Paris: Publications de la Sorbonne, 1983, pp. 475–479.

137. Yacoub (Jacques) Abraham.

138. The appendices in Mgr Ephrem II Rahmani's letter to the President of the Council of Ministers (18 June 1919) are reproduced in Sébastien de Courtois, *Le Génocide oublié. Chrétiens d'Orient, les derniers Araméens*, Paris: Ellipse, 2002, pp. 231–236.

139. See Weibel Yacoub, *op. cit.*, pp. 146–147.

140. Rockwell, *op. cit.*, p. 50.

141. *Ibid.*, pp. 58–66.

142. Armenian Bureau, *The Plight of Armenian & Assyrian Christians: report of public meeting organised by the Lord Mayor's fund, held at Central hall, Westminster, on December 4, 1918*, London: Spottiswoode, Ballantyne and Co., 1918.

143. "For Aid to Assyrians. American Bishops Urge their Claims be Heard", *The New York Times*, 26 January 1919.

144. Randall Davidson, "Distressed Assyrian Christians", *The Times*, London, 10 November 1915.

145. "Armenians and Serbians: The Primate's Appeal. The Archbishop of Canterbury has issued a statement, in which he says", *The Times*, London, 15 December 1915.

146. "Chaldean Relief Committee: A Mansion House Meeting", *The Tablet*, London, 17 January 1920. Two articles were devoted to the meeting in this issue.

147. Quoted by *L'Action assyro-chaldéenne*, Beirut, May 1920, pp. 21–22.

148. Rockwell, *op. cit.*, pp. 42–43.

149. Eyler, *op. cit.*, pp. 111–113. In pp. 113–115, Eyler quotes passages from letters from Mgr Sontag to Father Abel Zaya, pointing out the needs of the Persian Christians and thanking benefactors.

150. Letter from Mgr Thomas Bajari to His Holiness Benedict XV, Constantinople, 9 July 1919, Archivio Segreto Vaticano du Vatican, AA.EE.SS, rubric 12, fasc. 1, 1919, p. 131.

151. "Says Turks advise Christians to flee", *The New York Times*, 11 January 1915.

152. "Massacre in Urumiah", *The New York Times*, 24 March 1915; "Women taken as slaves", 26 March 1915; "Turks continue Urumiah slaying", 27 March 1915.

153. "Great Exodus of Christians: Thousands suffered Greatest Hardships to Escape Enemies", *The New York Times*, 26 April 1915.

154. "Says Turks aided Recent Massacres, Troops allowed Kurds to kill Hundreds, American Missionary Reports. Russia the Sole Hope. Occupation of Persia alone can save Situation, a Missionary writes", *The New York Times*, 29 April 1915.

155. "Allies to Punish Turks who Murder. Notify Porte that Government Heads must answer for Armenian Massacres", *The New York Times*, 24 May 1915.

156. "Russians occupy Urumiah, Drive Turks from District where Massacres took Place", *The New York Times*, 29 May 1915.

157. "25000 Syrians starving. Mountaineers take Refuge in a Persian Town. Americans aid them", *The New York Times*, 30 October 1915.

158. "The Massacres in Persia", *The Guardian*, 5 November 1915; "Urumiah Massacre, Death of 12000 Nestorian Christians. A Letter from Miss Barclay received by Rev. Gabriel Alexander", *The Times*, 9 October 1915.

159. Frédéric Masson, "Ce qui vient de Chaldée", *Le Gaulois*, Paris, 25 July 1916.

160. Pierre Aziz, "Mémoire sur les massacres survenus dans les diocèses de Salmas et d'Ourmiah", *L'Action assyro-chaldéenne*, Beirut, February 1920, pp. 4–16; "Dans la Haute Mésopotamie. Tristes drames", July 1920, pp. 123–143; Paul Béro, "Disparition d'un illustre archevêque chaldéen. Dans les massacres de 1915", December 1920, pp. 255–258.

161. FO 608/82, *Peace Congress, Political Middle East*; the document attached by Sir P. Cox in Dispatch 71 of 9 November 1918 is by Basil Nikitin and mentions the two newspapers and their articles on 15 March 1915.

162. "Want 50000 $ for Urumiah", *The New York Times*, 10 April 1915.

163. "Turkish Horrors in Persia. American Educated Native asks Aid for Thousands of Victims", *The New York Times*, 11 October 1915.

164. "Ask war relief for the Persians. Episcopal Bishops issue Appeal for funds for Native Christians. Three Ambulances sent. Rockefeller Foundation gives another $100,000 for Armenian Red Cross work". *The New York Times*, 9 July 1916; "Bishops appeal for Nestorians, ask American help for 100,000 Christians who are Victims of Moslems. Are dying of Starvation. Their plight Parallels that of the Serbs and Armenians, Bishop Greer's Committee reports", 13 November 1916.

165. "Distressed Assyrian Christians. To the Editor of the Times", *The Times*, London, 10 November 1915; "Decline of an Ancient Christian Church", *ibid.*, 13 November 1915.

166. "Assyria's call for help. A princess delegate", *The Guardian*, 27 October 1919.
167. "Reception at Lambeth Palace", *The Times*, 15 March 1920.
168. Letter from Mgr Emmanuel II Thomas to Cardinal Gasparri, Baghdad, 17 February 1919, Archivio Segreto Vaticano, AA.EE.SS, Affari Ecclesiastici Straordinari Stati Ecclesiastici, 1919, rubrica 12, fasc. 1, p. 114.
169. Letter from Mgr Thomas Bajari to His Holiness Pope Benedict XV, Constantinople, 9 July 1919, *ibid.*, p. 131.

2. THE SCENES AND ACTS OF THE TRAGEDY

1. *Lives of Saints, Acta Martyrum et Sanctorum*, 7 vols. Leipzig: Imprimerie Wilhem E. Drugulin, 1890–97.
2. See *An Introduction to the History of the Assyrian Church or the Church of the Sassanid Persian Empire 100–640 A.D.*, London: Society for Promoting Christian Knowledge (SPCK), 1910.
3. See Abbé F. Lagrange, *Les Actes des martyrs d'Orient*, translated into French from the Latin transcription of Aramaic manuscripts by Stefano Evodio Assemani, Tours: Alfred Mame et Fils, 1852.
4. See Paul Bedjan, *Lives of Saints* (Aramaic), Leipzig: Otto Harrassowitz, 1912, pp. 242–501; Abraham Yohannan, *A Church of Martyrs*, New York: Putman's, 1917; Albert Abouna, *Martyrs of the East* (Arabic), vol.i, Baghdad, 1985.
5. Rubens Duval, "Les Actes de Scharbil et les actes de Barsamya", *Journal asiatique*, July–August 1889, pp. 40–55.
6. Jean-Baptiste Chabot, *Littérature syriaque*, Paris: Bloud et Gay, 1934, p. 42.
7. Jérôme Labourt, *Le Christianisme dans l'Empire perse sous la dynastie sassanide (224–632)*, Paris: Victor Lecoffre, 1904, pp. 74–77
8. *History of the Church of the East* (in Aramaic), vol. i: *The Age of the Sassanid Kings*, Urmia: Archbishop of Canterbury's Assyrian Mission Press, 1907.
9. Lagrange, *op. cit.*, p. 34.
10. Sozomen, *Histoire ecclésiastique*, books I and II, trans. into French from Greek by André-Jean Festugière, Paris: Cerf, 1983, pp. 287–293.
11. Lagrange, *op. cit.*, p. 34.
12. Theodoret of Cyrus, *The Ecclesiastical History*, vol. 5, chapter 38, http://www.newadvent.org/fathers/27025.htm, last accessed 18 February 2016.

13. Jean-Baptiste Chabot (trans. & ed.), *Synodicon orientale ou Recueil des Synodes nestoriens*, Paris: Imprimerie Nationale, 1902, p. 254.

14. Eugène Griselle, *Syriens et Chaldéens, leurs martyres, leurs espérances, 1914–1917*, Paris: Ed. Bloud & Gay, 1918, p. 19.

15. *Ibid.*, p. 18.

16. Edmond Rabbath, *La question d'Orient sous l'Empire ottoman (1789–1919)*, Beirut: Bureau Mandia, 1958, p. 111.

17. The village of the celebrated fifth-century Bishop Marutha.

18. Joseph Naayem, *Les Assyro-Chaldéens et les Arméniens massacrés par les Turcs*, Paris: Bloud & Gay, 1920, p. 2.

19. Griselle, *op. cit.*, p. 19.

20. Gustave Meyrier to Paul Cambon, "Massacre at Diyarbakir", report no. 18, 18 December 1895. See Gustave Meyrier, *Les massacres de Diarbékir. Correspondance diplomatique du Vice-Consul de France (1894–1896)*, Paris: L'Inventaire, 2000, pp. 125–139.

21. Basil Nikitin, "Une petite nation victime de la guerre: les Chaldéens", *Revue des sciences politiques*, XLIV, October–December 1921, p. 609.

22. André N. Mandelstam, *La Société des Nations et les puissances devant le problème arménien*, Paris: Pédone, 1926, pp. 20–21 and p. 28.

23. William A. Wigram, *The Assyrians and their Neighbours*, London: G. Bell and Sons, 1929, p. 175.

24. See "Un rapport secret sur les massacres d'Adana", *L'Asie française*, Paris, March 1913, pp. 135–137.

25. Audrey R. Vine, *The Nestorian Churches: A Concise History of Nestorian Christianity in Asia from the Persian Schism to the Modern Assyrians*, London: Independent Press, 1937, pp. 194–195.

26. See Joseph Yacoub, *The Assyrian Question*, Chicago; Alpha Graphic, 1986 (reprinted 1993), pp. 57–102.

27. Jacques Rhétoré, *"Les Chrétiens aux bêtes": Souvenirs de la guerre sainte proclamée par les Turcs contre les Chrétiens en 1915*, Paris: Cerf, 2005, p. 173.

28. On the Siirt massacres, see Naayem, *op. cit.*, pp. 48–96.

29. On the Diyarbakir massacres, see *ibid.*, pp. 152–168

30. Rhétoré, *op. cit.*, p. 136.

31. Johannes Lepsius, *Le Rapport secret du Dr Johannès Lepsius, président de la Deutsche Orient Mission et de la Société germano arménienne sur les Massacres d'Arménie*, Paris: Payot & Cie, 1919, pp. 86 and 88.

32. Rhétoré, *op. cit.*, p. 130.

33. Naayem, *op. cit.*, p. 148.

34. *Ibid.*, pp. 153–154.

35. Johannes Lepsius, *Archives du Génocide des Arméniens, Recueil de documents diplomatiques allemands extraits de "Deutschland und Armenien 1914–1918" par le Dr Johannès Lepsius*, Paris: Fayard, 1986, p. 143.

36. Jakob Künzler, *Im Lande des Blutes und der Tränen. Erlebnisse in Mesopotamien während des Weltkrieges*, Potsdam: Tempel, 1921 pp. 49–50.

37. Naayem, *op. cit.*, pp. 28–30.

38. *Ibid.*, p. 190.

39. R. S. Stafford, *The Tragedy of the Assyrians*, George Allen and Unwin: London, 1935, p. 28.

40. Lepsius, *Archives du Génocide, op. cit.*, pp. 93–94.

41. William A. Wigram, *Our Smallest Ally: A Brief Account of the Assyrian Nation in the Great War*, London: Society for Promoting Christian Knowledge (SPCK), 1920, pp. 7–8.

42. *The Treatment of Armenians in the Ottoman Empire, 1915–16*, London: HM Stationery Office, p. 104.

43. William Walker Rockwell, *The Pitiful Plight of the Assyrian Christians in Persia and Kurdistan, Described from the Reports of Eye-witnesses*, New York: The American Committee for Armenian and Syrian Relief, 1916, p. 30.

44. *Ibid.*, p. 52. See *The Treatment of Armenians, op. cit.*

45. Anahit Khoesrova, "The Assyrian Genocide in the Ottoman Empire and Adjacent Territories", in Richard G. Hovannisian (ed.), *The Armenian Genocide: Cultural and Ethical Legacies*, Rutgers, NJ: Transaction, 2007, p. 270.

46. David Gaunt, "The Ottoman Treatment of the Assyrians", in Ronald Grigor Suny *et al.* (eds.), *A Question of Genocide: Armenians and Turks at the End of the Ottoman Empire*, New York: Oxford University Press, 2011, p. 257.

47. There are texts in Aramaic that describe this tragedy.

48. See Naayem, *op. cit.*, pp. 169–176.

49. Letter from Mgr Suleiman Sabbagh, Archbishop of Diyarbakir, "Les Missions catholiques, Un petit peuple en détresse", March 1919, p. 242.

50. Deputy Feizi Bey is described as "one of the most influential members of the committee, and one of the chief instigators of the massacre".

51. *The Treatment of Armenians, op. cit.*, p. 180.

52. Naayem, *op. cit.*, p. 86.
53. *Ibid.*, p. 86.
54. *Ibid.*
55. *Ibid*, p. 92.
56. This term is mentioned in several documents.
57. Joseph Yacoub, "Le génocide syriaque de 1915", Gamk, Paris, 27 December 1985. This article was translated into Arabic by Joseph Zeytoun and was published in Södertälje, Sweden, in the Assyrian monthly *Hujâdâ*, December 1986.
58. See the article "Manarat Antaquia al-Suryania" (The Lighthouse of Christian Antioch) dedicated to him in Arabic by Gregorius Yohanna Ibrahim, Metropolitan of Aleppo, in *La Revue patriarcale*, June 1992, no. 116, Damascus, pp. 363–375. Mor Ephrem Barsoum became patriarch in 1933.
59. Memorandum, "Claims to Consideration by Peace Conference put forward by Archbishop Barsaum", February 1920, F.O, E. 1221/E1242/96/44, nos. 22 and 23, Damascus-Homs: Syrian Archbishopric of Syria, pp. 108–112.
60. On the Christian cultural heritage of Tur Abdin, see Helga Anschütz, *Die syrischen Christen vom Tur 'Abdin. Eine altchristliche Bevölkerungsgruppe zwischen Beharrung, Stagnation und Auflösung*, Würzburg: Augustinus-Verlag, 1985.
61. On the work of the TMS Association, see Eugène Boulos Mnoufer Barsoum, "Pour qu'on n'oublie pas ce que l'orphelinat T.M.S. a réalisé. La promotion des écoles syriaques", *La Revue patriarcale*, Damascus, October–December 1989, pp. 453–458.
62. Naayem, *op. cit.*, pp. 177–219. Chapter 10 is entirely devoted to the massacres in Trebizond.

3. STRATEGY AND METHODOLOGY OF ERADICATION

1. Hyacinthe Simon, *Mardine, la ville héroïque: autel et tombeau de l'Arménie (Asie Mineure) durant les massacres de 1915*, Aleppo, 1919, pp. 1–6.
2. "Christians in Great Peril", *The New York Times*, 13 January 1915.
3. *The Treatment of Armenians in the Ottoman Empire*, London: HM Stationery Office, p. 175.
4. Abraham Yohannan, *The Death of a Nation*, New York & London; G.P. Putnam's Sons, 1916, p. 149.
5. *Ibid.*, pp. 150–151.

6. Joel E. Warda, *The Flickering Light of Asia, or the Assyrian Nation and Church*, New Jersey: published by the author, 1924, p. 208.

7. Ibid., p. 208.

8. Jacques Rhétoré, *"Les Chrétiens aux bêtes": Souvenirs de la guerre sainte proclamée par les Turcs contre les Chrétiens en 1915*, Paris: Cerf, 2005, p. 177.

9. See Joseph Yacoub, *The Assyrian Question*, Chicago; Alpha Graphic, 1986 (reprinted 1993), p. 63.

10. *Ibid.*, pp. 103–104.

11. Isaac Armalet dedicates pp. 148–157 to them in his book *Al-Qousara fi Nahabat Annasara*, Beirut, 1919 (in Arabic). Further details are to be found in the works of Joseph Naayem, Hyacinthe Simon and Jacques Rhétoré.

12. Joseph Naayem, *Shall This Nation Die?*, New York: Chaldean Rescue, 1921, pp. xi-xii.

13. *The Treatment of Armenians, op. cit.*, pp. 651–653.

14. Yohannan, *op. cit.*, p. 138.

15. *Ibid.*, pp. 138–139.

16. *Ibid.*, p. 146.

17. Armalet, *op. cit.*, p. 151.

18. Rhétoré, *op. cit.*, p. 27.

19. Naayem, *op. cit.*, p. 158.

20. *Ibid.*, pp. 158–162

21. Quoted in Sébastien de Courtois, *Le Génocide oublié, Chrétiens d'Orient, les derniers Araméens*, Paris: Ellipse, 2002, p. 233.

22. Rhétoré, *op. cit.*, p. 32.

23. Naayem, *op. cit.*, pp. 153–154.

24. Simon, *op cit.*, p. 11.

25. By "Catholics", Simon refers to the Syriacs and Chaldeans and by "schismatics" to Syriac Orthodox and Nestorian Assyrians.

26. Rhétoré, *op. cit.*, p. 37.

27. Simon refers to the existence of sixty-five wells, "deep and filled with corpses", from Ras al-Ayn to Nusaybin. He adds that one should "ask all the harems of Mardin and Diyarbakir for the boys and girls that they conceal, and roam the desert of Mesopotamia in search of victims." Simon, *op. cit.*, p. 12.

28. *Ibid.*, p. 94.

29. *Ibid.*, p. 94.

30. *Ibid.*, pp. 94.

31. *Ibid.*, pp. 94–95.

32. *Ibid.*, p. 95.
33. *Ibid.*, p. 95.
34. *Ibid.*, p. 95.
35. *Ibid.*, p. 11.
36. *The Treatment of Armenians, op. cit.*, p. 103.
37. Yohannan, *op. cit.*, p. 140.
38. *The Treatment of Armenians, op. cit.*, p. 161.
39. Naayem, *op. cit.*, p. 30.
40. Johannes Lepsius, *Le Rapport secret du Dr Johannès Lepsius, président de la Deutsche Orient Mission et de la Société germano arménienne sur les Massacres d'Arménie*, Paris: Payot & Cie, 1919, pp. 287–88.
41. *The Treatment of Armenians, op. cit.*, p. 181.
42. Jean-Maurice Fiey, "Hakkari", *Dictionnaire d'histoire et de géographie ecclésiastique*, vol. 23, Paris: Letouzey & Ané, 1990, col. 120.
43. Basil Nikitin, "Nestoriens", *Encyclopédie de l'Islam* (1st ed.), Leiden: E.J. Brill, 1935, vol. III, pp. 965–968. By the same author, see also "Les Kurdes et le christianisme", *Revue de l'histoire des religions*, Paris: Annales du Musée Guimet—Ernest Leroux, 1922, pp. 148–156.
44. Surma d'Bait Mar Shimun, *Assyrian Church Customs and the Murder of Mar Shimun*, London: Faith Press, 1920, republished New York: Vehicle Editions, 1983, p. 67.
45. Basil Nikitin, "Une petite nation victime de la guerre: les Chaldéens", *Revue des sciences politiques*, XLIV, October–December 1921, p. 618.
46. William A. Wigram, *Our Smallest Ally: A Brief Account of the Assyrian Nation in the Great War*, London: Society for Promoting Christian Knowledge (SPCK), 1920, p. 20.
47. *Ibid.*, pp. 19–20.
48. D'Bait Mar Shimun, *op. cit.*, p. 67.
49. Basil Nikitin, "Le problème assyrien", *Bulletin de l'Académie diplomatique internationale*, 4, October–December 1933, p. 230.
50. The town of Mosul was the *vali*'s base, and headquarters of the military division of the province of the same name.
51. The district of Diz is situated in Hakkari. On leaving the isolated village of Kotchanes in May 1915, the patriarch had taken refuge among the *achiret* Assyrians in Diz, where important decisions were taken for the remainder of the war.
52. Soldiers.
53. Two Assyrian tribes in Hakkari.
54. On the Oramar tribe, see Basil Nikitin, "Oramar", *Encyclopédie de*

l'Islam (2nd ed.), vol. viii, Leiden: E.J. Brill, 1995, pp. 175–176. Situated in the far south-east of Turkey and to the north of the border with Iraq, the Oramar district has a rich Christian history under the Church of the East. The name of Oramar itself is Aramaic-sounding, and two Nestorian churches were recorded there. At Nov Gund was the church of Mar Daniel, transformed into a mosque by the Kurds at the end of the nineteenth century. Nikitin cites the geographer Vital Cuinet, who wrote in his book *La Turquie d'Asie* (vol. II, p. 757) that "The 40 Nestorian *rayats* living in Oramar are tasked with looking after the two Nestorian churches situated in this Kurdish town."

55. The history of the flight from Hakkari is told in detail by an eye-witness to the tragedy, Abraham Shlemon, originally from Barwar. It was translated into English by Paul Shimun and published under the name of William Walker Rockwell as *The Pitiful Plight of the Assyrian Christians in Persia and Kurdistan, Described from the Reports of Eye-witnesses*, New York: The American Committee for Armenian and Syrian Relief, 1916, pp. 29–42.

56. Rockwell, *op. cit.*, pp. 32–33.

57. *Ibid.*, p. 34.

58. *Ibid.*, p. 40.

59. *Ibid.*, pp. 44–49.

60. *Encyclopédie de l'Islam* (2nd ed.), vol. vi, Leiden: E.J. Brill, 1991, p. 527.

61. In 1920, the publication *L'Action assyro-chaldéenne* announced: "We are currently busy searching for the manuscript of the third volume which the Turks took at the time when Addaï Scher was murdered in Siirt in August 1915."

62. Naayem, *op. cit.*, p. 89.

63. Patriarch Rahmani, 1919.

64. Nikitin, "Nestoriens", *op. cit.*, p. 967.

65. Wigram, *op. cit.*, p. 20.

66. Nikitin, "Les Kurdes", *op. cit.*, p. 149.

67. See the film *La Complainte du Firmin. Génocide de 1915*, by Father Aziz Yalap, Sarcelles, 2013. The author of this lament, Kasha Yonan Bidawid, was active from the 1890s until 1930–40. In touch with the Assyrians of Hakkari, he preached among those of Baz and Tkhuma, becoming chorbishop of the Chaldean community in Zakho. He wrote several essays, including one on the existence of God. Father Yalap's paternal grandmother, Wardé, belonged to the

Bidawid tribe from the village of Bedare, and subsequently family ties linked Yalap's father, who was the *agha* and *moukhtar* of Ischy, with the former Chaldean patriarch, Mar Raphael I Bidawid, Kasha Yonan's great-nephew. Yalap, born in the Hakkari village of Ischy in 1947, studied in Istanbul at the St Michel and St Joseph Colleges and at the Notre-Dame-de-Sion and Atatürk lycées. He was then a seminarist with the Capuchin Fathers at the St Louis seminary, and was ordained as a priest in Istanbul in 1975. Today priest of the St Thomas parish in Sarcelles, he explains that he found the *complainte* in a book of ancient songs, a manuscript that he entrusted to a *shamasha* (deacon) to be transcribed into print. He recalls that it was sung in the 1960s, when he was serving as deacon with Father Yawsep Harbolaya (from the village of Harbol) in the Bohtan area, but that it faded into obscurity in subsequent decades. He had the idea of giving the *complainte* new life in the form of a DVD to rescue it from its fifty-year oblivion. His aim was also to educate the young and not so young of the French Assyrian community about the genocide through this lament and its melody. I would like to express my sincere thanks to my friend Antoni Yalap, graduate in Oriental languages, translator-interpreter in Turkish and son of Father Aziz Yalap, for introducing me to this DVD and for the information concerning Kasha Yonan Bidawid and his father.

68. Abboud Zeytoun, *Music Pearls of Beth-Nahrain: An Assyrian/Syriac Discography*, Wiesbaden, 2007, p. 437. This book-catalogue contains the names of other composers and vocalists on the genocide of 1915.

69. Israel Audo, *Histoire des persécutions des chrétiens de Mardin, de Amid, de Siirt, de Djéziré et de Nisibine en 1915*, pp. 166–183. Translated into western Aramaic on the occasion of the ninetieth commemoration of the 1915 genocide (Jönköping: Assyriska Riksförbundet I Sverige/Ashurbanipal bokförlag, 2004)

70. On Tuma Nahroyo, see Zeytoun, *op. cit.*, pp. 516–519.

71. Armalet, *op. cit.*, pp. 326–331.

72. A version in four-line stanzas appears in Wigram, *op. cit.*, pp. 15–16.

73. *Genocide, Talk by Professor Raphael Lemkin* (duration 5, 36), p. 2. Archives UNESCO 341.48—Genocide (Box 176).

74. League of Nations, *The Settlement of the Assyrians, a Work of Humanity and Appeasement*, Geneva, 1935, p. 8.

75. *Ibid.*, p. 3.

4. AFTER 1915: THE TRAGEDY CONTINUES

1. League of Nations, *The Settlement of the Assyrians, a Work of Humanity and Appeasement*, Geneva, 1935, p. 12.
2. Paul Caujole, *Les Tribulations d'une ambulance française en Perse*, Paris: Les Gémeaux, 1922.
3. Paul Caujole, "La situation des Assyro-Chaldéens", *Le Fanion*, Paris, 10 June 1922.
4. Basil Nikitin, "La Perse que j'ai connue, 1909–1919", typed memoir, Paris: Bibliothèque INALCO, 1941, p. 177.
5. Aristide Châtelet, "La mission de Perse", *Annales de la Congrégation de la Mission*, 88, 1923, pp. 635–636.
6. Caujole, "La situation des Assyro-Chaldéens", *op. cit.*
7. Nicolas Gasfield, "Au front de Perse pendant la Grande Guerre. Souvenir d'un officier français", *Revue d'histoire de la Guerre mondiale*, 3, July 1924, Paris: Alfred Costes", pp. 128 & 150–151.
8. Joseph Naayem, *Shall This Nation Die?*, New York: Chaldean Rescue, 1921, preface, p. iv.
9. Herbert Henry Austin, *The Baqubah Refugee Camp, An Account of Work on Behalf of the Persecuted Assyrian Christians*, London: Faith Press, 1920
10. Brigadier J. Gilbert Browne, *The Iraq Levies, 1915–1932*, London: The Royal United Service Institution, 1932.
11. Solomon "Sawa" Solomon, *The Assyrian Levies*, ATOUR Publications, 1996.
12. These documents, dated 28 and 31 January 1925, are reproduced in Yusuf Malek, *Le drame assyrien*, Geneva, 1934, pp. 24–25.
13. Yusuf Malek, *The British Betrayal of the Assyrians*, Chicago: Assyrian National Federation, 1935, pp. 31–32.
14. "A Discussion on the Assyrian Problem: the Case for the Assyrians", *Journal of the Royal Central Asian Society*, XXI, 1934, p. 41.
15. At the time of that the Turkey-Iraq border issue was resolved, the Assyro-Chaldean lobby, particularly Malik Cambar, was active in Geneva.
16. League of Nations, *Question of the Frontier between Turkey and Iraq: Report Submitted to the Council Instituted by the Council Resolution of September 30th, 1924*, Geneva, 1925, p. 90. See also "L'Irak et la question assyrienne", *L'Asie française*, December 1933, p. 345, and Basil Nikitin, "Quelques observations sur la question de Mossoul", *L'Asie française*, March 1924, pp. 115–118.

17. League of Nations, *Question of the Frontier, op. cit.*, pp. 79–84.
18. Louis Le Fur, "L'affaire de Mossoul", *Revue générale de droit international public (RGDIP)*, Paris: Pédone, 1927, pp. 60–103 & 209–245.
19. League of Nations, *Question of the Frontier, op. cit.*, pp. 88–89.
20. Quoted in William Chauncey Emhardt and George M. Lamsa, *The Oldest Christian People: A Brief Account of the History and Traditions of the Assyrian People and the Fateful History of the Nestorian Church*, New York: Macmillan, 1926, p. 131.
21. The section on the deportation of Christians is fully reproduced in Le Fur, *op. cit.*, pp. 63–64. See also Basil Nikitin, "Le problème assyrien", *Bulletin de l'Académie diplomatique internationale*, 4, October–December 1933, pp. 231–232.
22. *League of Nations Official Journal*, Annex 789C, 6/10, Geneva, October 1925, p. 1436.
23. *Ibid.*, annex 789, g., p. 1439. All these documents appear in the *League of Nations Official Journal*, which reproduced the proceedings of the thirty-fifth session of the Council, held in Geneva between 2 and 28 September 1925.
24. *Ibid.*, annex 791, d.p., p. 1447.
25. *Ibid.*, annex 789, d.p., p. 1441.
26. Le Fur, *op. cit.*, p. 72.
27. For the entire text of Paulus Bédaré's report, see Le Fur, *op. cit.*, pp. 72–76.
28. J.T. Delos, "Les Assyriens d'Irak", *Revue générale de droit international public*, July–August 1934, p. 7.
29. *Ibid.*.
30. Le Fur, *op. cit.*, pp. 76–77.
31. R. S. Stafford, *The Tragedy of the Assyrians*, London: Allen and Unwin, 1935, pp. 174–175.
32. *Ibid.*, p. 81.
33. For a detailed study, see Joseph Yacoub, "Les Réfugiés assyro-chaldéens de Turquie", Forcalquier: Comité européen de défense des réfugiés et immigrés, 1986, and *Babylone chrétienne. Géopolitique de l'Église de Mésopotamie*, Paris: DDB, 1996; *Menaces sur les chrétiens d'Irak*, Chambray-lès-Tours: CLD, 2003; updated Italian translation, *I Cristiani d'Iraq*, Milan: Jaca Book, 2006, pp. 239–276.
34. Joseph Yacoub, "Les Assyro-Chaldéens originaires de Turquie: une communauté en situation migratoire", *Les Annales de l'autre Islam*, 3, Paris: INALCO-ERISM1995, pp. 451–466.

35. See *Solidarité-Orient*, Ath, Belgium, June–August–September 1994, p. 46.

36. Florian Kuntner, "Un évêque en visite chez les chrétiens oubliés", *Droits de l'homme sans frontières*, Braine-le-Comte, Belgium, December 1992, p. 9.

37. See Gary Neil Smith, "From Urmia to Stanislaus: A Cultural-Historical Geography of Assyrian Christians in the Middle East and America", dissertation submitted for the degree of Doctor of Philosophy in Geography, University of California, Davis 1981

38. See *The Assyrian National Directory in the United-States of America for 1960*, New Jersey: The Assyrian National Association of Chicago/Kimball Press, 1960.

39. Formerly the *Persian American Courier*.

40. Joseph Yacoub, "La communauté assyro-chaldéenne en France", *Accueillir*, 154, Paris: SSAE, December 1988, pp. 10–13.

41. See the author's book, *Menaces sur les chrétiens d'Irak*, Chambray: CLD-Témoignage Chrétien, 2003, pp. 173–174.

42. Yacoub, "Les Réfugiés assyro-chaldéens", *op. cit.*; Yacoub, "Ils seront des Chaldéens de France", special edition of *La Pastorale des migrants*, 43, 1991.

43. Ulf Björklund, "North to Another Country: the Formation of a Suryoyo Community in Sweden", University of Stockholm, Department of Social Anthropology, and Swedish Commission on Immigration Research, May 1981; see also Stefan Andersson, *Assyrierna*, Stockholm: Tidens Förlag, 1983.

44. Gabriele Yonan, *Assyrer Heute: Kultur, Sprache, Nationalbewegung der aramäisch sprechenden Christen im Nahen Osten*, Hamburg & Vienna: Gesellschaft für bedrohte Völker, Reihe Pogrom, 1978.

45. "Turquie. Les Assyriens, un peuple en voie d'extinction", *Droits de l'homme sans frontières*, November–December 1992, pp. 2–10; "Heurs et malheurs de la minorité assyrienne au Proche-Orient et en Belgique", Brussels: *Droits de l'homme sans frontières* & Assyrian Democratic Organisation (ADO), 1994.

46. Guillaume Perrier, "À Karakoch, les chrétiens irakiens vivent sous la protection des peshmergas", *Le Monde*, 22–23 June 2014.

47. Joseph Yacoub, "C'est une politique d'épuration à caractère génocid-aire", interview with Jennifer Chainay, *Ouest-France*, 2 September 2014.

CONCLUSION: RETURNING TO THE STAGE OF HISTORY

1. Joseph Naayem, *Shall This Nation Die?*, New York: Chaldean Rescue, 1921, p. xxx.
2. See "Mémoire sur les massacres survenus dans les diocèses de Salamas et d'Ourmiah", *L'Action assyro-chaldéenne*, no. 7, Beirut, 1920, pp. 5–16.
3. The modern Assyrian language was standardized in Urmia from 1840.
4. Died May 2014.
5. Toma Mikho (ed.), *Un village chaldéen: Ischy*, Sarcelles, p. 4.
6. *Ibid.*, p. 68.
7. *Ibid.* See the website www.ischy.fr.
8. Zackarie Yaramis, *Gaznakh: nid de civilisations*, Paris: Transversales Éditions, 2010.
9. *Ibid.*, pp. 19–57.
10. Ibid., p. 185.
11. Edited by Bedri Hurmuz Diril.
12. See Joseph Yacoub, "La marginalisation des chrétiens d'Irak", in *Confluences Méditerranée*, 66, summer 2008, pp. 83–98.
13. See Joseph Yacoub, "How does the Arab World Perceive Multiculturalism and Treat its Minorities? The Assyro-Chaldeans of Iraq as a Case Study", in Will Kymlicka and Eva Pföstl (eds.), *Multiculturalism and Minority Rights in the Arab World*, Oxford: Oxford University Press, 2014, pp. 271–277.
14. Iraq is divided into eighteen provinces and a single autonomous region, Kurdistan, which in turn contains three provinces: Duhok, Erbil and Sulaymaniyah.

BIBLIOGRAPHY

This book contains some 400 notes and references. Listed here are works of importance on the genocide, the diaspora and the Assyrian question. Literature in Aramaic on the genocide is widely cited in the body of the text.

Alichoran, Joseph, "Du génocide à la diaspora: les Assyro-Chaldéens au XXè siècle," *Istina*, 4, October–December 1994.

Anschütz, Helga, *Die syrischen Christen vom Tur 'Abdin: Eine altchristliche Bevolkerungsgruppe zwischen Beharrung, Stagnation und Auflosung,* Würzburg: Augustinus-Verlag, 1985.

Armalet, Isaac, *Al-Qousara Fi Nakabat Annasara* (The Calamities of the Christians, in Arabic), Beirut, 1919.

Assyrians. National Archives of the United States, Inquiry Documents, 629, Washington DC, 1918.

Audo, Israel, *Histoire des persécutions des chrétiens de Mardin, de Amid, de Séert, de Djéziré et de Nisibine en 1915,* Translated into western Syriac, Jönköping: Assyriska Riksförbundet I Sverige/Ashurbanipal bokvörlag, 2004.

Badger, George Percy, *The Nestorians and their Rituals: with the Narrative of a Mission to Mesopotamia and Coordistan in 1842–1844, and of a late visit to those countries in 1850; also, researches into the present condition of the Syrian Jacobites, papal Syrians, and Chaldeans, and an inquiry into the religious tenets of the Yezeedees,* London, 1852.

Berré, Marie Dominique, Jacques Rhétoré and Hyacinthe Simon, *Nous avons vu l'enfer. Trois Dominicains, témoins directs du génocide des Arméniens,* Paris: Cerf, 2015.

Cambar, Malek, *La question assyro-chaldéenne et la Société des*

Nations. Rapports et Documents, Jerusalem: Ratisbonne Printing Press, 1933.

Caujole, Paul, *Les Tribulations d'une ambulance française en Perse*, Paris: Les Gémeaux, 1922.

Chevalier, Michel, *Les montagnards chrétiens du Hakkari et du Kurdistan septentrional*, Paris: Publications du Département de Géographie de l'Université de Paris-Sorbonne, 13, 1985.

Christensen, Arthur, *L'Iran sous les Sassanides*, Paris: Annales du Musée Guimet, Librairie Orientaliste Paul Geuthner, 1936, Paris.

Courtois, Sébastien de, "Une communauté syriaque orthodoxe en péril à la fin de l'Empire ottoman, Diarbékir, Mardine et le Tur Abdin (1880–1919)", Paris: Ecole Pratique des Hautes Etudes (EPHE), June 2001.

—— *Le génocide oublié. Chrétiens d'Orient, les derniers Araméens*, Paris; Ellipse, 2002.

Delos, Joseph-Thomas, "Les Assyriens d'Irak et la Société des Nations", *Revue générale de droit internaional public*, Paris: Pédone, July–August 1934.

Gasfield, Nicolas, "Au front de Perse pendant la Grande Guerre. Souvenirs d'un officier français," *Revue d'histoire de la guerre mondiale*, 3, Paris: Alfred Coste, July 1924.

Gaunt, David, *Massacres, Resistance, Protectors: Muslim-Christian relations in Eastern Anatolia during World War I*, New Jersey: Gorgias Press, 2006.

Griselle, Eugène, *Syriens et Chaldéens, leurs martyres, leurs espérances, 1914–1917*, Paris: Bloud & Gay, 1918.

Heazell, F. N., *The Woes of a Distressed Nation: Being an Account of the Assyrian People from 1914 To 1934*, London: Faith Press, 1934.

Journal of the Royal Central Asian Society, 1916–47. This publication offers many valuable studies of the Assyrian question.

Labourt, Jérôme, Le christianisme dans l'Empire perse sous la dynastie sassanide (224–632), Paris: Librairie Victor Lecoffre, 1904.

Le Fur, Louis, "L'affaire de Mossoul", *Revue générale de droit international public*, Paris: Pédone, 1927.

League of Nations, *The Settlement of the Assyrians: A Work of Humanity and Appeasement*, Geneva, 1935.

Lepsius, Johannes, *Le Rapport secret du Dr Johannès Lepsius, président de la Deutsche Orient Mission et de la Société germano arménienne sur les Massacres d'Arménie*, Paris: Payot & Cie, 1919.

—— *Deutschland und Armenien 1914–1918. Sammlung diplomatischer Aktenstücke*, Potsdam: Tempelverlag, 1919.

—— *Archives du Génocide des Arméniens, Recueil de documents diplomatiques allemands extraits de "Deutschland und Armenien 1914–1918" par le Dr Johannès Lepsius*, Paris: Fayard, 1986.

Livingstone, Elizabeth A. (ed.), *The Concise Oxford Dictionary of The Christian Church*, third edition, Oxford: Oxford University Press, 1987.

Longrigg, Stephen Hemsley, *Iraq 1900 to 1950: A Political, Social and Economic History*, Oxford: Oxford University Press, 1953.

Magie, David, "Report on the Assyrian Christians", National Archives and Record Service, *Records of the American Commission to Negotiate Peace*. Inventory of Record Group, 256, ed. Sandra K. Rangel, Washington DC, 1918.

Main, Ernest, *Iraq from Mandate to Independence*, London: G. Allen and Unwin, 1935.

Malek, Yusuf, *The British Betrayal of the Assyrians*, Chicago: Assyrian National Federation, 1935.

Mandelstam, André N., *Le sort de l'Empire ottoman*, Lausanne & Paris: Payot, 1917.

—— *La Société des Nations et les Puissances devant le problème arménien*, Paris: Pédone, 1926.

Naayem, Joseph, *Les Assyro-Chaldéens et les Arméniens, massacrés par les Turcs*, Paris: Bloud & Gay, 1920; translated into English as *Shall This Nation Die?*, New York: Chaldean Rescue, 1921.

Nikitin, Basil, "La Perse que j'ai connue, 1909–1919," typescript, Paris: INALCO, 1941.

———— "Une petite nation victime de la guerre: les Chaldéens", *Revue des sciences politiques*, XLIV, October–December 1921.

———— "Les Kurdes et le christianisme", *Revue de l'histoire des religions*, Annales du Musée Guimet, Paris: Ernest Leroux, 1922.

———— "Le problème assyrien", *Bulletin de l'Académie diplomatique internationale*, 4, October–December 1933.

———— "La question des Assyriens", *Bulletin de l'Académie diplomatique internationale*, 3, 1937.

Pinon, René, *La suppression des Arméniens*, Paris: Librairie académique Perrin, 1916.

Rhétoré, Jacques, *"Les chrétiens aux bêtes". Souvenirs de la guerre sainte proclamée par les Turcs contre les chrétiens en 1915*, Paris: Cerf, 2005.

Rockwell, William Walker, *The Pitiful Plight of the Assyrian Christians in Persia and Kurdistan, Described from the Reports of Eye-witnesses*, New York: The American Committee for Armenian and Syrian Relief, 1916.

Sanders, J.C.J, *Assyrian-Chaldean Christians in Eastern Turkey and Iraq: Their Last Homeland Re-Charted*, Kasteel Hernen, Holland: A.A.Brediusstichting, 1999.

Schauffler Platt, Mary, *The War Journal of a Missionary in Persia* (preface by William Shedd), Chicago: Woman's Presbyterian Board of Missions of the Northwest, 1915.

Shabaz, Yonan H., *The Rage of Islam*, Philadelphia: Roger William Press, 1918.

Shimun, Mar Eshai, *The Assyrian Tragedy*, 1934, republished Turlock, CA: Mar Shimun Memorial Foundation, 2010.

Shimun, Paul, *Massacres of Syrian Christians in N.W. Persia and Kurdistan*, New York: Columbia University Press, 1916.

Simon, Hyacinthe, *Mardine, la ville héroïque: autel et tombeau de l'Arménie (Asie Mineure) durant les massacres de 1915*, Aleppo, 1919.

Stafford, Ronald Semphill (Lt.), *The Tragedy of the Assyrians*, London: Allen and Unwin, 1935.

Surma d'Bait Mar Shimun, *Assyrian Church Customs and the*

Murder of Mar Shimun, London: Faith Press, 1920, republished Turlock, CA: Mar Shimun Memorial Foundation, 1983.

The Treatment of Armenians in the Ottoman Empire, 1915–16, Documents presented to Viscount Grey of Fallodon, Secretary of State for Foreign Affairs by Viscount Bryce, With a Preface by Viscount Bryce, London; HM Stationery Office, 1916.

Vine, Audrey R., *The Nestorian Churches: A Concise History of Nestorian Christianity in Asia from the Persian Schism to the Modern Assyrians*, London: Independent Press, 1937.

Warda, Joel E., The *Flickering Light of Asia or the Assyrian Nation and Church*, New Jersey: published by the author, 1924.

Weibel Yacoub, Claire, *Surma l'Assyro-Chaldéenne (1883–1975): Dans la tourmente de Mésopotamie*, Paris: L'Harmattan, 2007.

——— *Le rêve brisé des Assyro-Chaldéens. L'introuvable autonomie*, Paris:.Cerf, 2011.

Wigram, William A., *An Introduction to the History of the Assyrian Church or the Church of the Sassanid Persian Empire 100–640 A.D.*, London: Society for Promoting Christian Knowledge, 1910.

——— *Our Smallest Ally: A Brief Account of the Assyrian Nation in the Great War*, London, Society for Promoting Christian Knowledge, 1920.

——— *The Assyrians and their Neighbours*, London: G. Bell and Sons, 1929

Wigram, William A. and Edgar T. A. Wigram, *The Cradle of Mankind: Life in Eastern Kurdistan*, London, 1914.

Yacoub, Joseph, *The Assyrian Question*, Chicago: Alpha Graphic, 1986; republished 1993.

——— *Les Réfugiés assyro-chaldéens de Turquie*, Forcalquier: Comité européen de défense des réfugiés et immigrés, 1986.

——— "Les Assyro-Chaldéens d'aujourd'hui," *L'Afrique et l'Asie modernes*, 151, Paris: CHEAM, winter 1986–1987.

——— *Les Assyro-Chaldéens. Un peuple oublié de l'histoire*, Paris: Groupement pour les droits des minorités, 1987.

——— "La question assyro-chaldéenne, les puissances européennes et la Société des nations", *Guerres mondiales et conflits contemporains*, 151, July 1988.

——— *Diasporas et Développement, Histoires de développement*, special issue 6, *Cahiers de l'Institut d'études sociales de Lyon*, Lyon: Université catholique de Lyon, June 1989.

——— "Les Assyro-Chaldéens, une minorité dispersée," *Minorités au Proche-Orient*, special issue of *Hommes et Migrations*, January–February 1994.

——— "De Babylone à Paris: la diaspora assyro-chaldéenne", *L'Espace géographique*, 23/1, Paris & Montpellier: Doin & Reclus, 1994.

——— "Les Assyro-Chaldéens originaires de Turquie: une communauté en situation migratoire," *Les Annales de l'autre Islam*, 3, Paris: INALCO-ERISM, 1995.

——— *Les minorités. Quelle protection?* Paris: DDB, 1995.

——— *Babylone chrétienne. Géopolitique de l'Eglise de Mésopotamie*, Paris: DDB, 1996.

——— *Les minorités dans le monde. Faits et analyses*, Paris: DDB, 1998.

——— *Au-delà des minorités. Une alternative à la prolifération des Etats*, Paris: L'Atelier, 2000.

——— *Menaces sur les chrétiens d'Irak*, Chambray-lès-Tours: CLD, 2003.

——— *L'Humanisme réinventé*, Paris: Cerf, 2012.

——— "How Does the Arab World Perceive Multiculturalism and Treat its Minorities? The Assyro-Chaldeans of Iraq as a Case Study", in Kymlicka, Will and Eva Pföstl (eds.), *Multiculturalism and Minority Rights in the Arab World*, Oxford: Oxford University Press, 2014.

Yohannan, Abraham, *The Death of a Nation or the ever-persecuted Nestorians or Assyrian Christians*, London & New York: G. P. Putnam's Sons, 1916.

Yonan, Gabriele, *Ein vergessener Holocaust: Die Vernichtung der christlichen Assyrer in der Türkei*, Göttingen & Vienna: Reihe Bedrohte Völker, 148/49, May 1989.

BIBLIOGRAPHY

Filmography

Alaux, Robert, *Les derniers Assyriens*, Paris: Lieurac productions, 2005.

Alaux, Robert and Beth-Kinne, Nahro, *Seyfo, l'Elimination*, self-production, 2006.

Beth-Kinne, Nahro and Halleux Vincent, *Diaspora et renaissance assyriennes*, Brussels: Assyrian Voice Production, 2010.

Halleux, Vincent, *La Turquie des Empires et des Hommes*, Brussels, 2008.

Yakubova, Lina, *Assyrians in Armenia*, Yerevan: State Institute of Theatre Art and Cinematography, 2005.

INDEX

INDEX

INDEX

INDEX

275